THE BEST BUSINESS BOOKS EVER

THE BEST BUSINESS BOOKS EVER

THE 100 MOST INFLUENTIAL MANAGEMENT BOOKS YOU'LL NEVER HAVE TIME TO READ

PERSEUS
PUBLISHING

A Member of the Perseus Books Group

Copyright © 2003 by Bloomsbury Publishing Plc

Cataloging-in-Publication Data is available from the Library
of Congress

ISBN 0-7382-0849-3

Perseus Publishing is a Member of the Perseus Books Group
Find us on the World Wide Web at
http://www.perseuspublishing.com

Perseus Publishing books are available at special discounts
for bulk purchases in the U.S. by corporations, institutions,
and other organizations. For more information, please
contact the Special Markets Department at the Perseus
Books Group, 11 Cambridge Center, Cambridge, MA 02142,
or call (800) 255-1514 or (617) 252-5298, or e-mail
j.mccrary@perseusbooks.com.

Text design by Fiona Pike, Pike Design, Winchester, U.K.
Typeset by RefineCatch Limited, Bungay, Suffolk, U.K.
Printed in the United States of America

First printing May 2003

1 2 3 4 5 6 7 8 9 10–06 05 04 03

For more information about *Business: The Ultimate Resource*
and related titles, and to register for your free electronic
upgrades, please visit:
www.ultimatebusinessresource.com. At the subscriber
registration page enter your name, e-mail address, and your
password: **mybiz**

Contents

User's Guide

There is a vast literature of business and the world of work, and thousands of new publications emerge each year. *The Best Business Books Ever* aims to distill in an accessible format the main lessons from the best and most influential titles ever published.

Taking in the perspectives of authors, practitioners, and theorists around the world and across the centuries, the contents range from timeless texts on strategy such as *The Art of War* and *The Prince*, to the management classics *The Principles of Scientific Management* and *The Human Problems of an Industrial Civilization*, to contemporary titles such as *The Practice of Management*, *The Age of Unreason* and *Blur*.

A two-page digest of each work contains the following features:

- a capsule introduction describing the book's key contribution to management thought and practice
- **Getting Started**– an introduction to the main themes that each author sets out to address
- **Contribution**– a detailed summary of the book's most important points
- **Context**–an overview of both the immediate reaction to the book and its long-term significance
- **For More Information**–essential bibliographic information on each title

THE BEST
BUSINESS BOOKS
EVER

Action Learning
by Reg Revans

What is the difference between a puzzle and a problem? According to Revans, there is an existing solution to a puzzle and it simply needs to be found. There is no existing solution to a problem. The solution has to be worked out by a process of inquiry that begins at the point where one does not know what to do next and expertise is no help. *Action Learning* explains that process and offers an alternative method of learning to the traditional one, which is based on programmed knowledge instead of encouraging students to ask questions and roam widely around a subject.

Getting Started

As a young man, Reg Revans competed in the 1928 Olympics and worked in the famous Cavendish laboratories at Cambridge, England, alongside such fathers of nuclear physics as Ernest Rutherford and J. J. Thompson. Action learning is his systematization of the methods used by the Cambridge team to deal with problems. He developed them further when working for the National Coal Board after World War II. He also later went on to become Britain's first professor of industrial administration at the University of Manchester.

Action Learning is all about an alternative to traditional education and training. The method it sets out is a form of "learning by doing," but its proponents are careful to distinguish it from simply "learning on the job" or "learning by experience." It involves a collaborative effort, humility, a "trading of one's confusion with that of others," and deep reflection on one's experience and on the nature of the problem. Its outcome is personal growth as much as a way out of a current difficulty.

> *Action Learning* is all about an alternative to traditional education and training.

Contribution

Action Learning. The concept of "action learning" is based on a simple equation: $L = P + Q$. Learning (L) occurs through a combination of programmed knowledge (P) and the ability to ask insightful questions (Q).

It does not deny all usefulness to existing knowledge, but its focus is on asking questions. Learning must be opened up. Programmed knowledge is one-dimensional and rigid; the ability to ask questions opens up other dimensions and is free-flowing.

The first step toward asking constructive questions is to acknowledge one's own ignorance. Too many people are concealing their ignorance under a veneer of knowledge. Instead of hiding our ignorance, according to Revans, we should be bartering it.

The essence of action learning is to become better acquainted with the self through observing what one actually tries to do, endeavoring to ascertain the reasons for attempting it, and tracing the consequences that result from it. Revans said he sought "to focus [his] own doubt by keeping away from experts with prefabricated answers."

The Importance of Small Team Learning. The structure linking the two elements in the equation is the small team or set. The central idea of this approach is collaboration within the set; its members strive to learn with and from each other as they confess failures and expand on victories.

A Better Way to Develop Managers. Action learning is also the antithesis of the traditional approach to developing managers. We keep solving the same problems because we do not learn from them. We bring in consultants to provide solutions or send managers on courses where they are taught a lot but learn little. Action learning is about teaching little and learning a lot.

Collaboration Counts. In industry, managers and workers need to acknowledge the problems they face and then attempt to solve them. When doctors listen to nurses, patients recover more quickly. If mining engineers pay more attention to their workers than to their machinery, the pits are more efficient. It is neither books nor seminars from which managers learn much, but from here-and-now exchanges about the operational job in hand.

According to Revans, "The ultimate power of a successful general staff lies not in the brilliance of its individual members, but in the cross-fertilization of its collective abilities."

Context

For a long time Revans's ideas were comparatively little known and comparatively undervalued—at least in the English-speaking world. His ideas were received much better in mainland Europe (and in Belgium in particular), however, and he himself spent the final period of his working life there. Many management ideas that are currently fashionable, however, such as teamworking, reengineering, and the learning organization, contain elements of "action learning."

One of the critical points about action learning is its relation to action. In a way it appears misnamed. The name at first sight suggests learning in practical situations or performing tasks rather than studying theory. It tends to conceal the centrality of reflection, questioning, especially questioning one's own actions in a deliberate and precise way, ignorance-bartering, and collaborative effort to the process. The solutions that are eventually arrived at must be tested in action, but that is very much the final stage.

Interest in Revans's ideas nevertheless continues to grow. The Pentagon is said to be enthusiastic; the ANC has taken up action learning; General Electric uses action teams to tackle particular problems. There is also a Revans Centre at the University of Salford in England, where the theory and practice of action learning are particularly studied.

For More Information

Revans, Reg. *Action Learning*. London: Blond & Briggs, 1974.

Administrative Behavior

by Herbert Simon

Decision making, according to Simon, is synonymous with management. But what is decision making, how are decisions made? Simon realized that most people's assumptions were hopelessly unrealistic. He set out to inject some realism into the subject, but not in a merely reductive way; he also elaborated a very modern concept of the organization as an interrelated and intercommunicating body. He also said that the ability to make decisions effectively made the difference between effectiveness and ineffectiveness in organizations. On that basis alone, his book must be worth reading.

Getting Started

Herbert Simon, the son of German immigrants to Milwaukee and a graduate of the University of Chicago, won the Nobel prize for economics in 1978 for his work on administrative behavior, the subject of his doctoral thesis and this book. He is said to have been inspired to write it by observations made while working part-time for the Milwaukee municipal authority while a student. He is also said to have told the Nobel committee, when collecting his award, that his real interest was in artificial intelligence the field into which his interest in how decisions and choices are made ultimately led him.

In *Administrative Behavior: A Study of Decision-making Processes in Administrative Organization* (to give the book its full title), he developed a theory of human choice or decision making that aimed to be sufficiently broad and realistic to accommodate both the rational views of economists and the human concerns of psychologists and practical decision makers.

Contribution

The Problems of Organizational Theory. According to *Administrative Behavior*, the way in which administration is usually described suffers from superficiality, oversimplification, and a lack of realism. Theorists have refused to undertake the tiresome task of studying the actual allocation of decision-making functions. Instead, they have been satisfied with talking loosely about authority, centralization, span of control, function, and the like, without seeking operational definitions of these terms.

Classic economic theory also suggests that decisions are made by obtaining all the available information, assessing it, and coming to an objective and rational conclusion as to how the best result can be achieved. In reality, nobody has the time and the mental resources to do this. Instead of aiming for "the best," administrators are content with what is "good enough," a solution that is "satisficing" (that satisfies and suffices).

Organization is Important. Organization is important, first, because in our society, people spend most of their waking adult lives in organizations, and this environment provides much of the force that molds and develops personal qualities and habits.

Second, because it provides those in responsible positions with the means for exercising authority and influence over others.

The Complexity of Organizational Interaction. It is not sufficient to regard organizational behavior as a matter of understanding people or measuring the performance of people more effectively. Each act in an organization exists in a complex interaction with the organizational system as a whole.

Understanding Decision Making. A complex decision is like a great river, drawing from its many tributaries the innumerable component premises of which it is constituted.

Many individuals and organization units contribute to every large decision, and the problem of centralization and decentralization is a problem of arranging the complex system into an effective schema.

The Importance of Relationships. An organization is not an organizational chart, but a complex pattern of communications and other relationships in a group of human beings.

This pattern provides the members of the group with much of the information, assumptions, goals, and attitudes that enter into the decisions made by each and every one of them. It also provides them with a set of stable and comprehensible expectations as to what the other members of the group are doing and how they will react to what any individual says and does.

Context

Simon later observed that he must have had a prophetic gift when he included the words "behavior," "decision-making," and "organization" in the book's full title as they quickly became the fashionable phrases of social science.

> Organizational theory had remained deeply bedded in vagueness before the publication of *Administrative Behavior*.

Organizational theory had remained deeply bedded in vagueness before the publication of *Administrative Behavior*. Its clearest proponent up to that time had been Chester Barnard, who contributed the foreword to Simon's book.

In response, Simon developed a theory of human choice or decision making that aimed to accommodate:

- the rational aspects of choice that have been the principal concern of the economist;
- and the properties and limitations of the human decision-making mechanisms that have attracted the attention of psychologists and practical decision makers.

He thus formed a bridge between the humanists and engineers in management thinking.

His views were ahead of their time. For the next 40 years, organization, in the West at least, continued to be seen as an act of ordering, simplifying, and categorizing rather than as a powerful dynamic and ever-changing force.

Only in the early 1990s, partly through the success of Senge's *The Fifth Discipline*, did systems thinking make the leap from academic obscurity to the executive agenda.

For More Information

Simon, Herbert. *Administrative Behavior: A Study of Decision-making Processes in Administrative Organization*. New York: Macmillan, 1947.

The Age of Discontinuity

by Peter F. Drucker

Drucker predicted the rise of the knowledge worker long before the term came into common usage. His definition is much broader than the IT-led version that is currently used. The book gives a valuable insight into the changing nature of management roles and responsibilities in the knowledge economy.

Getting Started

According to Drucker, the manager as knowledge worker was a new breed of thoughtful, intelligent executive. The manager was reincarnated as a responsible individual, paid for applying knowledge, exercising judgment, and taking responsible leadership.

The knowledge worker sees him or herself as another professional. While dependent on the organization for access to income and opportunity, the organization equally depends on him or her.

In this book we read that knowledge, rather than labor, is the new measure of economic society—and the knowledge worker is the true capitalist in the knowledge society. Knowledge is not only power, but also ownership of the means of production.

Contribution

The Manager as Knowledge Worker. Drucker coined the term "knowledge worker." This was a new breed of executive—a highly trained, intelligent managerial professional who realized his or her own worth and contribution to the organization. Drucker bade farewell to the concept of the manager as mere supervisor or paper shuffler. The manager was reincarnated as a responsible individual.

Though the knowledge worker is not a laborer, and certainly not proletarian, he or she is not a subordinate (in the sense that he or she can be told what to do). The knowledge worker is paid, on the contrary, for applying his or her knowledge, exercising judgment, and taking responsible leadership.

The Nature of the Knowledge Worker. According to Drucker, the knowledge worker sees him or herself just as another professional, no different from the lawyer, the teacher, the preacher, the doctor, or the government servant of yesterday. He or she has the same education, but more income—and probably greater opportunities as well.

The knowledge worker may well realize that he or she depends on the organization for access to income and opportunity, and that without the organization, there would be no job. But there is also the realization that the organization depends equally on him or her.

Drucker effectively wrote the obituary for the obedient, gray-suited, loyal, corporate man and woman. The only trouble was, it took this corporate creature another 20 years to die.

The Impact of Knowledge Workers. The social ramifications of this new breed of corporate executive were significant. If knowledge, rather than labor, was the new measure of economic society then the fabric of capitalist society had to change.

The knowledge worker is both the true capitalist in the knowledge society and dependent on his or her job.

Collectively the knowledge workers—the employed, educated middle class of today's society—own the means of production through pension funds, investment trusts, and so on.

Knowledge was not only power, but it was also ownership.

Context

The book effectively mapped out the demise of the age of mass, labor-based production and the advent of the knowledge-based, information age. Drucker's realization that the role of the manager had fundamentally changed was not a sudden one. The foundations of the idea of the knowledge worker can be seen in his description of management by objectives in *The Practice of Management* (1954). Knowledge management, intellectual capital and the like are now the height of corporate fashion. The modern idea of the knowledge worker is a creature of the technological age, the mobile executive, the hot-desker. Drucker provided a characteristically broader perspective. He placed the rise of the knowledge worker in the evolution of management into a respectable and influential discipline.

Drucker has since developed his thinking on the role of knowledge, most notably in his 1992 book, *Managing for the Future*, in which he observed, "From now on the key is knowledge. The world is becoming not labor intensive, not materials intensive, not energy intensive, but knowledge intensive."

The Age of Discontinuity was startlingly correct in its predictions. Much of it would fit easily into business books of today.

Management guru Gary Hamel said, "Peter Drucker's reputation is as a management theorist. He has also been a management prophet. Writing in 1969, he clearly anticipated the emergence of the knowledge economy. I'd like to set a challenge for would-be management gurus: try to find something to say that Peter Drucker has not said first, and has not said well. This high hurdle should substantially reduce the number of business books clogging the bookshelves of booksellers, and offer managers the hope of gaining some truly fresh insights."

For More Information

Drucker, Peter F. *The Age of Discontinuity*. Woburn, MA: Butterworth-Heinemann, 1969.

The Age of Unreason
by Charles Handy

Written in 1989, this book includes a number of incisive predictions about the way work would develop. The author provides valuable insights into changing organizational structures and developments such as knowledge working, outsourcing, and strategic alliances—the hallmarks of the new economy.

Getting Started

In the author's view, the age of unreason is a time when the future is shaped by us and for us. At such a time, a number of organizational forms will emerge, as will new working patterns, such as outsourcing, telecommuting, the intellectual capital movement, and the rise of knowledge workers.

The portfolio worker will become more important, contributing to a greater work/life balance. A work portfolio is a way of describing how the different bits of work in our lives fit together to form a balanced whole. Portfolio work includes wage work and fee work, homework, gift work, and study work.

Handy goes on to state that the social changes resulting from these developments will be reflected in changing patterns of business, with a mix of small enterprises and large conglomerates. There will also be temporary alliances of large and small organizations to deliver a particular project.

Contribution

The Concept of an Age of Unreason. The age of unreason is a time when the future, in so many areas, is to be shaped by us and for us. The only prediction that will hold true is that no predictions will hold true. It will be a time for thinking the unlikely and doing the unreasonable.

New Organizational Forms. The author suggests that a number of organizational forms will emerge in an age of unreason:

- the shamrock organization
- the federal organization
- the Triple I organization

The shamrock organization is a form of organization based around a core of essential executives and workers supported by outside contractors and part-time help.

The federal organization is a form of decentralized setup, in which the center's powers are given to it by the outlying groups; the center therefore coordinates, advises, influences, and suggests rather than directs or controls. Federalism is the way to combine the autonomy of individual parts with the economics of coordination.

The Triple I organization is based on Information, Intelligence, and Ideas. This type of organization will resemble a university and will seek to make added value out of knowledge. To achieve this, the Triple I organization increasingly uses smart machines, with smart people to work with them.

New Working Patterns. Handy anticipated the growth of outsourcing, telecommuting, the intellectual capital movement, and the rise of knowledge workers. He also foresaw how these developments might impact on the individual. His concept of the portfolio worker helped redefine the nature of work, as well as questions of work/life balance.

Portfolio Working. A work portfolio is a way of describing how the different bits of work in our life fit together to form a balanced whole. There are five main categories of portfolio work:

- wage work and fee work, which are both forms of paid work;
- homework, gift work, and study work, which are all free work.

Wage (or salary) work represents money paid for time given.

Fee work is money paid for results delivered. Employees do wage work; professionals, craftspeople, and freelancers do fee work. Fee work is increasing as jobs move outside the organization. Some employees now get fees (bonuses) as well as wages.

Homework includes that whole catalog of tasks that go on in the home, from cooking and cleaning, to children and carpentry. Done willingly or grudgingly, it is all work.

Gift work is work done for free outside the home, for charities and local groups, for neighbors, or for the community.

Study work done seriously is a form of work, not recreation.

A Broader Portfolio. In the past, for most people, the work portfolio has had only one item in it—their career. This was a risky strategy. Few people would put all their money into one asset, yet that is what most people were doing with their lives. The career had to provide many things at once—interest or satisfaction in the work, interesting people and good company, security, money, and the opportunity for development.

Funding the Portfolio. Portfolio people think in terms of portfolio money, not salary money. Money comes in fits and starts from different sources, for example, a bit of a pension, some part-time work, some fees to charge, or things to sell. They lead cash-flow lives not salary lives, planning always to have enough in-flows to cover out-flows.

Portfolio people think in terms of barter and know that most skills are saleable if you want to sell them.

Changing Patterns of Business. It will be a world of "fleas and elephants"—large conglomerates and small individual entities, or large political and economic blocs and small countries.

A small enterprise can be global as easily as a large conglomerate, but can more easily be swept away. Conglomerates are a guarantee of continuity, but small enterprises provide the innovation.

There will also be ad hoc organizations, temporary alliances of large and small organizations to deliver a particular project.

Context

The book predicts many of the important changes in working patterns which are now commonplace, including outsourcing, telecommuting, and virtual project teams from different organizations.

It also recognized the growing importance of knowledge workers and intellectual capital.

For More Information

Handy, Charles. *The Age of Unreason*. Boston: Harvard Business School Press, 1990.

The Art of Japanese Management
by Richard Pascale and Anthony Athos

This book was one of the first business bestsellers. It played a crucial role in the discovery of Japanese management techniques. In its comparisons of Japanese and U.S. companies, it provides rare insights into the truth behind the mythology of Japanese management and the inadequacy of much Western practice.

Getting Started

By the late 1990s, growing Japanese superiority threatened the United States' dominant position in world markets. In the authors' view, a major reason for the superiority of the Japanese is their managerial skill. Japanese managers have vision, something notably lacking in the West. In Japan, visions are dynamic, rather than generic statements of corporate intent. U.S. managers are constrained by their beliefs and assumptions. The seven S framework (strategy, structure, skills, staff, shared values, systems, and style) represents the key categories requiring managers' attention. The Japanese succeeded through attention to the "soft" Ss—style, shared values, skills, and staff, while the West remained preoccupied with the "hard" 3s of strategy, structure, and systems.

> In Japan, managers enhance their modus operandi via dynamic visions rather than pallid or generic statements of corporate intent.

Contribution

Growing Japanese Superiority. In 1980, Japan's GNP was third highest in the world. Extrapolating trends at the time, it looked likely to be the highest by the year 2000.

For the U.S. readership, *The Art of Japanese Management* contains some hard-hitting truths.

If anything, the extent of Japanese superiority over the United States in industrial competitiveness is underestimated.

Managerial Skills. A major reason for the superiority of the Japanese is their managerial skills. Among the key components of Japanese management is vision, something they found to be notably lacking in the West, where the tools are there but vision is limited.

Beliefs, assumptions, and perceptions about management frequently constrain U.S. managers. The Western vision of management circumscribes our effectiveness.

In Japan, managers enhance their modus operandi via dynamic visions rather than pallid or generic statements of corporate intent.

The Seven S Framework. The book is best known for its central concept: the seven S framework.

As a generic statement of the issues facing organizations the seven S framework is unremarkable, though it did gain a great deal of attention. It simply lists the seven important categories that managers should take into account—strategy, structure, skills, staff, shared values, systems, and style.

According to Pascale, the value of a framework such as the seven Ss is that it imposes an interesting discipline on the researcher.

Comparing Management Styles. The seven Ss presents a framework for comparing Japanese and U.S. management approaches.

The Japanese succeeded largely because of the attention they gave to the "soft" Ss—style, shared values, skills, and staff.

The West remained preoccupied with the "hard" Ss of strategy, structure, and systems.

Since the book's publication, the general trend of Western managerial thinking has been directed toward the soft Ss.

Context

The book played a crucial role in the discovery of Japanese management techniques by the West. Its roots lie in Pascale's work with the U.S. National Commission on Productivity. Having initially thought that lessons from Japan were limited for cultural reasons, Pascale decided it would be more productive to look at Japanese companies in the United States. The research for the book eventually covered 34 companies over six years.

The authors' championing of vision proved highly influential. It was Athos who really started the entire "visioning" industry in the United States. Soon after *The Art of Japanese Management*, a flurry of books appeared highlighting so-called visionaries. Today, corporate visions are a fact of life.

Leading author Gary Hamel commented, "Japan-phobia has subsided a bit, helped by a strong yen, inept Japanese macroeconomic policy, and the substantial efforts of many Western companies to rebuild their competitiveness. While Pascale and Athos undoubtedly overstated the unique capabilities of Japanese management (is Matsushita really that much better managed than Hewlett-Packard?), they successfully challenged the unstated assumption that the United States was the font of all managerial wisdom. Since *The Art of Japanese Management* hit the bookstores, U.S. companies have learned much from Japan. Pascale and Athos deserve credit for setting the learning agenda."

For More Information

Pascale, Richard Tanner, and Anthony Athos. *The Art of Japanese Management*. New York: Simon & Schuster, 1981.

The Art of the Long View
by Peter Schwartz

It may be impossible to predict the future, but it *is* possible to prepare for it and lessen the degree of any shocks it may bring. The "scenario method," presented in this book by Peter Schwartz, enables managers to cover the possible outcome of their actions and take account of external events outside their control. It has been widely used in major corporations to prevent problems caused by unexpected developments.

Getting Started

The book describes the use of scenarios to investigate and test decisions about the future. A scenario is a way of looking ahead, a description of how the world might turn out to be in the future, if certain events take place. Schwartz believes that scenarios enable an organization to plot routes through necessarily uncertain terrain. They are not predictions—accurate predictions are impossible. Nor are they extrapolations of trends. Scenarios, according to the author, are an approach to making better decisions about the future.

Contribution

What Type of Scenario? The author highlights three possible scenarios for the future:

- more of the same, but better;
- worse, leading to decay and depression;
- different, but better with profound social changes.

It is possible to identify what types of business would succeed in each of those scenarios.

The Problem of Denial. Schwartz explains that some scenarios predict situations that people are not prepared to contemplate. He refers to this as a state of denial. Scenarios, he suggests, need to be treated as stories to overcome the problem of denial. Putting figures in the scenario makes them believable. With stories, readers can suspend belief.

Responses to Scenarios. People have different mindsets and so respond to scenarios differently. Schwartz puts people into three main categories: optimists, pessimists, and people who prefer the status quo. Some commentators dismiss scenarios as impossible dreams, but the author believes it is important to ask awkward questions and be prepared for the unexpected.

The Right Perspective. Schwartz recommends changing focus between the broad picture and the specific area of concern. For someone looking at the future prospects for an industry, it is important to take account of global developments as well as industry trends.

Wide-Ranging Research. Research into areas such as science, technology, politics, and economics underpins the development of scenarios, but conventional research sources may simply point to the continuation of the status quo. The author believes that "fringe research" may be equally important.

Certainty and Uncertainty. The author explains how the building blocks of scenarios are society, technology, economics, politics, and the environment. Looking at developments in each area gives the scenario builder a series of useful perspectives. The author describes how Shell established the Global Business Network to bring together people with different perspectives. Scenario builders use multiple perspectives to create a series of challenges and possible responses and identify potential winners and losers.

Context

The book draws on the author's wide-ranging experience in scenario development within Shell. He uses real-life examples to demonstrate the importance of scenarios in an industry like energy that is influenced by technology, politics, and economic and environmental factors. He explains how unexpected events such as war or major political change could have had a significant impact on the industry if it had not prepared for change through the use of scenarios.

Schwartz is careful to highlight the difference between scenarios and predictions about the future. His book is not a prediction about the way the world might look, but a method for assessing what might change if unforeseen circumstances occur. In that sense, the book is a valuable complement to books on strategy development based on "business as usual."

For More Information

Schwartz, Peter. *The Art of the Long View.* New York: John Wiley, 1997.

The Art of War
by Sun Tzu

When the postwar achievements of Japanese industry began to make a significant impression in the West, and Western businesspeople began to inquire into the thinking that underlay the success of their Far Eastern counterparts, Sun Tzu's *The Art of War* was a book that was often mentioned. This may seem surprising as it was probably written some 2,500 years ago. But military language and imagery have played an important role in the development of management thinking, and if you wish to gain an insight into strategy, leadership, and survival in a hostile, competitive environment, who better to turn to than a general whose name is a byword for sagacity?

Getting Started
Sun Tzu is thought to have lived over 2,400 years ago, at roughly the same time as Confucius. Historians are generally agreed that he was a general who led a number of successful military campaigns in present-day Anhui Province; the state of Wu, under whose sovereign he served, became a dominant power at that time. Since then, it has become standard practice for Chinese military chiefs to familiarize themselves with his writings.

The Art of War (the book's actual title is *Sun Tzu Ping Fa*, literally "The Military Method of Mr. Sun") is a compilation of the legendary general's thinking on the strategies that underlie military success. His anecdotes and thoughts, which fill no more than about 25 pages of text in all, are divided into 13 sections. Not all of them are relevant to modern-day concerns, but some strike a significant chord. Rather like a proponent of judo, Sun Tzu particularly recommends using the momentum of your enemies' own moves to defeat them.

Contribution
Get the Strategy Right. Sun Tzu, like most good and seasoned generals, is anything but an adventurer and anything but gung-ho. "Why destroy", he asks, "when you can win by stealth and cunning? To subdue the enemy's forces without fighting is the summit of skill."

His advice shows subtlety and restraint: "A sovereign should not start a war out of anger, nor should a general give battle out of rage. While anger can revert to happiness and rage to delight, a nation that has been destroyed cannot be restored, nor can the dead be brought back to life."

He continues: "The best approach is to attack the other side's strategy; next best is to attack his alliances; next best is to attack his soldiers; the worst is to attack cities."
Get Information From the Right Sources. Sun Tzu also gives sound advice on knowing your markets, saying: "Advance knowledge cannot be gained from ghosts and spirits, but must be obtained from people who know the enemy situation."
Stay Focused. His view on strategy leaves no room for sentiment or distraction.

"Deploy forces to defend the strategic points; exercise vigilance in preparation, do not be indolent. Deeply investigate the true situation, secretly await their laxity. Wait until they leave their strongholds, then seize what they love."

Context

So what does *The Art of War* have to offer the manager of a small components factory in, say, Peoria? Sun Tzu's admirers argue that his pithy sayings encapsulate basic and eternal truths. According to Gary Hamel, "Strategy didn't start with Igor Ansoff; neither did it start with Machiavelli. It probably didn't even start with Sun Tzu. Strategy is as old as human conflict . . . ." Anyone, therefore, who has to devise a plan, anyone who has to give a lead, can do with all the help they can get.

Hamel goes on to add " . . . and, if the stakes are high in business, they're rather higher in the military sphere." One of the attractions of the military analogy and the military role model in business is that they elevate proceedings to a loftier plane. Not only are the issues larger, and the scale more heroic, but it is clear who your enemy is, and when your enemy is clear, the world appears clearer whether you are a military general or a managing director.

Embattled managers, in particular, may benefit from the stimulus that military authors, like Sun Tzu, Clausewitz, or Liddell-Hart, and the writings of modern military leaders, like Colin Powell or Norman Schwarzkopf, can give to their civilian imaginations.

Finally, as has often been pointed out, Sun Tzu has long been revered in the Far East. He is said to be required reading not only for Eastern military tacticians but also for Eastern businesspeople. To know your enemies—or indeed to know your friends, partners, and colleagues—it is useful to have read what they read.

For More Information

Sun Tzu. *The Art of War* (trans. Griffith). Oxford: Oxford University Press, 1963.

A Behavioral Theory of the Firm
by Richard Cyert and James March

The book is a powerful introduction to the complex world of decision making. One of its authors, James G. March, is one of the foremost decision-making theorists of the 20th century. The book evaluates traditional approaches to decision making and puts forward real-world alternatives.

Getting Started

An entire academic discipline, decision science, is devoted to understanding management decision making. Early thinkers believed that the decision process could be rationalized and systematized, and that decision making can therefore be distilled into a formula. However, reality is often more confused and messy, and managers make decisions based on a combination of intuition, experience, and analysis.

Contribution

The Evolution of Decision-Making Theory. Early theories were based on the premise that, under a given set of circumstances, human behavior is logical and therefore predictable.

A profusion of models, software packages, and analytical tools followed, seeking to distill decision making into a formula. The danger is in concluding that the solution provided by a software package is the answer.

The Rational Theory of Decision Making. The authors suggest that the rational, or synoptic, model of decision making involves a series of steps:

- identifying and clarifying the problem;
- prioritizing goals;
- generating and evaluating options;
- comparing predicted outcomes of each option with the goals;
- choosing the option that best matches the goals.

These models rely on a number of assumptions about the way in which people will behave when confronted with a set of circumstances. The assumptions allow mathematicians to derive formulas based on probability theory. The decision-making tools include such things as cost/benefit analysis, which aims to help managers evaluate different options.

Problems in the Rational Theory. Reality is often more confused and messy than a neat model can allow for. Underpinning the mathematical approach are a number of flawed assumptions. The model assumes that decision making is:

- consistent;
- based on accurate information;
- free from emotion or prejudice;
- rational.

Real-world Decision Making. According to the authors, the reality is that managers make decisions based on a combination of intuition, experience, and analysis. As intuition and experience are impossible to quantify, the temptation is to focus on the analytical side of decision making.

The Relevance of Decision-Making Models. This does not mean that decision theory is redundant or that decision-making models should be cast to one side.

A number of factors mean that decision making is becoming ever more demanding. The growth in complexity means that companies no longer encounter simple problems. Complex decisions are now not solely the preserve of senior managers but the responsibility of many others. Managers are having to deal with a flood of information: a 1996 Reuters survey of 1,200 managers worldwide found that 43% thought important decisions were delayed and their ability to make decisions affected as a result of having too much information.

Decision theory and the use of models are reassuring, as they lend legitimacy to decisions that may be based on prejudices or hunches. However, no models are foolproof; none is universally applicable, and none can yet cope with the idiosyncrasies of human behavior.

The Challenge for Organizational Decision Making. Business decision-making theory faces a crucial and immediate problem: individuals have goals; collective groups do not. There is a need, therefore, is to create useful organizational goals, while not believing there is such a thing as an organizational mind.

Organizations should be regarded as coalitions that negotiate goals.

Creating goals requires three processes:
- bargaining, which establishes the composition and general terms of the coalition;
- internal organizational control, which clarifies and develops the objectives;
- adjustment to experience, which alters agreements in accord with changing circumstances.

Goals are inconsistent for three reasons:
- decision making being decentralized;
- short-term goals taking most managerial attention;
- the resources available to the organization being insufficient to maintain the coalition.

A New Decision-Making Model. The authors assert that the five principal goals of the modern organization are production, inventory, sales, market share, and profit. There are nine steps in the decision process: forecast competitors' behavior; forecast demand; estimate costs; specify objectives; evaluate plans; reexamine costs; reexamine demand; reexamine objectives; select alternatives. To work successfully, this decision-making model demands that there are standard operating procedures. The procedures can be divided into general ones based on avoiding uncertainty, maintaining the rules, and using simple rules. There are also specifics, such as task performance rules, continuing records and reports, information-handling rules, and plans.

Context

Much of decision science is built on the foundations set down by early business thinkers, such as computer pioneer Charles Babbage and scientific management founder Frederick W. Taylor, who believed that, under a given set of circumstances, human behavior was logical and therefore predictable. Based on this premise, models emerged to explain the workings of commerce which, it was thought, could be extended to the way in which decisions were made.

For More Information

Cyert, Richard M., and James G. March. *A Behavioral Theory of the Firm*. New York: Prentice Hall, 1963.

Being Digital

by Nicholas Negroponte

This book explains why knowledge is more important than physical commodities. Although it argues that organizations of any size can break into the new economy, this is not a book that offers practical guidelines.

Getting Started

Negroponte was a regular contributor to *Wired* magazine and provided many insights into the digital world. He introduced the terms "bits" and "atoms" that are used to describe the elements of the digital world. He explains that most information, despite being digital, is delivered to us in the form of atoms, that is to say, as newspapers, magazines, and books.

Economists still measure trade and write balance sheets with atoms in mind, he points out. But looking ahead, he explains why bits are easy to make and keep. They can travel easily around the world, he argues, and they are the basis of a global economy that allows the smallest company to participate.

Contribution

The Concept of "Bits" and "Atoms." According to Negroponte, the best way to appreciate the merits and consequences of being digital is to reflect on the difference between "atoms" and "bits." Atoms, he explains, are the elements of the old economy. Bits are digital. However, he points out that while we are undoubtedly in a new digital age, most information is still delivered to us in the form of atoms: newspapers, magazines, and books.

The author argues that, although the economy may be moving toward an information economy, we measure trade and we write our balance sheets in the traditional way, using atoms as the measure.

Describing the Digital World. According to Negroponte the bits and atoms distinction has improved, not weakened, over time. He claims that people quickly grasp the idea of bits that have no weight, no size, no shape, no color, and can travel at the speed of light.

The Value of Bits. Bits, claims Negroponte, are the key elements of the new information economy. He explains how the marginal cost of making more bits is zero, and you need no inventory. It is possible to sell bits and keep them for yourself at the same time because the originals and the copies are indistinguishable.

Toward a Global Marketplace. The author believes that bits will form the basis of a global marketplace that is accessible to even the smallest company. That is because bits don't stop at customs. Governments cannot tell where they are, and regulators cannot determine their appropriate jurisdiction.

Context

The book consists of a "repurposing" of many of the themes first visited in the author's monthly *Wired* column in the early- to mid-1990s. The book offers practical insights into the future of communications, but allows little opportunity for considered reflection of big-picture issues.

According to critics, Negroponte seems content to describe rather than to analyze, and the book lacks an incisive conclusion bringing together the key themes that he touches on but never really makes explicit.

For More Information

Negroponte, Nicholas. *Being Digital.* New York: Knopf, 1995.

Blur

by Stan Davis and Christopher Meyer

Blur is a book about the future, but the authors do not offer prescriptions. Instead they offer a starting point: provocative ideas, observations, and predictions to get you to think creatively about your business and your future.

Getting Started

At the heart of *Blur* are three forces—connectivity, speed, and intangibles—that are redefining businesses and destroying solutions that worked for the industrial world. The forces are known as the blur of desires, the blur of fulfillment, and the blur of resources.

A product offer and exchange were once clear-cut, but buyers and sellers are now in a constantly evolving relationship. The entire theory and practice of competitive strategy is changing, and intellectual capital has emerged as the key resource.

Change no longer carries the huge weight it did only a few years ago, and connectivity is speeding the economy up and changing the way it works.

Contribution

The Nature of *Blur*. At the heart of the authors' Blur theory are three forces, connectivity, speed, and intangibles. These forces are blurring the rules and redefining our businesses and our lives. They are destroying solutions, such as mass production, segmented pricing, and standardized jobs, that worked for the relatively slow, unconnected industrial world.

> Intellectual capital has emerged as the key resource. Hard assets have become intangibles; intangibles have become your only assets.

The three forces are shaping the behavior of the new economy and are affecting what Davis and Meyer label the blur of desires, the blur of fulfillment, and the blur of resources.

The Blur of Desires. The blur of desires has two central elements—the offer and the exchange that were once clear-cut.

In the product-dominated age, a company offered a product for sale. Money was exchanged and the customer disappeared into the distance. Now, however, products and services are often indistinguishable from each other. Buyers and sellers are in a constantly evolving relationship—a mutual exchange—which is driven by information and emotion as well as by money.

The Blur of Fulfillment. As organizations change to meet changing demands, so too must the entire theory and practice of competitive strategy.

Connectivity produces different forms of organization operating according to different first principles.

The blur of businesses has created a new economic model in which returns increase rather than diminish; supermarkets mimic stock markets, and you want the market, not your strategy, to price, market, and manage your offer.

The Blur of Resources. Intellectual capital has emerged as the key resource. Hard assets have become intangibles; intangibles have become your only assets.

Change is Less Critical. The authors assert that "built to last" now means "built to change." However, change, and the ambiguity it brings, no longer carry the huge weight it did only a few years ago.

The Impact of Connectivity. In the information economy, small things are connected in myriad ways to create a complex adaptive system.

Instantaneous, myriad connections are speeding the economy up and changing the way it works. The problem is that the connections are so many and so complex, that they can bring things to a grinding, inexplicable halt.

Context

From Dale Carnegie to Stephen Covey, Frederick Taylor to Michael Porter, business book readers have been weaned on a diet of prescriptions for success. Books are distilled down to a handful of key points or simple models. The trouble is that lists of the essential ingredients for success are becoming increasingly more questionable.

Uncertainty is uncharted territory and *Blur* is a book of the new breed. *Blur* would not even have been considered as a possible title just a few years ago when blind faith and certainty ruled. It would have been too weak, too suggestive of managerial confusion and impotence, too realistic.

For More Information

Davis, Stan, and Christopher Meyer. *Blur: The Speed of Change in the Connected Economy*. Reading, MA: Perseus Publishing, 1998.

The Borderless World

by Kenichi Ohmae

Like *The Mind of the Strategist*, the book gives valuable insights into the strategic thinking behind Japanese corporate success. The author adds new elements to the structure of business strategy, showing how it operates on a global scale.

Getting Started

According to Ohmae, in the global marketplace, the concepts of country and currency are important to business strategy. Fluctuations in trade policy or exchange rates can affect an otherwise brilliant strategy. Strategy is about more than being better than the competition. Big companies must relearn the art of invention in global industries. Customers are not driven to purchase things through nationalistic sentiments, therefore strategy should be formulated around a determination to create value for customers. Global business balances world-scale economies with products tailored to key markets. The role of central governments must change to allow individuals access to the best and cheapest goods and services from anywhere in the world.

Contribution

The Key Elements of Business Strategy. To the three Cs of his previous works (commitment, creativity, and competitiveness), Ohmae adds:

- country—the government-created environments in which global organizations must operate;
- currency—the exposure of such organizations to fluctuations in foreign exchange rates.

These two additional elements are now key to the formulation of any strategy.

An otherwise brilliant strategy can be ruined by a sudden fluctuation in trade policy or exchange rates, leading to a seemingly irreparable hemorrhage of cash.

Making arrangements to deal with fluctuations must lie at the very heart of strategy.

Strategy is creating sustained values for the customer more effectively than the competitors.

Invention is Critical. In the author's view, invention and the commercialization of invention are essential. Most people in big companies have forgotten how to invent, but they must relearn the art of invention. This time they must learn to manage invention in industries or businesses that are global, where it is necessary to achieve world-scale economies and yet tailor products to key markets.

Going Beyond the Competition. Strategy is about more than simply being better than the competition, which only encourages companies to become fixated on the competition. This fixation drives them to formulate their strategy according to the strategy of their competitors.

Possible strategies should be tested against competitive realities.

Tactical responses to what competitors are doing may be appropriate, but they should come second to your real strategy.

Before you test yourself against the competition, your strategy should encompass the determination to create value for customers.

The Interlinked Economy. In the author's view, countries are merely government creations.

In the interlinked economy (made up of the Triad of the United States, Europe and Japan) consumers are not driven to purchase things through nationalistic sentiments, no matter what politicians may say.

At the cash register, people don't care about country of origin or country of residence. They don't think about employment figures or trade deficits.

This also applies to industrial consumers.

Declaration of Interdependence. The role of central governments must change to:

- allow individuals access to the best and cheapest goods and services from anywhere in the world;
- help corporations provide stable and rewarding jobs anywhere in the world, regardless of the corporation's national identity;
- coordinate activities with other governments to minimize conflicts arising from narrow interests;
- avoid abrupt changes in economic and social fundamentals.

Governments must deal collectively with traditionally parochial affairs, including taxation.

Context

The Borderless World explores the new logic of the global marketplace as well as what Ohmae calls power and strategy in the interlinked economy.

This manifesto for the future is as broad-ranging as it is, in political reality, unlikely.

The Borderless World has, however, fueled debates about the role of governments, as well as the relationship between governments and the business world, which have yet to be resolved.

Ohmae has since gone on to explore the role of nations still further and now suggests that we have reached a time when the end of the nation state is imminent (see *The End of the Nation State*, Free Press, 1996, and *The Invisible Continent*, HarperBusiness, 2001).

Leading business author Gary Hamel commented, "So the world is becoming interdependent. Hardly news to companies like Dow Chemical, IBM, Ford, or Nestlé. But in 1990 this was still news to Japanese companies (and politicians) who typically defined globalization as big open export markets, and maybe a factory in Tennessee. Kenichi challenged Japanese companies, and myopic executives elsewhere, to develop a more sophisticated view of what it means to be global. Just what balance will ultimately be struck between the forces of globalization and the forces of nationalism and tribalism remains to be seen."

For More Information

Ohmae, Kenichi. *The Borderless World: Power and Strategy in the Interlinked Economy*. New York: HarperBusiness, 1990.

Built to Last

by James Collins and Jerry Porras

According to the authors, companies that enjoy enduring success have core values and a core purpose that remain fixed, while their business strategies and practices endlessly adapt to a changing world. The book shows the importance of developing and sticking to a set of guiding principles, and identifies the qualities essential to building a great and enduring organization.

Getting Started

Values are important in the context of business and corporations, and many companies have long recognized the importance of possessing a set of guiding principles.

In the authors' view, enduring organizations with strong guiding principles have outperformed the general stock market by a factor of 12 since 1925.

Core values are the organization's essential and enduring tenets, and drive the way the company operates at a level that transcends strategic objectives. Such values don't change, although strategies and practices adapt endlessly to change.

Core ideology defines what the company stands for and why it exists. It complements the envisioned future—what the company aspires to become. Any effective vision must embody the core ideology of the organization.

Contribution

The Importance of Corporate Values. Honesty, integrity, wealth, fairness are all values that we may be able to relate to on an individual personal basis. But what about values in the context of business and corporations?

While the term "corporate values" is a relative newcomer to the business lexicon, the concept of values as an important aspect of corporate life is not. Many companies have long recognized the importance of possessing a set of guiding principles, and the evolution of the concept can be traced through some of the most influential business books over the last 50 years.

> Honesty, integrity, wealth, fairness are all values that we may be able to relate to on an individual personal basis. But what about values in the context of business and corporations?

Thomas Watson, Jr., C.E.O. of IBM, observed that any great organization that has lasted over the years owes its resiliency to the power of its beliefs and the appeal these beliefs have for its people.

The Qualities of an Enduring Organization. The book sets out to identify the qualities essential to building a great and enduring organization—the successful habits of visionary companies.

The 18 companies chosen as subjects had outperformed the general stock market by a factor of 12 since 1925.

Core values are the organization's essential and enduring tenets. These are a small set of guiding principles (not to be confused with specific cultural or operating practices) which are never to be compromised for financial gain or short-term expediency.

Values are timeless guiding principles that drive the way the company operates at a level that transcends strategic objectives. For Hewlett-Packard, for example, values include a strong sense of responsibility to the community. For Disney, they include creativity, dreams, and imagination and the promulgation of wholesome American values.

Core Values Don't Change. Companies that enjoy enduring success have core values and a core purpose that remain fixed while their business strategies and practices endlessly adapt to a changing world. This is a key factor in the success of companies such as Hewlett-Packard, Johnson & Johnson, Procter & Gamble, Mercke, and Sony.

A Model for Core Values. The authors recommend a conceptual framework to cut through some of the confusion swirling around the issues.

In their model, vision has two components—core ideology and envisioned future. Core ideology, the Yin in their schema, defines what the company stands for and why it exists. Yin is unchanging and complements Yang, the envisioned future.

The envisioned future is what the company aspires to become, to achieve, to create—something that will require considerable change and progress to attain. Core ideology provides the glue that holds an organization together through time.

An Effective Vision. Any effective vision must embody the core ideology of the organization. This has two components—core values (a system of guiding principles and tenets) and core purpose (the organization's most fundamental reason for existence).

Context

Built to Last set out to identify the qualities, or corporate values, essential to building a great and enduring organization.

The evolution of the concept of corporate values can be traced through some of the most influential business books over the last 50 years.

In *A Business and Its Beliefs*, published in 1963, Thomas Watson, Jr. observed, "Consider any great organization—one that has lasted over the years—I think you will find it owes its resiliency not to its form of organization or administrative skills, but to the power of what we call beliefs and the appeal these beliefs have for its people."

In the early 1980s, Tom Peters and Robert Waterman thought corporate values important enough to warrant an entire chapter in *In Search of Excellence*.

For More Information

Collins, James, and Jerry Porras. *Built to Last*. New York: HarperBusiness, 1994.

A Business and Its Beliefs

by Thomas Watson, Jr.

> *A Business and Its Beliefs: The Ideas That Helped Build IBM* was written by the son of the founder of IBM's commercial greatness, who himself led the company into the computer age. It describes the origins of one of the world's most successful corporations and shows how its achievements were built on a strong corporate culture and a passionate commitment to customer service.

Getting Started

Thomas Watson, Jr. went to work for IBM in 1946 as a salesman. He was appointed chief executive in 1956 and retired in 1970, after presiding over IBM's rise to international preeminence at the beginning of the computer age.

IBM's origins lay in the Computing-Tabulating-Recording Company, which Thomas Watson, Sr. joined in 1914. The company initially made everything from butcher's scales to meat slicers, but gradually concentrated on tabulating machines that processed information mechanically on punched cards. It changed its name to International Business Machines in 1924.

> A company's central beliefs (what would now be called its core values) are central to its success.

IBM's development was helped by the 1937 Wages-Hours Act, which required U.S. companies to record hours worked and wages paid. The existing machines couldn't cope; Watson, Sr. developed a solution, the Mark 1, which was subsequently followed by the Selective Sequence Electronic Calculator in 1947. By then IBM's revenues were $119 million and it was set to make the great leap forward to become the world's largest computer company.

As far as management thinking is concerned, what IBM stood for is more important than what it did. Thomas Watson, Jr. took on a hugely successful company with a strong corporate culture built around salesmanship and service. Thomas Watson, Sr. had emphasized people and service obsessively. IBM was a service star in an era of machines that performed badly. This is where the heart of the message of *A Business and Its Beliefs* lies.

Contribution

Core Values Are Critical. A company's central beliefs (what would now be called its core values) are central to its success. Watson believed that these beliefs help people find common cause with each other, and sustain this common cause and sense of direction through the many changes that take place from one generation to another.

Success, in his view, comes through a sound set of beliefs, on which the corporation premises all its policies and actions. Beliefs must always come before policies, practices, and goals. The latter must always be altered if they are seen to violate fundamental beliefs.

Not only should the beliefs be sound, they should be stuck to through thick and thin. The most important single factor in corporate success is faithful adherence to those beliefs. Beliefs never change. Change everything else, but never the basic truths on which the company is based.

However, Watson argued for flexibility in all other areas. If an organization, he asserted, is to meet the challenges of a changing world, it must be prepared to change everything about itself except beliefs as it moves through corporate life. The only sacred cow in an organization should be its basic philosophy of doing business.

Develop a Corporate Culture. The beliefs that mold great organizations frequently grow out of the character, the experience, and the convictions of a single person. In IBM's case that person was Thomas Watson, Sr.

The Watsons created a corporate culture that lasted. IBM, "Big Blue," became the archetypal modern corporation and its managers the ultimate stereotype, with their regulation somber suits, white shirts, plain ties, zeal for selling, and company song.

A Passion for Competing. Behind the corporate culture lay a belief in competing vigorously and providing quality service. Later, competitors complained that IBM's sheer size won it orders. This was only partly true. Its size masked a deeper commitment to managing customer accounts, providing service, and building relationships, and to the values laid out by the Watsons.

People Matter. The real difference between success and failure in a corporation can very often be traced to the question of how well the organization brings out the great energies and talents of its people. Giving full consideration to the individual employee was one of the enduring beliefs on which IBM's success was built.

Context

In this book, the author codified and clarified what IBM stands for. The book is a statement of business philosophy, an extended mission statement for IBM.

Though it was published in the same year as Alfred P. Sloan, Jr.'s *My Years with General Motors*, it could not be more different. While Sloan sidelines people, Watson celebrates their potential; while Sloan espouses systems and structures, Watson talks of values.

Guru Gary Hamel commented, "Never change your basic beliefs, Watson argued. He may be right. But the dividing line between beliefs and dogmas is a fine one. A deep set of beliefs can be the essential pivot around which the company changes and adapts; or, if endlessly-elaborated, overly-codified, and solemnly worshipped, the manacles that shackle a company to the past."

For More Information

Watson, Thomas Jr. *A Business and Its Beliefs: The Ideas That Helped Build IBM*. New York: McGraw-Hill, 1963.

Capital

by Karl Marx

In the capitalist world human labor itself becomes a commodity. *Capital*, the major work by the social philosopher Karl Marx (1818–83), is a thoroughgoing critique of capitalism. Marx recognized the dynamics of the economic process, foresaw economic cycles, and developed a closed theory of economic activity. He was also the first economist to bring economics and history into relation with each other, and *Capital* was the book in which he did it.

Getting Started

Marx describes the capitalist method of production in its overall context. He follows David Ricardo in positing that only labor can produce value, then develops a theory of added value as the difference between the use value and the exchange value of labor as a commodity. Workers do only a portion of their work for themselves; a large portion goes to create added value, which falls entirely to the capitalist. Capitalists, Marx suggests, attempt to increase added value either by making their workers work longer or by reducing the amount of work time necessary for their workers' subsistence. Workers, therefore, have to earn their livelihoods in a shorter time, so that they can produce more added value. This leads to the exploitation of the working class.

Contribution

Volume One: The Production Process of Capital. Volume One deals with the development of the laws of added value production. This is the part of *Capital* that has always played the largest role in public discussion of the book.

Capitalist production, for Marx, is the production of goods, that is, production for the market. It is not conducted by small independent producers such as craftspeople, but by non-working entrepreneurs, who control the means of production and who therefore have the ability to make others work for them and to exploit them.

Every commodity, Marx argues, has two characteristics: usefulness (equivalent to its use value) and the property of being produced by human labor. Since use value varies depending on persons, time, and circumstances, it cannot be the basis of price. Labor must therefore be the criterion of value.

With the development of the exchange of goods, Marx continues, trade emerges as an independent function. In trade, consumption is not the purpose of the act of exchange, as it is in a simple exchange of goods, profit is.

The following paradox, according to Marx, then emerges. The law of value regulating the exchange of goods knows only the exchange of equal values. But in exchange transactions in trade, on the other hand, an inequality must come into play. This can only stem from production. For this to be possible, the capitalist must discover a commodity whose use value is that it creates more value than it actually possesses. That commodity is labor.

Volume Two: The Circulation Process of Capital. In the second volume, Marx deals with the circulation of capital as it passes through various stages. Capital must, he says, continually take on and then divest itself of three separate forms in order to be able to function and be of use: money capital, productive capital, and commodity capital. Money capital constantly transforms itself into the elements of the production process—labor and the means of production—and the result of its functioning appears in the form of commodities, endowed with added value, which are once again transformed into money. Acts involving the circulation of commodities take place continually, sales and purchases are always being transacted, goods and money are constantly brought into conjunction. But it is, says Marx, the fact that these acts are transition stages in the circulatory process of capital that makes them functions of capital; it is precisely that that transforms a sum of money into money capital, that makes commodities either productive capital or commodity capital. It is not their material nature that gives them this character, but the economic and historical conditions under which the process takes place. Commodities are not by nature capital, any more than workers are.

> It is a mighty intellectual construct made up of historical, sociological, and economic ideas and propaganda.

Volume Three: The Overall Process of Capitalist Production. In this volume, Marx brings volumes one and two into unity. The theoretical category of value, he asserts, is of interest to the capitalist. What the capitalist looks at is the capital advance that must be made to bring about production of a particular commodity. The advance is made up of constant and variable capital and represents, for the capitalist, the cost of the commodity. Capitalists do not calculate added value achieved in relation to the capital used, they simply calculate the surplus achieved against aggregate costs when the goods are sold, the profit.

Added value, says Marx, interests capitalists as little as does value per se. They expect a gain not on the variable capital they advance, but on aggregate capital. The added value on aggregate capital is profit; the numerical relationship of the one to the other is the profit rate.

Context

Marx came to economics after his political party failed to achieve power in the revolution of 1848/49. *Capital*, published in 1867, became the cornerstone of Marxism, the political doctrine and system named after him. It is, of course, more than pure economic theory. It is a mighty intellectual construct made up of historical, sociological, and economic ideas and propaganda. It was to provide the groundwork for socialism and give a theoretical basis to Marx's other major work, the *Communist Manifesto*. Marx's guiding light was the classless society, communism. As a result, while some honor him as the prophet and advocate of the working class, others refuse to take him seriously as an economist. He has also been blamed for the fact that, while concerned in theory with the working class, he avoided actual contact with the object of his investigations and never once saw a factory from the inside.

For More Information

Marx, Karl. *Capital: A Critique of Political Economy.* (trans. David Fernbach). New York: Penguin USA, 1992.

The Change Masters
by Rosabeth Moss Kanter

This book is regarded as an authoritative work on the factors behind successful corporate change. Kanter's work takes a human relations perspective, and was one of the earliest books to focus on the importance of empowerment.

Getting Started

According to the author, "change masters" are adept at anticipating the need for, and leading, productive change. Companies with a commitment to human resources were significantly ahead in long-term profitability and financial growth.

Kanter goes on to suggest that growth problems in American companies are due to suffocation of the entrepreneurial spirit—innovation is the key to growth. New skills are required to manage effectively in innovation-stimulating environments: power skills, the ability to manage employee participation, and an understanding of how change is managed. Empowerment is critical to corporate success.

Contribution

The Nature of Change Masters. Change masters are those people and organizations adept at the art of anticipating the need for, and leading, productive change. Change resisters are intent on reining in innovation.

The Importance of Managing People. A research program asked 65 human resource directors in large organizations to name companies that were progressive and forward-thinking in their systems and practices, in relation to people. Forty-seven companies emerged as leaders in the field. They were then compared to similar companies. The companies with a commitment to human resources were significantly ahead in long-term profitability and financial growth.

> The message is that if you manage your people well, you are probably managing your business well.

The message is that if you manage your people well, you are probably managing your business well.

Innovation As the Key to Growth. Kanter places responsibility for company growth problems on the quiet suffocation of the entrepreneurial spirit in segmentalist companies. She identifies innovation as the key to future growth. The way to develop and sustain innovation is to adopt an integrative approach rather than a segmentalist one.

Three new sets of skills are required to manage effectively in such integrative, innovation-stimulating environments:

- the ability to persuade others to invest information, support, and resources in new initiatives driven by an entrepreneur
- the ability to manage problems associated with increased use of teams and employee participation
- an understanding of how change is designed and constructed in an organization: how the microchanges introduced by individual innovators relate to macrochanges or strategic reorientation

The Importance of Empowerment. The extent to which individuals are given the opportunity to use power effectively influences whether a company stagnates or innovates. In an innovative company, people are at center stage.

Context

Rosabeth Moss Kanter began her career as a sociologist before her transformation into international business guru. *The Economist* (October 15, 1994) commented, "Kanter-the-guru still studies her subject with a sociologist's eye, treating the corporation not so much as a micro-economy, concerned with turning inputs into outputs, but as a mini-society, bent on shaping individuals to collective ends."

Kanter's work is a development of the Human Relations School of the late 1950s and 1960s. Through *The Change Masters* (1983) and *When Giants Learn to Dance* (1989), she was partly responsible for the increased interest in empowerment, if not its practice.

The Change Masters has been called "the thinking man's *In Search of Excellence*."

Author Gary Hamel said: "In a turbulent and inhospitable world, corporate vitality is a fragile thing. Yesterday's industry challengers are today's laggards. Entropy is endemic. Certainly *The Change Masters* is the most carefully researched, and best argued, book on change and transformation to date. While Rosabeth may not have discovered the eternal fountain of corporate vitality, she certainly points us in its general direction."

For More Information

Kanter, Rosabeth Moss. *The Change Masters*. New York: Simon & Schuster, 1983.

The Changing Culture of a Factory
by Elliot Jaques

This book is based on an extensive study of industrial democracy in practice at the United Kingdom's Glacier Metal Company beginning in 1948. The company introduced a number of highly progressive changes in working practice that were ahead of their time and set a pattern for future practice.

Getting Started

The Glacier Metal Company introduced a number of highly progressive changes in working practice, resulting in a form of industrial democracy that was ahead of its time. According to the study, the emphasis was on granting people responsibility and giving them a say in every problem. The project highlighted the shortcomings of conventional industrial relations practice, and showed that managers should be measured by the long-term impact of their decisions.

> The project was a decade ahead of any form of organizational development.

Contribution

Introducing Industrial Democracy. The Glacier Metal Company introduced a number of highly progressive changes in working practice:

- a works council was introduced. This was far removed from the usually toothless attempts at worker representation;
- no change of company policy was allowed unless all members of the works council agreed. Any single person on the council had a veto;
- "clocking on," the traditional means of recording whether someone had turned up for work, was abolished.

Contrary to what experts and observers anticipated, the company did not grind to an immediate halt.

Increasing Personal Responsibility. The emphasis was on granting people responsibility and of understanding the dynamics of group working. Everybody should be encouraged to accept the maximum amount of personal responsibility, and should be allowed to have a say in every problem in which they could help.

Anticipating Organizational Developments. The project was a decade ahead of any form of organizational development. It highlighted a number of issues:

- the redundancy of conventional organization charts;
- the potential power of corporate culture (a concept then barely understood);
- the potential benefits of running organizations in a fair and mutually beneficial way.

Theory of the Value of Work. "The manifest picture of bureaucratic organization is a confusing one," according to Jaques. "There appears to be no rhyme or reason for the structures that are developed, in number of levels, in titling, or even in the meaning to be attached to the manager–subordinate linkage."

A solution, labeled "the time span of discretion," contended that levels of management should be based on how long it was before their decisions could be checked. Managers should be paid in accordance with that time, and measured by the long-term impact of their decisions.

Context
The practices introduced at the Glacier Metal Company were almost a decade ahead of their time. However, they did not ensure the company's survival.

The study's progressive views on the importance of motivation at work have undoubtedly influenced other management writers and practitioners, such as Mary Parker Follett and Frederick Herzberg. Jaques' work was based on long-term scientific observation, in contrast to what he terms the "fantasy fads," the "waffle and fiddling around" of management consultants.

For More Information
Jaques, Elliot. *The Changing Culture of a Factory*. London: Tavistock Publications, 1951.

Competing for the Future

by Gary Hamel and C. K. Prahalad

Competing for the Future, named by *BusinessWeek* as the best management book of 1994, is regarded as the definitive book on strategy for contemporary business. It criticizes the narrow mechanistic view of strategy and calls for a broader approach that recognizes a company's core competencies.

Getting Started

This book argues that traditional strategy is too narrow in its perspective. Far from being a simple annual exercise, strategy is multifaceted, emotional as well as analytical, and concerned with meaning, purpose, and passion. Managers must look to the future and adopt "strategizing"—a new approach for developing complex, robust strategies, focusing on core competencies.

Today the onus is on transforming not just individual organizations, but entire industries. The true challenge is to create revolutions when you are large and dominant. Small entrepreneurial offshoots are not the route to organizational regeneration. Downsizing is an easy option—growth comes from creating a difference, and vitality comes from within, if only executives would listen.

Contribution

The Narrow Focus of Traditional Strategy. The authors assert that strategy has tied itself into a straitjacket of narrow, and narrowing, perspectives:

- a huge proportion of strategists, perhaps 95%, are economists and engineers who share a mechanistic view of strategy;
- strategy is multi-faceted, emotional as well as analytical, concerned with meaning, purpose, and passion;
- strategy should be looked on as a learning process.

Strategy is not Simple. In the authors' view, executives perceive that the problem with strategy is not creating it, but implementing it. Strategy is not a ritual or a once-a-year exercise. As a result, managers are bogged down in the nitty-gritty of the present—spending less than 3 percent of their time looking to the future.

Adopt Strategizing. Instead of talking about strategy or planning, companies should talk about strategizing and ask, "What are the fundamental preconditions for developing complex, variegated, robust strategies?"

Strategizing is part of the new managerial argot of strategic intent, strategic architecture, foresight (rather than vision), and the idea of core competencies.

Focus on Core Competencies. Core competencies represent the collective learning in the organization, especially how to coordinate diverse production skills and integrate multiple streams of technologies.

Organizations should see themselves as a portfolio of core competencies as opposed to business units. Core competencies are geared to growing opportunity share whereas business units are narrowly focused on market share.

Different Approaches to Strategy. There is a thin dividing line between order and chaos. Neither Stalinist bureaucracy nor Silicon Valley provides an optimal economic system. Silicon Valley is extraordinarily good at creating new ideas, but in other ways is extraordinarily inefficient.

Small or Large Organizations? Small entrepreneurial offshoots are not the route to organizational regeneration. They are too random, inefficient, and prone to becoming becalmed by corporate indifference. Smaller companies have had a revolutionary impact (IKEA, Body Shop, Swatch, and Virgin), but the true challenge is to create revolutions when you are large and dominant. American companies such as Motorola and Hewlett-Packard are more successful at this than their European counterparts. We are moving to more democratic models of organization, to which U.S. corporations appear more attuned. In Europe and Japan there is a more elitist sense of knowledge residing at the top—a hierarchy of experience, not of imagination.

Rules for Success.

- A company surrenders today's businesses when it gets smaller faster than it gets better.
- A company surrenders tomorrow's businesses when it gets better without getting different.
- Downsizing is an easy option.
- Growth (the authors prefer to speak of vitality) comes from difference, though there are as many stupid ways to grow as there are to downsize.
- The pressure for growth is usually ignited by a crisis.
- Vitality comes from within, if only executives would listen.
- Companies will pay millions of dollars for the opinions of McKinsey's bright 29-year-old, but ignore their own bright 29-year-olds.

Context

The debate on the meaning and application of strategy is long-running. The 1960s gave us the resolutely analytical Igor Ansoff; the 1970s, Henry Mintzberg with his cerebral and creative crafting strategy; the 1980s, Michael Porter's rational route to competitiveness.

Nominations for the leading strategic thinkers of the 1990s would certainly include Gary Hamel and C. K. Prahalad. *Competing for the Future* has been called the blueprint for a new generation of strategic thinking. *BusinessWeek* (September 19, 1994) said: "At a time when many companies continue to lay off thousands in massive re-engineering exercises, this is a book that deserves widespread attention. It's a valuable and worthwhile tonic for devotees of today's slash-and-burn school of management."

The surge of interest in core competencies has tended to enthusiastic over-simplification. Commentators believe companies need to be cautious about where core competencies will lead. They are a very powerful weapon, but can encourage companies to get into businesses simply because they see a link between core competencies rather than ones where they have an in-depth knowledge.

The authors' strategic prognosis falls between two extremes. At one extreme are the arch-rationalists, insisting on a constant stream of data to support any strategy. At the other is the thriving-on-chaos school, with its belief in freewheeling organizations where strategy is a moveable feast.

For More Information

Hamel, Gary, and C. K. Prahalad. *Competing for the Future*. Boston: Harvard Business School Press, 1994.

The Competitive Advantage of Nations

by Michael Porter

Many consider *The Competitive Advantage of Nations* to be one of the most ambitious books of our times. Said to do "for international capitalism what Marx did for the class struggle," it reexamines the nation state, suggesting that its basic role today is an economic one, and that, even in a global economy, it has a key role to play by ensuring the competitiveness of the companies operating within its borders who are the actual wealth producers for the population.

Getting Started

Michael Porter, author of the modern business classic *Competitive Strategy*, has a good deal of experience as a consultant to national governments. *The Competitive Advantage of Nations* emerged from his work on Ronald Reagan's Commission on Industrial Competitiveness. The research for the book encompassed ten countries: the United Kingdom, Denmark, Italy, Japan, Korea, Singapore, Sweden, Switzerland, the United States, and Germany (then West Germany).

The book can be read on three levels:

- as a general inquiry into what makes national economics successful;
- as a detailed study of eight of the world's main modern economies;
- as a series of prescriptions about what governments should do to improve their country's competitiveness.

It asks crucial questions. What makes a nation's firms and industries competitive in global markets and what propels a whole nation's economy to advance? Why are firms based in a particular nation able to create and sustain competitive advantage against the world's best competitors in a particular field? Why is one nation often the home for so many of an industry's world leaders? Why, for example, is Switzerland the home base for international leaders in pharmaceuticals, chocolate, and trading?

At its heart is a radical new perspective of the role of nations. From being military powerhouses they are now economic units whose competitiveness is the key to power.

Contribution

Nations, Competition, and Productivity. According to the author, "Nations don't compete. Companies compete. Nations can make it hard or easy for them to do so." When governments deliberately set out to help companies compete, however, their efforts are often counterproductive. The principal economic goal of a nation is to produce a high and rising standard of living for its citizens. The ability to do so depends not on the amorphous notion of competitiveness but on the productivity with which a nation's labor and capital resources are employed.

The Paradox of Globalization. Companies and industries have become globalized and more international in their scope and aspirations than ever before. This would appear to suggest that the nation has lost its role in the international success of its firms. Companies, at first glance, seem to have transcended countries.

While the globalization of competition might appear to make the nation less important, instead it seems to make it more so. With fewer impediments to trade to shelter uncompetitive domestic firms and industries, the home nation takes on growing significance because it is the source of the skills and technology that underpin competitive advantage.

In addition, it is the intensity of domestic competition that often fuels success on a global stage.

The National Diamond. To make sense of the dynamics behind national or regional strength in a particular industry, Porter developed the concept of the national diamond.

This is made up of four forces.

- Factor conditions—these would once have been largely restricted to natural resources and plentiful supplies of labor; now they also embrace data communications, university research, and the availability of scientists, engineers, or experts in a particular field.
- Demand conditions—if there is strong national demand for a product or service, this can give the industry a head start in global competition. The United States, for example, is ahead in health services due to heavy national demand.
- Related and supporting industries—industries which are strong in a particular country are often surrounded by successful related industries.
- Firm strategy, structure, and rivalry—domestic competition fuels growth and competitive strength.

Together, these four determine whether a nation has competitive advantage or not.

Clusters. "Nations succeed not in isolated industries, but in *clusters* of industries connected through vertical and horizontal relationships." Groups of interconnected firms, suppliers, and related industries arising in particular locations contribute substantially to national success. Porter shows how such clusters come into being.

Context

According to *The Economist* (October 8, 1994), "The book that projected Mr. Porter into the stratosphere, read by aspiring intellectuals and despairing politicians everywhere, was *The Competitive Advantage of Nations*."

Not everyone, however, agrees with Porter on the relationship between the nation and the globalized economy. Kenichi Ohmae believes that the nation state is on its way out, and Gary Hamel commented: "While *The Competitive Advantage of Nations* provides a good account of why particular industry clusters emerged in some countries and not others, it is essentially backward-looking. In a world of open markets, and mobile capital, technology, and knowledge, no firm need be the product of its geography."

Yet on balance, readers around the world have embraced the challenges outlined in Porter's book, and its status and impact as a classic business text cannot be overestimated.

For More Information

Porter, Michael. *The Competitive Advantage of Nations*. New York: Free Press, 1990.

Competitive Strategy

by Michael Porter

Competitive Strategy is a modern classic. It claims to provide a solution to a long-running strategic dilemma, and certainly put strategy at the forefront of management thinking.

Getting Started

In 1973 Michael Porter became one of the youngest professors ever at the Harvard Business School. He has since acted as a strategy counselor to many leading U.S. and international companies, besides playing an active role in economic policy with the U.S. Congress, business groups, and as an adviser to foreign governments.

Competitive Strategy is one of those books that bases its message around significant numbers—in this case three and five, the three generic strategies (every company must adopt one or lose out to its competitors) and the five competitive forces (that determine what a company must do to remain competitive). Over 20 years after its first publication, the current critical consensus seems to be that the competitive forces are truer to reality than the generic strategies. But strategy, having gone out of fashion in the 1980s and 1990s, may be making a comeback.

Contribution

Resolving the Strategy Dilemma. *Competitive Strategy* presents a rationalist's solution to a long-running strategic dilemma. At one end of the spectrum are the pragmatists, who contend that companies have to respond to their own specific situations. Competitive advantage emerges from immediate, fast-thinking responsiveness. There is no pat formula for achieving sustainable competitive advantage.

At the other end are those who, like the Boston Consulting Group, think that market knowledge is all-important. Any company that masters the intricacies of a particular market can reduce prices and increase market share. Porter proposes a logical compromise, arguing that there are three generic strategies for dealing with competitive forces: differentiation, overall cost leadership, and focus.

Differentiation. Differentiation entails competing on the basis of value added to customers (quality, service, differentiation) so that customers will pay a premium to cover higher costs. It requires creative flair, research capability, and strong marketing.

Overall Cost Leadership. Cost-based leadership involves offering products or services at the lowest cost. Quality and service are not unimportant, but cost reduction provides focus to organization.

Focus. Focus involves combining elements of the previous two strategies and targeting a specific market intensively.

Combining the Strategies. Companies with a clear strategy outperform those whose strategy is unclear or those that attempt to achieve both differentiation and cost leadership.

Sometimes the firm can successfully pursue more than one approach, though this is rarely possible. Effectively implementing any of these generic strategies usually requires total commitment, and organizational arrangements are diluted if there is more than one primary target.

The Risks of Ignoring Generic Strategies. If a company fails to focus on any of the three generic strategies it is liable to encounter problems. The firm stuck in the middle is almost guaranteed low profitability. It either loses the high-volume customers who demand low prices or must bid away its profits to get this business away from low-cost firms. It also loses high-margin businesses, the cream, to the firms who are focused on high-margin targets. In addition, it will also probably suffer from a blurred corporate culture and a conflicting set of organizational arrangements and motivation systems.

The Five Competitive Forces. In any industry, whether domestic or international or product- or service-oriented, the rules of competition are embodied in five competitive forces.

- The entry of new competitors. New competitors necessitate some competitive response, which will inevitably use resources and reduce profits.
- The threat of substitutes. If there are viable alternatives to your product or service in the marketplace, the prices you can charge will be limited.
- The bargaining power of buyers. If customers have bargaining power they will use it. This will reduce profit margins.
- The bargaining power of suppliers. Given power over you, suppliers will increase their prices and adversely affect your profitability.
- The rivalry among the existing competitors. Competition leads to the need to invest in marketing or R&D, or to price reductions. These will reduce profits.

The collective strength of these five competitive forces determines the ability of firms in an industry to earn, on average, rates of return on investment in excess of the cost of capital.

Context

When *Competitive Strategy* was published, it offered a rational and straightforward method for companies to extricate themselves from strategic confusion. The reassurance proved short-lived. Less than a decade later, companies were having to compete on all fronts. They had to be differentiated, through improved service or speedier development, and be cost leaders, cheaper than their competitors.

Porter's other contribution proved more robust. The five forces are a means whereby a company can begin to understand its particular industry. Initially passively interpreted as statements of the facts of competitive life, they are now usually seen as the rules of the game, which may have to be changed and challenged if an organization is to achieve any impact.

Influential author Gary Hamel commented, "In *Competitive Strategy*, Michael Porter did a masterful job of synthesizing all that economists know about what determines industry and firm profitability. While *Competitive Strategy* isn't much help in discovering profitable strategies, it is an unfailing guide to whether some particular strategy, once articulated, can be counted on to produce worthwhile profits. What distinguishes *Competitive Strategy* from many other contemporary business books is its strong conceptual foundation. Every MBA graduate in the world can remember Porter's five forces. How many can recall the eight rules of excellence?"

For More Information

Porter, Michael. *Competitive Strategy*. New York: Free Press, 1980.

Complexity

by M. Mitchell Waldrop

The science of complexity is now recognized as important to the study and development of economics and business strategy. This book is regarded as one of the most influential in the field. Complexity is based on mathematical theories that show how random events can quickly organize into complicated structures. In a business context, the theory can be used to gain an insight into the interdependencies of an organization and the potential impact of change.

Getting Started

The science of complexity shows how, in any system, there are a vast number of independent agents interacting with each other in different ways. In many cases, the author claims, individual elements are interdependent. In a simple model of a market, for example, there may be thousands of buyers and sellers.

According to the author, the complexity theory also indicates that these systems are self-organizing and adaptive. In the market example, groups or sectors will emerge and these groups will change or adapt to external conditions. Waldrop explains that the order emerging from these groupings can be contrasted with a state of chaos, where there is no interaction or dependency.

The complexity theory also suggests that a random event, such as a fall in the price of a single stock or share, can impact on the whole market. In that particular example, a single share price change has the potential to trigger a stock market crash because of the interdependencies in the market.

Contribution

Complexity in Economics. An economy, according to the author, is a web of transformations among goods and services. A producer extracts raw materials and converts them into a useful product. As an economy grows more complex, he explains, the number of possible combinations expands.

New technologies can accelerate the process even more. However, economies that depend on a single industry are likely to stagnate and decline. The author also describes a process called "economic take-off" where an economy reaches a critical point of complexity. Trade and mergers, he explains, can stimulate the complexity of different countries or organizations. The process can also lead to the phenomenon of "boom and bust."

The Problem of Predictability. Waldrop introduces game theory and chess analogies to describe economics. Players in a market, he explains, will not necessarily take predictable positions. They may change their roles. He points out that this runs counter to traditional economic theories that players make decisions based on analytical reasoning.

Traditional theory suggests that stock exchange behavior should be predictable. Prices should move up and down in line with the laws of economics. On that basis, he argues, crashes and booms should not occur. The new theory of economics, based on complexity, says that the stock market is a living thing. It would adapt to new pricing levels.

The End of Equilibrium. The author argues that it is hard to follow economic theory when things are not in equilibrium, because change is occurring all the time. This means that:

- problems are not well defined;
- the environment is not well defined;
- the environment might be changing;
- changes are totally unknown.

The implication, according to Waldrop, is that an economy can never be in equilibrium. The real world, he claims, is never that well defined.

A New Approach to Economics. Waldrop uses the terms "evolutionary economics" or "increasing return economics" to describe a new approach based on complexity theory. He points out that traditional economic theory is based on equilibrium, the balance of supply and demand in the marketplace. New economics looks at the phenomenon of increasing returns—the more you have, the more you'll get. This is in stark contrast to the traditional theory of diminishing returns.

Increasing Returns. The author cites examples of increasing returns such as Silicon Valley, Microsoft Windows, or VHS video technology. Silicon Valley attracts more technology startups because the early technology companies are established there. Companies build to the Microsoft Windows standard because it is so widely adopted by computer users. VHS eliminated the technically superior Betamax video format because more people were buying VHS.

This is also known as positive feedback. Waldrop shows how new technology developments emerge from an interconnected web of dependencies. A new technology spawns other new developments and the market becomes a self-organizing entity.

Context

Complexity theory has many other applications beyond economics. However, it is beginning to be accepted as part of mainstream management thinking.

Richard Pascale is another author to apply the theory to business. In a *Sloan Management Review* article, "Surfing the Edge of Chaos," he looks at the challenges posed to organizations by continuous change. Pascale uses complexity theory to explain why it is important for companies to increase the number of winning business strategies they pursue.

Pascale seeks to explore the process of change by trying to understand its complexities and interrelationships. He argues:

- complex adaptive systems cannot be directly controlled;
- a complex adaptive system is at risk when it is interfered with and controlled;
- complex adaptive systems are capable of self-organization and of generating new methods of operating.

Kevin Kelly's 1994 book, *Out of Control: The New Biology of Machines*, explores the organic nature of human-made systems. Kelly's view is that our technological future is headed toward a neobiological civilization.

The concept of positive feedback and the interdependencies among technology companies is also explored in *Information Rules* by Carl Shapiro and Hal R. Varian. The authors describe the development of networks fueled by positive feedback, though they base their views on observation, rather than complexity theory.

For More Information

Waldrop, M. Mitchell. *Complexity*. New York: Simon & Schuster, 1992.

Co-opetition

by Barry J. Nalebuff and Adam M. Brandenburger

The authors claim that this is the first book to adapt game theory to business strategy. Combining cooperation with competition to produce "co-opetition" is, they claim, an innovative business strategy that will give companies a winning advantage. It is a technique for making the right strategic business decisions in complicated business situations.

Getting Started

The authors explain why game theory provides a valid basis for thinking about business. The theory states that nothing is static; markets are dynamic and evolutionary. Companies can create new models or take on different roles to succeed. Nothing is taken as given. According to the authors, players in the game of business can change the rules to succeed. *Co-opetition* uses game theory to show how companies who cooperate can influence each other's success. Software, for example, becomes more valuable when a complementary company produces more powerful computers. Co-opetition strengthens the interdependence between companies.

Contribution

The Game of Business. Nalebuff and Brandenburger believe that co-opetition depends on complementary activities. When products stimulate demand for complementary products, companies should cooperate.

They show how the game of business includes customers, suppliers, competitors, and complementors. These organizations form part of a value net with integral dependencies. The value net expands the concept of a company's customers. By taking a multiple perspective, they argue, companies can redefine the role of a customer in a value net.

> To succeed in a game, companies must be able to offer added value.

The authors explain how film companies initially saw video as a threat to their business. Now, they recognize video as complementary to film distribution. Similarly, computers did not create a paperless office, they made it easier to create paper.

The Importance of Added Value. To succeed in a game, companies must be able to offer added value. However, say the authors, this must represent what a customer or competitor regards as valuable. If the value is not sufficient, the company can change the game by playing a different role or changing the rules. Perception therefore plays an important part in co-opetition; recognizing what other people believe is important.

Companies must recognize the boundaries of their business. According to the authors, companies operating in a lower segment can easily harm their core business by attempting to move into a higher segment.

Changing the Rules. The authors suggest a number of ways to change the rules.

A company entering a monopoly market may create competition, but if the incumbent has strong brand values, the new entrant may not gain sales. In those circumstances they recommend "getting paid to play." The new entrant should gain some benefit from entering a market, rather than just acting as a makeweight competitor.

The authors suggest that a company needing sales of complementary products to boost its own sales can influence a market by negotiating favorable prices for its own customers.

As the authors point out, a dominant supplier can exercise a monopoly position: limiting development and supplies to keep customers and suppliers hungry strengthens its own position.

Changing the Game. Nalebuff and Brandenburger recommend an action plan for bringing about change:

- look at your own value net;
- identify opportunities for cooperation and competition;
- change the players;
- identify the implications if the players change;
- identify added value;
- see how you can add further value;
- identify the other players' added value;
- see which roles are hindering or helping you;
- identify roles you would like to adopt;
- decide whether you can change the rules;
- understand how other players perceive the game.

Context

Game theory began in the 1950s with the publication of the book *Theory of Games and Economic Behavior* by Neumann and Morgenstern. Their theories were applied to economics, military strategy, computer science, and evolutionary biology. Game theory has been used more widely in business since the 1990s.

Co-opetition is the first book to use game theory to demonstrate business strategy. Its publication is timely as industry commentators from leading companies believe that the idea of complementary business is still not widely understood.

For More Information

Nalebuff, Barry J., and Adam M. Brandenburger. *Co-opetition.* New York: Harper-Collins Business, 1996.

Corporate Strategy
by Igor Ansoff

In *Corporate Strategy*, Ansoff codifies and generalizes his experiences as a strategist at Lockheed. The book develops a series of concepts and procedures that managers can use to develop a practical method for strategic decision making within an organization.

Getting Started

Corporate Strategy integrated strategic planning concepts invented independently in leading American firms. The book provided a powerful, rational model by which strategic and planning decisions could be made. Ansoff saw strategic planning as a complex sequence, or cascade, of decisions and defined two main concepts which are essential to understanding its nature, and therefore to implementing it successfully. The first of these was "gap analysis"—the "gap" being the difference between the current position of an organization and its strategic objectives. The second was "synergy"—the concept that 2 + 2 = 5.

Contribution

Integrating Strategic Planning Concepts. *Corporate Strategy* integrated strategic planning concepts which were invented independently in a number of leading U.S. firms, including Lockheed.

Ansoff saw strategic management as a powerful applied theory, offering a degree of coherence and universality lacking in the functionally-dominated management theorizing. **New Theoretical Concepts.** The book presented several new theoretical concepts such as partial ignorance, business strategy, capability and competence profiles, and synergy. One particular concept, the product-mission matrix, became very popular, because it was simple and—for the first time—codified the differences between strategic expansion and diversification.

A Rational Model for Planning Decisions. *Corporate Strategy* provided a rational model by which strategic and planning decisions could be made. The model concentrated on corporate expansion and diversification, rather than on strategic planning as a whole.

> *Corporate Strategy* provided a rational model by which strategic and planning decisions could be made. The model concentrated on corporate expansion and diversification, rather than on strategic planning as a whole.

The Ansoff Model of Strategic Planning was a complex sequence, or cascade, of decisions. The decisions started with highly aggregated ones and proceeded toward the more specific.

The Introduction of Gap Analysis. Central to the cascade of decisions is the concept of gap analysis, which can be summarized as: see where you are, identify where you wish to be, and identify the tasks that will take you there.

The procedure within each step of the cascade is similar.

- A set of objectives is established.
- The difference (the gap) between the current position of the organization and the objectives is estimated.

- One or more courses of action (strategy) are proposed.
- These are tested for their gap-reducing properties.

A course is accepted if it substantially closes the gap; if it does not, new alternatives are tried.

The Concept of Synergy. *Corporate Strategy* introduced the word "synergy" to the management vocabulary. Although the term has become overused, Ansoff's explanation (2 + 2 = 5) remains memorably simple.

Context

Corporate Strategy was published at a time of widespread enthusiasm for strategic planning, and an increasing number of organizations were joining the ranks of its users. Until its publication, strategic planning was a barely understood, ad hoc concept. It was practiced, while the theory lay largely unexplored. Ansoff also examined corporate advantage long before Michael Porter's dissection of the subject in the 1980s.

While *Corporate Strategy* was a remarkable book for its time, its flaws have been widely acknowledged, most honestly by Ansoff himself. It is highly prescriptive and advocates heavy reliance on analysis.

Some companies have encountered what Ansoff calls "paralysis by analysis"— the more information they possess, the more they think they need. This vicious circle dogs many organizations that embrace strategic planning with enthusiasm.

Ansoff regards strategic planning as an incomplete invention, though he is convinced that strategic planning was an inherently useful management tool. He has spent the last 40 years attempting to prove that this is the case and that, rather than being prescriptive and unwieldy, strategic management can be a dynamic tool able to cope with the unexpected twists of turbulent markets.

Business guru Gary Hamel described Ansoff as "truly the godfather of corporate strategy," and said, "Though Ansoff's approach may now appear overly-structured and deterministic, he created the language and processes that, for the first time, allowed modern industrial companies to explicitly address the deep questions of corporate strategy: how to grow, where to coordinate, which strengths to leverage, and so on."

For More Information

Ansoff, Igor. *Corporate Strategy*. New York: McGraw-Hill, 1965.

Corporate-Level Strategy

by Michael Goold, Marcus Alexander, and Andrew Campbell

Although large conglomerates claim to add value through synergy and economies of scale, the authors suggest this is not the case. They recommend that multi-business organizations should aim for a tighter fit between individual company strategies and the overall corporate strategy. The book introduces the concept of heartland businesses and shows how it can help corporations improve their overall performance.

Getting Started

The authors argue that most large companies are now multibusiness organizations. Research indicates that the benefits of economies of scale and synergy do not, in reality, exist.

While individual businesses within the organization often have strategies, the corporation as a whole may not. Only a tight fit between the parent organization and its businesses will add value.

There must be a clear insight about the role of the parent organization. "Parents" must concentrate on heartland businesses that they understand. The parent must only intervene on limited issues, and corporate strategy should be driven by parenting advantage.

Contribution

The Value of Multibusiness Organizations. Multibusiness companies, by virtue of their very size, should offer economies of scale and synergy between the various businesses, which can be exploited to the overall good. The authors' research suggests that in reality this is not the case.

They calculate that in over half of multibusiness companies, the whole is worth less than the sum of its parts. Instead of adding value, the corporation actually detracts from its value. Its influence, though pervasive, is often counterproductive.

This condemnation is not restricted to conglomerates. The influence of the corporate parent is also felt in companies with portfolios in a single industry, or in a series of apparently related areas.

Lack of Overall Strategy. A primary cause of this phenomenon is that while individual businesses within the organization often have strategies, the corporation as a whole may not. The proclaimed strategy is often an amalgam of the individual business strategies given credence by general aspirations.

Need for a Tight Fit. According to the authors, if corporate-level strategy is to add value, there needs to be a tight fit between the parent organization and its businesses.

Successful corporate parents focus on a narrow range of tasks and create value in those areas, and align the structures, processes, and central functions of the parent accordingly. Rather than being all-encompassing and constantly interfering, the center is akin to a specialist medical practitioner—intervening in its areas of expertise when it knows it can suggest a cure.

Success Factors for Multibusiness Organizations. From their analysis of 15 successful multibusiness corporations, the authors identify three essentials for successful corporate strategies:

- there must be clear insight about the role of the parent. If the parent does not know how or where it can add value, it is unlikely to do so;
- the parent must have distinctive characteristics. It, too, has a corporate culture and personality;
- it must be recognized that each parent will only be effective with certain sorts of business—described as their "heartland."

The Importance of Heartland Businesses. "Heartland businesses are well understood by the parent; they do not suffer from inappropriate influence and meddling that can damage less familiar businesses," say the authors. "The parent has an innate feel for its heartland that enables it to make difficult judgments and decisions with a high degree of success."

> The concept of heartland businesses is distinct from core businesses.

Heartland businesses are broad ranging and can cover different industries, markets, and technologies. Given this complexity, the ability of the parent to intervene on a limited number of issues is crucial.

Core Businesses. The concept of heartland businesses is distinct from core businesses. "A core business is often merely a business that the company has decided to commit itself to," they say. Though core businesses may be important and substantial, the parent may not be adding a great deal to them.

Building Parenting Advantage. The authors continue: "In contrast, the heartland definition focuses on the *fit* between a parent and a business: do the parent's insights and behavior fit the opportunities and nature of this business? Does the parent have specialist skills in assisting this type of business to perform better?"

Corporate strategy should be driven by "parenting advantage" to create more value in the portfolio of businesses than would be achieved by any rival. To do so requires a fundamental change in basic perspectives on the role of the parent and on the nature of the multibusiness organization.

Context

Most large companies are now multibusiness organizations. The logic behind this fact of business life is generally assumed rather than examined in depth.

The authors' research runs counter to the findings of authors such as Alfred Chandler in *Strategy and Structure* and Peter Drucker in *The Practice of Management*.

Gary Hamel said: "Chandler and Drucker celebrated large multidivisional organizations, but as these companies grew, decentralized, and diversified, the corporate center often became little more than a layer of accounting consolidation. In the worst cases, a conglomerate was worth less than its break-up value. In writing the definitive book on corporate strategy, Goold, Alexander, and Campbell gave hope to corporate bureaucrats everywhere. Maybe it really was possible for the corporate level to add value."

For More Information

Goold, Michael, Marcus Alexander, and Andrew Campbell. *Corporate-Level Strategy*. New York: John Wiley, 1994.

The Discipline of Market Leaders

by Michael Treacy and Fred Wiersema

The authors suggest that no company can become a market leader until it learns certain key disciplines. They provide a broad variety of examples of winning companies that used these disciplines to reinvent the rules of competition in their chosen markets. The book, they claim, will make it impossible for companies to compete on the old terms.

Getting Started

The authors have identified three value disciplines that they believe are essential to success—operational excellence, product leadership, and customer intimacy. By focusing on the most suitable discipline for their marketplace, a company can achieve leadership in its chosen field. That discipline, say the authors, should shape all the company's other plans and activities.

Contribution

Improving Value. According to the authors, market leaders don't excel at everything. They have achieved a level of excellence in one value discipline that puts them ahead of competitors.

Treacy and Wiersema believe that there are now new rules of competition. Successful companies must change customer expectations. They explain how customers buy different types of value, such as product quality, expert advice, or personalized service.

The authors advise companies to continue improving value year after year to meet rising customer expectations. However, producing ever-increasing value requires a superior operating model that can deliver results.

Winners, they suggest, concentrate on the competencies that are core to their value proposition. This determines their operating model.

Product Leadership. Product leaders, say the authors, focus on investment, product development, and market exploitation. They tend to have a loose-knit organizational structure that encourages enterprise.

They believe that companies who compete on premium product performance need to have a good basis of design and quality management. They also educate and prepare the market for new products, reducing risk and uncertainty for customers.

They demonstrate how product leadership companies are driven by vision and concept. Such companies cultivate talent who can turn ideas into marketable products. Talent is their most important asset, so they spend a great deal of time recruiting and retaining the right people. They create a culture for innovation by giving their people personal challenges.

Despite product leadership, they argue, companies have to adjust prices to market conditions. Brand leadership no longer provides price protection. If price is a chosen weapon, it requires an integrated system to sustain the advantage.

Service-Driven Organizations. Treacy and Wiersema show how service-driven organizations recognize and reward employees, get the supply position right, and deliver first-class service. Time, they believe, is critical to a market leader. Customers are no longer prepared to wait for slow service. Customers expect support as well as an excellent product, and that, the authors argue, makes service an integral part of any market-leading offer.

Leadership Through Customer Intimacy. The authors explain that companies who lead through customer intimacy build strong relationships and aim to achieve high levels of customer lifetime value. Their employees are empowered to deliver great levels of personal service to customers throughout the relationship.

> Treacy and Wiersema show how service-driven organizations recognize and reward employees, get the supply position right, and deliver first-class service.

This type of company, they argue, focuses on a hierarchy of customer needs. They go beyond the product and basic service to discover underlying problems and contribute to customer success. They leverage their understanding of customer problems and offer a variety of support services.

Frequently, they will manage customers' problems for them and mold their own organizations to those of their customers. The authors believe that customer intimacy requires the focus of all employees so that deep relationships can be formed throughout an organization.

Building on Operational Strengths. Companies who build on their operational strengths demonstrate a number of important characteristics, according to Treacy and Wiersema. They offer standard products, services, and operating procedures. They have developed tried and tested formulas for success and they simplify transactions. They also make extensive use of information technology to improve their efficiency.

Context

The book is one of many that look at successful companies and try to identify a formula for success. Many of the companies given as examples are similar to those found in other "success books."

Tom Peters and Robert Waterman first brought the technique to prominence with the publication of *In Search of Excellence*. Unfortunately, many of their excellent companies failed in subsequent years, but that did not prevent other authors from following similar investigations.

Treacy and Wiersema focus on three strands—operational excellence, product leadership, and customer intimacy. The themes of product leadership and customer intimacy are well covered by other authors.

Operational excellence is less of a recurring theme. However, the authors acknowledge a debt to Hammer and Champy's *Reengineering the Corporation* for examples of operational excellence at work.

For More Information

Treacy, Michael, and Fred Wiersema. *The Discipline of Market Leaders: Choose Your Customers, Narrow Your Focus, Dominate Your Market.* Reading, MA: Addison Wesley, 1997.

Dynamic Administration

by Mary Parker Follett

The book provides one of the earliest perspectives on business from the point of view of human relationships. It was written at a time when workers were seen simply as part of the mass-production process. The book provides useful background on the development of concepts such as empowerment and visionary leadership.

Getting Started

In the author's view, management is a social process and should have a special human dimension. The process is based in human emotions and in the interrelations created by working. The working environment has human problems, which have psychological, ethical, and economic dimensions.

She goes on to say that workers should be given greater responsibility, which is the great developer of people—and successful leaders must offer a vision of the future and train followers to become leaders.

Relationships, not just transactions, are important in organizations. Knowing this involves recognizing that conflict is a fact of life that we should use to work for us—but integration is the only positive way forward.

Contribution

Management As a Social Process. "We can never wholly separate the human from the mechanical sides," says Follett. The study of human relations in business and the study of the technology of operating are bound up together. The everyday incidents and problems of management reflect the presence or absence of sound principle.

Management has a special human character. Its nature as a social process is deeply embedded in human emotions and in the interrelations to which the everyday working of industry necessarily gives rise—both at manager and worker levels and, of course, between the two.

Toward Empowerment. Mary Parker Follett believed that, "we should undepartmentalize our thinking in regard to every problem that comes to us."

> Follett advocated giving greater responsibility to people at a time when the mechanical might of mass production was at its height. "Responsibility is the great developer of men," she said.

She continued, "I do not think that we have psychological and ethical and economic problems. We have human problems, with psychological, ethical, and economical aspects, and as many others as you like."

Follett advocated giving greater responsibility to people at a time when the mechanical might of mass production was at its height. "Responsibility is the great developer of men," she said.

Leadership Through Vision. The most successful leader of all is one who sees another picture not yet actualized—who sees the whole rather than the particular, organizes the experiences of the group, offers a vision of the future, and trains followers to become leaders.

Leading should be a two-way, mutually beneficial process. "We want worked out a relation between leaders and led which will give to each the opportunity to make creative contributions to the situation," Follett wrote.

Relationships Matter. Relationships, not just transactions, are important in organizations. The reciprocal nature of relationships means that a mutual influence is developed when people work together, however formal authority is defined.

Conflict is a fact of life that we should use to work for us. There are three ways of dealing with confrontation: domination; compromise; and integration. Integration is the only positive way forward. This can be achieved by first uncovering the real conflict and then taking the demands of both sides and breaking them up into their constituent parts.

Outlook is narrowed, activity is restricted, and chances of business success largely diminished when thinking is constrained within the limits of what has been called an either-or situation. "We should never allow ourselves to be bullied by an either-or," said Follett. There is often the possibility of something better than either of two given alternatives.

Context

Published eight years after her death, *Dynamic Administration* is a collection of Mary Parker Follett's papers on management gathered from 12 lectures given between 1925 and 1933. Her work stands as a humane counterpoint to that of Frederick Taylor and the proponents of scientific management. Follett was a female, liberal humanist in an era dominated by reactionary males intent on mechanizing the world of business.

Bearing in mind she was speaking of America in the early 1920s, her thinking can be described as little less than revolutionary, and certainly a generation ahead of its time. During her life, Mary Parker Follett's thinking on management was generally ignored—though in Japan there was a great deal of interest in her perspectives.

Leading commentator Gary Hamel said, "The work of Mary Parker Follett is refreshingly different from that of her peers. She was the first modern thinker to get us close to the human soul of management. She had the heart of a humanist, not an engineer."

To some, Follett remains a utopian idealist out of touch with reality; to others, she is a torchbearer of good sense whose ideas have sadly not had significant impact on organizations.

Henry Mintzberg commented, "Integration requires understanding, in-depth understanding. It requires serious commitment and dedication. It takes effort, and it depends on creativity. There is precious little of all of these qualities in too many of our organizations today."

For More Information

Follett, Mary Parker. *Dynamic Administration*. New York: Harper & Bros., 1941.

Emotional Intelligence
by Daniel Goleman

Daniel Goleman challenges traditional thinking, which claims that a high IQ is essential for success. He provides examples of people with high IQs and considerable academic achievement who have failed in business and in life, and, conversely, of those who, though apparently less gifted intellectually, were able to manage and harness their emotional intelligence in order to succeed. Although the book does not specifically relate to behavior in business, its conclusions highlight patterns that can be used to improve personal performance at work. Emotional intelligence is also referred to as the "soft skills," and these are increasingly regarded as important in business, particularly for people in sales, supervisory, or customer service roles.

Getting Started

Goleman describes the evolution of the brain and explains how the two main brain functions that influence behavior—emotion and intelligence—are situated in different parts of the brain. The part of the brain that controls emotions receives external signals before the intelligence functions, and that means that initial reactions to events may be emotional rather than rational. Goleman explains that the brain still retains a primitive "survival mode" that may trigger reactions and responses that are inappropriate. To succeed, he advises, we need to understand those reactions and learn how to control them.

> By looking at your strengths and weaknesses and learning from your experiences, you can gain self-confidence and certainty about your capabilities, values, and goals.

Contribution

Overcoming Impulses. According to Goleman, emotions have a wisdom of their own that can be harnessed. Although our natural reaction is to respond emotionally, it is important to make use of emotional intelligence to develop more positive responses.

A Framework of Emotional Intelligence. Goleman has developed a framework that explains emotional intelligence in terms of five elements:

- self-awareness
- self-regulation
- motivation
- empathy
- social skills

Self-awareness. According to Goleman, this element enables you to develop a better understanding of the way emotions affect your performance. You can also use your values to guide your decision making. By looking at your strengths and weaknesses and learning from your experiences, you can gain self-confidence and certainty about your capabilities, values, and goals.

Self-regulation. Goleman describes how this element can help you control your temper and reduce stress by acting in a more positive and action-oriented way. This enables you to retain your composure and improves your ability to think clearly under pressure. Through self-regulation, he claims, you can handle your impulses effectively and exercise self-restraint.

Motivation. According to the author, by harnessing this aspect of emotional intelligence, you can enjoy challenge and stimulation, and strive for achievement. You will be committed to the cause and seize the initiative. You will also be guided by your personal preferences in following one set of goals, rather than another.

Empathy. Empathy is the characteristic that enables you to understand other points of view, and behave openly and honestly.

Social Skills. Goleman describes how social skills such as persuasion, communication, listening, negotiating, and leading can be honed.

Emotional Intelligence and Management. Goleman claims that people with a higher degree of emotional intelligence are more likely to succeed in senior management. He also believes that emotional intelligence can be developed over a period of time, although this is disputed by a number of commentators.

Context

Daniel Goleman has built on the work in this book to research leadership styles based on different characteristics of emotional intelligence. These range from coercive leaders who are self-motivated and driven to succeed, to democratic leaders who are good at communication and listening, and coaching leaders who listen well and motivate others. The research is reported in the March–April 2000 issue of the *Harvard Business Review*.

Commentators point out a possible contradiction in Goleman's work. He claims that emotional intelligence is inherent, yet suggests that it can be developed.

Other studies of leaders have pointed out the relationship between high achievement and characteristics such as self-awareness and empathy. In *Emotional Intelligence*, Goleman does not specifically deal with the relationship between leadership and emotional intelligence. His subsequent research does, however, analyze the relationship further.

For More Information

Goleman, Daniel. *Emotional Intelligence.* New York: Bantam, 1997.

The Fifth Discipline

by Peter Senge

This is the book that popularized the concept of the learning organization. More philosophical in tone than the majority of business-oriented books, it adopts a holistic approach. Learning is an individual and a group experience, something, Senge would claim, much deeper than just taking information in. "It is about changing individuals so that they produce results they care about, accomplish things that are important to them."

Getting Started

Peter Senge is director of the Center for Organizational Learning at MIT. *The Fifth Discipline* emerged from extensive research by Senge and his team, but the germ of the idea came to him during his meditation, when he realized that "the 'learning organization' would likely become a new management fad."

The "fifth discipline" of the title is systems thinking. Of the five building blocks of a learning organization, systems thinking connects the other four and enables them to work together for the benefit of business.

Contribution

Learning Is Vital. In the author's view, as the world becomes more interconnected and business becomes more complex and dynamic, work must become more "learningful." It is no longer sufficient to have one person learning for the whole organization, a Ford, say, or a Sloan or a Watson. It is no longer possible to figure it out from the top, and have everybody else follow the orders of the grand strategist.

The organizations that will excel in the future will be those that can tap the commitment and capacity to learn of people at all levels within them.

Managers should therefore encourage employees to:

- be open to new ideas;
- communicate frankly with each other;
- understand thoroughly how their companies operate;
- form a collective vision;
- work together to achieve their goal.

The Five Disciplines. There are five components to a learning organization:

- systems thinking
- personal mastery
- mental models
- shared vision
- team learning

Systems Thinking. Systems thinking is a conceptual framework to make patterns clearer, claims Senge. It requires us to see interrelationships rather than linear cause and effect. It can help managers spot patterns, such as the way certain kinds of problems persist, or the way systems have their own in-built limits to growth.

Personal Mastery. This idea is based on familiar managerial competencies and skills. But it also includes spiritual growth—opening oneself up to a deeper reality and living life from a creative rather than a reactive viewpoint.

As part of this discipline, one must continually learn to see current reality more clearly; the ensuing gap between vision and reality produces the creative tension from which learning arises.

Mental Models. These are the organization's driving and fundamental values and principles. Senge emphasizes the power of patterns of thinking at the organizational level and the importance of nondefensive inquiry into the nature of these patterns.

Shared Vision. Senge stresses the importance of cocreation and the need to base shared vision on personal vision. Shared vision is present when the task that follows from the vision is no longer seen by the team members as separate from the self.

Team Learning. The discipline of team learning involves two practices: dialog and discussion. Dialog is characterized by its exploratory nature, discussion by the opposite process of narrowing down the field to the best alternative for the decisions that need to be made. The two are mutually complementary, but the benefits of combining them only come from having previously separated them.

Creating Learning Organizations. The author argues that transforming companies into learning organizations has proved problematical, principally because managers must surrender their traditional spheres of power and control to the people who are learning. If people are to learn, they must be allowed to experiment and fail. In a blame-oriented culture, this requires a major change in attitude.

The learning organization demands trust and involvement. Again, this is usually notable by its absence. Real commitment is rare in today's organizations. Experience indicates that 90% of the time what passes for commitment is compliance. One man reported to Senge that by adopting the learning organization model, he made what he called "job-limiting choices." What he meant was that he could have climbed the corporate ladder faster by rejecting Senge's theories and toeing the company line.

Context

Although the learning organization sounds like a product, it is actually a process, Phil Hodgson of Ashridge Management College commented: "Processes are not suddenly unveiled for all to see. Academic definitions, no matter how precise, cannot be instantly applied in the real world. Managers need to promote learning so that it gradually emerges as a key part of an organization's culture."

The Fifth Discipline has proved highly influential. Though the learning organization has rarely been converted into reality, the idea has fueled the debate on self-managed development and employability, and has affected the rewards and remuneration strategies of many organizations.

Gary Hamel observed that: "While Professor [Chris] Argyris put organizational learning on the management agenda, Peter Senge married it with systems thinking and created a language and approach that makes the whole set of ideas accessible to managers. Peter is no mere theorist, his Organizational Learning Center at MIT has helped launch thousands of in-company learning experiments. *The Fifth Discipline* would certainly be on my short list of the half dozen best business books of the last 25 years."

For More Information

Senge, Peter. *The Fifth Discipline: The Art and Practice of the Learning Organization.* New York: Doubleday, 1990.

The Functions of the Executive

by Chester Barnard

Barnard is regarded as an important management thinker who, according to Tom Peters and Robert Waterman in *In Search of Excellence*, created "a complete management theory." Though his language is dated, much of his thinking—particularly on the importance of communication—is relevant to modern management.

Getting Started

The author asserts that an organization allows people to achieve what they could not achieve as individuals, as they and their actions are interconnected. One essential ingredient for a successful organization is good, short lines of communication because communication enables everyone to be tied into the organization's objectives. It is also vital that chief executives nurture goals and values and translate them into action; executives should not just ensure conformance to a code of morals, they should create moral codes for others.

Contribution

People Are Interconnected in an Organization. Barnard rejected the concept of an organization as comprising a rather definite group of people whose behavior is coordinated with reference to some explicit goal or goals. "In a community," he argued, "all acts of individuals and of organizations are directly or indirectly interconnected and interdependent."

The Importance of Communication. Barnard highlights the need for communication. He argues that everyone needs to know what and where the communications channels are so that every single person can be tied into the organization's objectives.

Lines of communication should be short and direct. "The essential functions are, first, to provide the system of communications; second, to promote the securing of essential efforts; and third, to formulate and define purpose," he writes.

> An organization is simply a means of allowing people to achieve what they could not achieve as individuals. An organization is a system of consciously coordinated activities of forces of two or more persons.

The Need to Nurture Goals and Values. The chief executive is not a dictatorial figure geared to simple, short-term achievements. Part of his or her responsibility is to nurture the values and goals of the organization. Values and goals need to be translated into action rather than meaningless motivational phraseology—"strictly speaking, purpose is defined more nearly by the aggregate of action taken than by words," he writes.

A Holistic Approach to Management. An organization is simply a means of allowing people to achieve what they could not achieve as individuals. An organization is a system of consciously coordinated activities of forces of two or more persons.

A Code of Management Morality. In Barnard's view, the distinguishing mark of executive responsibility is that it requires not merely conformance to a complex code of morals, but also the creation of moral codes for others.

Context

Chester Barnard was a rarity: a management theorist who was also a successful practitioner. He won an economics scholarship to Harvard but, before finishing his degree, he joined American Telephone and Telegraph, eventually becoming president of New Jersey Bell in 1927.

The Functions of the Executive collected together his lectures on management. "It is doubtful if any other book since Taylor's *Scientific Management* has had a deeper influence on the thinking of serious business leaders about the nature of their work," observed Barnard's contemporary, Lyndall Urwick.

Although the language is dated, much of what Barnard argued strikes a chord with contemporary management thinking. His ideas on communication and the importance of short lines of communication remain relevant. In arguing that there was a morality to management, Barnard played an important part in broadening the managerial role from one simply of measurement, control, and supervision, to one also concerned with more abstract notions, such as values.

For More Information

Barnard, Chester. *The Functions of the Executive*. Boston: Harvard University Press, 1968.

General and Industrial Management

by Henri Fayol

Fayol created one of the first systems of management that put management at the center of the organization. His system divides a company's activities into six groups, in which managerial activities are distinct from the other five. The book provides a systematic analysis of the process of management, in which he anticipated most of the more recent analyses of modern business practice. His brief résumé of what constitutes management later largely held sway throughout the 20th century.

Getting Started

Fayol created a system of management in which management was the basis of the organization. His system focused on acceptance of, and adherence to, six different functions: technical, commercial, financial, security, accounting, and managerial activities.

He believed that to manage is to forecast and plan, to organize, to command, to coordinate, and to control. His view of forward planning was one of the first examples of business planning in practice.

Contribution

A System of Management. Fayol created a system of management encapsulated in *General and Industrial Management*.

"Management plays a very important part in the government of undertakings; of all undertakings, large or small, industrial, commercial, political, religious, or any other," he writes.

Division by Function. Fayol's system was based on acceptance of, and adherence to, different functions. He said that all activities to which industrial undertakings give rise can be divided into six groups. These are:

- technical activities
- commercial activities
- financial activities
- security activities
- accounting activities
- managerial activities

The Nature of Management. The management function is quite distinct from the other five essential functions. To manage is to forecast and plan, to organize, to command, to coordinate, and to control.

Fayol's view of what constitutes management has been highly influential throughout the late 20th century and has only recently been challenged.

Principles of Management. From his observations, Fayol also produces general principles of management:

- division of work
- authority and responsibility

- discipline
- unity of command
- unity of direction
- subordination of individual interest to general interest
- remuneration of personnel
- centralization
- scalar chain (line of authority)
- order
- equity
- stability of tenure of personnel
- initiative
- esprit de corps

Forward Planning. Fayol talks of ten-yearly forecasts, revised every five years—one of the first instances of business planning in practice.

The maxim "managing means looking ahead," gives some idea of the importance attached to planning in the business world. It is true that if foresight is not the whole of management, it is at least an essential part of it.

Context

Fayol created a system that put management at the center of the organization in a way never envisaged by contemporaries such as Frederick W. Taylor, author of *Scientific Management*.

Fayol's championing of management was highly important. While Taylor regarded managers as little more than overseers with limited responsibility, Fayol regarded their role as critical to organizational success.

In his faith in carefully defined functions, Fayol was systematizing business organization in ways that worked at the time, but proved too limiting and restraining in the long term.

In *The Principles and Practice of Management*, a 1953 study of early management thinking, E. F. L. Brech notes, "The importance of Fayol's contribution lay in two features: the first was his systematic analysis of the process of management; the second, his firm advocacy of the principle that management can, and should, be taught. Both were revolutionary lines of thought in 1908, and still little accepted in 1925."

Igor Ansoff has noted that Fayol anticipated imaginatively and soundly most of the more recent analyses of modern business practice. His brief résumé of what constitutes management has largely held sway throughout the late 20th century. Only now is it being seriously questioned and challenged.

An extrapolation of Fayol's methods was later exposed by Peter Drucker who observed, "If used beyond the limits of Fayol's model, functional structure becomes costly in terms of time and effort."

For More Information

Fayol, Henri. *General and Industrial Management*. London: Pitman, 1949.

General Theory of Employment

by John Maynard Keynes

Should the state intervene to combat unemployment? Governments today may ask themselves this question; governments were already asking themselves this question during the 1930s and had even more compelling reasons for doing so, perhaps. Keynes was the first to show convincingly why state intervention to boost employment is sensible and necessary. This book, first published in 1936, lays the foundations of Keynesianism, a demand-oriented doctrine that is still hotly debated and highly influential in both politics and economics today.

Getting Started

Keynes's *General Theory* shows how economic policy can overcome periods of stagnation. He argues in favor of investment being state-directed to ensure full employment. In contrast to the exponents of classical economic theory, he does not believe in the self-healing power of the market. Demand is, for him, the lever of the economy, and in times of crisis it is the state that must operate the lever.

Contribution

The Error in Classical Economics. According to Keynes, Adam Smith and David Ricardo start out from the assumption that the law of supply and demand regulates the price of goods and of labor. Workers, therefore, are only dismissed when their wages are too high. If they accept lower wages, they are reemployed. The classical economic model always returns to a state of balance: anyone who is unemployed, is so voluntarily.

The world economic crisis of the 1930s could not, however, be explained in this way, Keynes thought. Millions of workers were on the streets, although wages were sinking lower and lower. The "paradox of poverty in the midst of affluence" needed another explanation. Supply was not decisive in achieving economic success; demand was.

Aggregate Demand—Consumption and Investment. Demand across the entire economy—the sum of expenditure on consumer and investment goods—has one essential characteristic, Keynes argues: it is unstable. Expenditure on consumption depends on income: the higher the income the more money is spent. But above a particular level of income, the tendency to increase consumption declines. Part of the additional income is saved.

Investments are the second element in aggregate demand, because they increase the potential of businesses to produce. Investments, according to Keynes, depend on the "marginal efficiency of capital." If this is higher than the standard rate of interest in the market, the investor has an incentive to use credit to implement investment plans. In the opposite case, the costs of credit would be higher than the profit, and the investment would not be made.

Imbalance between the Markets for Goods and Capital. The market interest rate for investments, says Keynes, results from the population's inclination toward liquidity, that is, their demand for cash. People save for a variety for reasons, to purchase goods, to protect themselves against hard times, or in order to speculate.

Speculators keep their savings in cash until prices are low and a favorable opportunity arises to enter the stock market.

Harmonization between the goods and capital markets is the exception; equality of savings and investments is a rare and lucky chance. It is not the case, says Keynes, that people's savings decisions are solely dependent on the rate of interest and that the interest mechanism ensures that all savings are available to be loaned to businesses for the purchase of investment goods. Rather, he argues, businesses expand their production so long as they expect larger sales in the future. More and more investors try to attract the capital of the savers. Interest rates and production costs rise and reduce returns. The suppliers of capital get nervous. Panic grips the markets. The unrealistic expectations of the boom are followed by the hysteria of crisis. Investments fall, employment drops, purchasing power disappears, future prospects become more and more dismal. Businesses do not invest even when interest rates sink to zero. The national economy is caught in the "liquidity trap."

> Harmonization between the goods and capital markets is the exception; equality of savings and investments is a rare and lucky chance.

The State As Starter Motor of the Economy. To free the economy from this disastrous situation and turn it back in the direction of full employment, aggregate demand must rise, says Keynes, until increasing production by businesses offers all workers employment. If the demand for investment goods rises, this leads to more production, more work, and more income. Higher consumption boosts demand for goods and investment, which means that production and income rise further. A chain reaction begins, an "income multiplier"—an exogenous impulse, perhaps an extra boost to investment, gives rise to a multiple increase in income.

From this, Keynes draws the following conclusion. If entrepreneurs do not invest in sufficient amounts, the state must step forward as an investor to set the economy back in motion. To produce additional investment, the public purse accepts credit and uses it to finance, for example, roads, sewage systems, schools, or hospitals.

Context

The stock market crash of 1929, the crisis in the world economy, and the Great Depression of the 1930s threw up a number of crucial economic and political questions, which Keynes attempted to answer in this book. It made him the most famous national economist of the 20th century and initiated one of the most influential strands in modern economic thought, Keynesianism. Keynesian ideas provided the framework for the postwar recovery and held sway in many countries during the middle of the last century. Even President Richard Nixon remarked, "We are all Keynesians now." It was only in the 1970s that the "monetarist counterrevolution" began, eventually re-enthroning supply-side economics and the market forces whose fallibility it had been part of Keynes's purpose to demonstrate.

For More Information
Keynes, John Maynard. *The General Theory of Employment, Interest, and Money.* New York: Harcourt Brace, 1965.

Getting to Yes

by Roger Fisher and William Ury

Negotiation is an important skill in many aspects of business and personal life. The authors claim that people can become more effective negotiators by moving from adversarial haggling to constructive joint problem solving, a solution they call "principled negotiation." Both Fisher and Ury have conducted negotiations at extremely high levels in business, politics, diplomacy, law, and international relations. They write with authority and have the experience to offer practical advice and insight into each stage of the negotiating process.

Getting Started

The authors offer a number of negotiating principles that, they claim, will lead to successful outcomes:

- don't bargain over positions;
- separate the people from the problem;
- focus on interests, not positions;
- invent options for mutual gain;
- insist on objective criteria.

Contribution

The Importance of Effective Negotiation. Negotiation involves everyone, the authors claim. People use negotiation to handle their differences at work and in personal life. However, they believe that standard negotiating strategies tend to leave one or both parties dissatisfied. They describe two types of negotiators:

- soft negotiators who may make easy compromises to avoid conflict
- hard negotiators who want to win at all costs

The authors propose a third way, using what they call "principled negotiation." Its objective is to decide issues on their merits, rather than on will.

Avoid Bargaining over Positions. Fisher and Ury point out that, traditionally, people take positions and defend them. The matter is only resolved through concessions. This approach can harm relationships, and that can be damaging to future negotiations. In this approach, emotions become entangled with logic, so it is important to separate people from problems.

> Fisher and Ury point out that, traditionally, people take positions and defend them.

Separate People from Problems. The authors prompt us to remember that negotiators are people with emotions. Negotiators are therefore just as interested in ongoing relationships as in dealing with the immediate problem. Understanding the emotions of the other side is important, because they can act as a barrier to rational discussion. It is important to understand the other person's perspective and find out what is important to him or her. Listening actively and acknowledging the other party's perspective is critical.

The authors explain how successful negotiators try to make the other party own the problem so that they fully participate in reaching a satisfactory conclusion. Communication is an important part of this process, helping to build a working relationship that can reduce the element of confrontation.

Focus on Interests, Not Positions. Fisher and Ury recommend looking for the underlying interest in negotiations. Interests may not conflict, although positions do. They suggest finding out or asking why the other side takes a particular position, and acknowledging those interests as part of the problem.

Invent Options for Mutual Gain. The objective of negotiation is a single conclusion, say the authors. Introducing other options may appear to slow down the process, but, they claim, it can make the outcome easier to achieve. Enlarging the pie can help to provide what appears to be mutual gain. They believe that brainstorming can help to determine the options because during brainstorming, no decisions have to be made and creativity is encouraged.

Insist on Objective Criteria. Finally, according to Fisher and Ury, it may be possible to decide on the outcome by reference to an independent or objective authority. The standards should be fair and acceptable to both sides. Comparable criteria from other negotiations may also be acceptable.

Context

Negotiation is a critical element of business. The book looks at the process of negotiation independently of business processes such as sales, customer service, or union negotiations.

The authors build on their own experience of negotiations in politics, diplomacy, and the law. Although not all of the examples relate directly to business, it is possible to apply the same principles to business situations of many types.

For More Information

Fisher, Roger, and William Ury. *Getting to Yes.* Boston: Houghton Mifflin Company, 1981.

The Goal

by Eliyahu Goldratt and Jeff Cox

What goes on in modern manufacturing businesses is highly complex, and often very frustrating. Production problems and job delays are the order of the day, and attempts to improve the situation run up against the existing organizational setup and come to grief. This may sound like the starting point for a textbook on process optimization, but Eliyahu Goldratt, famous for his use of the fictional format, takes an inefficient factory threatened with closure and makes it the setting for a novel as fast-paced and gripping as the average thriller. Many books are said to be entertaining as well as instructive, but Goldratt, here writing with Jeff Cox, does more than most to optimize the entertainment process.

Getting Started

Plant manager Alex Rogo is handed an ultimatum by his bosses: either he makes a clear improvement in the profitability of his factory within three months, or the factory closes. For Rogo, it's then a race against time. In order not to fail, he has to change his ideas radically. He meets Jonah, the authors' spokesman in the novel, who helps him to break free of traditional ways of thinking and recognize what needs to be done. Jonah knows the solution to the factory's problems and enables Alex to discover it for himself by providing him with questions instead of guidelines. In this way the authors show that management can only learn by deductive insight.

Contribution

Goldratt and Cox set out an important principle of product organization in their novel. The story deals with people who want to understand how business processes function. Because they think about their problems logically, they manage to establish cause-and-effect relations between their actions and the changes that result from them. From these they gradually derive the underlying principles that enable them to turn their factory around and finally achieve success.

Alex Rogo is the novel's narrator, the "I" of the story. It begins on the day when Bill Peach, the division vice president, walks into his factory and demands "to be shown the status of Customer Order Number 41427." It turns out that nobody knows anything about this order, which happens to be a fairly big one, and also a late one. Rogo sums up the situation in the factory like this: "Everything in this plant is late. Based on observation, I'd say this plant has four ranks of priority for orders: Hot . . . Very Hot . . . Red Hot . . . and Do It NOW. We just can't keep ahead of anything."

Rogo meets Jonah, his former math teacher who is now a specialist in production organization. When Jonah asks him whether productivity has risen in the plant since industrial robots were put in, he says that it has—by 36%. In response to further questions, however, Rogo reveals that the 36% increase applies only to one section. Jonah than tells him that if he hasn't slimmed down his inventory and reduced his wage costs, and if the plant is not selling more product than before, the robots cannot have increased its productivity.

Rogo speaks to Lou, the plant controller. Together they establish benchmark figures for turning the business around. These should be, they decide, the net profit, the return on investment, and cash flow, because negative cash flow would kill off the business.

But these figures are not enough in themselves. They are the ones that the people in division management use to measure progress. At the level of the individual factory, these figures do not make much sense. Jonah prompts Rogo to look at three more figures: throughput, inventory, and operating costs. Goldratt, speaking through Jonah, defines throughput as the amount of money per time unit that the system earns by sales, stressing the fact that sales are what counts, not production. Inventory, he says, is all the money that is invested in the system for the purchase of things that are intended for sale. And operating costs are all the money that the system spends to turn inventory into throughput.

Rogo starts thinking about what goes on in his factory in these terms. He then moves on to what is very much home territory for Goldratt, the exponent of the "Theory of Constraints." He decides that he has to find the *bottlenecks*, production units whose capacity is equal to or less than the market requirement allotted to them. He says he would like to organize everything so that the production unit with the smallest capacity has the top place in any work plans.

Eventually, Rogo gets to the point where he can go to the managing director with a five-step program to save the plant:

1. Identify the regulating factor in the system.
2. Decide how the bottlenecks in the system can be used.
3. Make everything else subordinate to the above decision.
4. Free up the bottlenecks in the system.
5. Set the changed procedures in motion.

Context

The Goal is an economics textbook on the natural laws of business life in the form of a novel. It has attained cult status. One the two authors, Eliyahu Goldratt, has been reckoned an industrial guru and cultural revolutionary. He is an expert on production management. He created the mathematical and philosophical bases on which the OPT (Optimized Production Technology) system of planning and organizing production processes is built and leads a management organization, OPT Management Systems. Goldratt's appearances as a speaker are feared by many in business, because he tends to pillory firms and their practices in public.

For More Information

Goldratt, Eliyahu, and Jeff Cox. *The Goal: A Process of Ongoing Improvement*. 2nd ed. Great Barrington, MA: North River Press, 1994.

How to Win Friends and Influence People
by Dale Carnegie

Dale Carnegie was a highly successful public speaker and author of books on public speaking and confidence development. *How to Win Friends and Influence People* provides practical advice on the universal challenge of face-to-face communication. As the familiarity of the title proves, the book has had a great impact. The first edition had a print run of mere 5,000, but the book has since sold over 15 million copies.

Getting Started
Carnegie holds that it is essential to handle people effectively, and to make them like you to ensure your own success. His book is littered with illustrative anecdotes from the lives of the famous—Clark Gable, Marconi, Franklin D. Roosevelt, Mary Pickford—and the not so famous.

Contribution
Handle People Effectively. Carnegie presented the fundamental techniques in handling people:
- don't criticize, condemn, or complain;
- give honest and sincere appreciation;
- arouse in the other person an eager want.

Make People Like You. He added advice on other ways to make people like you:
- become genuinely interested in other people;
- smile;
- remember that a person's name is to that person the sweetest and most important sound in any language;
- be a good listener;
- encourage others to talk about themselves;
- talk in terms of the other person's interests;
- make the other person feel important, and do it sincerely.

Context
How to Win Friends and Influence People is the original self-improvement book, and Carnegie was the first superstar of the self-help genre. Cashing in on his success, he wrote a plethora of other titles on similar themes, including *Public Speaking and Influencing Men in Business*, *How to Stop Worrying and Start Living*, *How to Enjoy Your Life and Your Job*, and *How to Develop Self-confidence and Influence People by Public Speaking*. His successors included Anthony Robbins and Stephen Covey, who studied American success literature (of which Carnegie is a prime example) before coming up with *The Seven Habits of Highly Effective People*.

How to Win Friends and Influence People is the original self-improvement book, and Carnegie was the first superstar of the self-help genre.

Carnegie had done much the same 50 years before, and his principles have a similar homely ring to those of Covey. Carnegie's books and his company's training programs continue to strike a chord with managers and aspiring managers, because they deal with the universal challenge of face-to-face communication.

Carnegie was notable in being the first to create a credible long-term business out of his ideas. In creating a flourishing business, Carnegie ensured that his name and ideas should continue to live on and make money after his death.

For More Information

Carnegie, Dale. *How to Win Friends and Influence People*. New York: Simon & Schuster, 1937.

The HP Way
by David Packard

David Packard was half of the partnership that created one of the business and management benchmarks of the 20th century—Hewlett-Packard. In 1937, with a mere $538 and a rented garage in Palo Alto, Bill Hewlett and David Packard created one of the most successful corporations in the world. This book tells the story behind the company.

Getting Started

According to Packard, the HP secret lay in a simple approach to business. The HP way reflected the culture of the company and the management style the partners used to run it. It was based on openness and respect for the individual, which was key to the company's success. Management was always available and involved, and conflict had to be tackled through communication and consensus rather than confrontation. Their commitment to people fostered commitment to the company, and HP people at all levels show boundless energy and enthusiasm. The recipe for growth was to make products leaders in their markets. They kept divisions small and didn't do anything too risky. These values worked to save the company when times were hard.

Contribution

A Simple Approach to Business. HP's secret lay in the simplicity of its methods.

"Professors of management are devastated when I say we were successful because we had no plans. We just took on odd jobs," said Bill Hewlett.

Their legacy lies in the culture of the company they created and the management style they used to run it—the HP way.

From the very start, Hewlett-Packard worked to a few fundamental principles:

- it did not believe in long-term borrowing to secure the expansion of the business;
- its recipe for growth was simply that its products needed to be leaders in their markets;
- it got on with the job.

"Our main task is to design, develop, and manufacture the finest [electronic equipment] for the advancement of science and the welfare of humanity. We intend to devote ourselves to that task", said Packard in a 1961 memo to employees.

> HP believed that management should be available and involved— "Managing by wandering about" was the motto.

The duo eschewed fashionable management theory: "If I hear anybody talking about how big their share of the market is or what they're trying to do to increase their share of the market, I'm going to personally see that a black mark gets put in their personnel folder."

Respect for the Individual. The company believed that people could be trusted and should always be treated with respect and dignity.

"We both felt fundamentally that people want to do a good job. They just need guidelines on how to do it."

HP believed that management should be available and involved—"Managing by wandering about" was the motto.

Rather than the administrative suggestions of management, Packard preferred to talk of leadership.

If there was conflict, the company decided, it would be tackled through communication and consensus rather than confrontation.

Their legacy, and Packard's proudest achievement, is a management style based on openness and respect for the individual.

Keeping It Small. Hewlett-Packard was a company built on very simple ideas. While competitors were turning into conglomerates, Hewlett and Packard kept their heads down and continued with their methods.

When their divisions grew too big (around 1,500 people) they split them up to ensure that they didn't spiral out of control.

They didn't do anything too risky or too outlandish. Packard was skeptical about pocket calculators though in the end the company was an early entrant into the market.

They didn't risk the company on a big deal or get into debt.

Commitment to Values. Their values worked to save the company when times were hard. During the 1970s recession, Hewlett-Packard staff took a 10% pay cut and worked 10% fewer hours.

As the book documents, if the company hadn't had a long-term commitment to employee stock ownership, perhaps employees wouldn't have been so willing to make sacrifices. Packard claims that commitment to people clearly fostered commitment to the company.

Context

Hewlett-Packard has pulled off an unusual double—it is admired and successful. When they were assembling their list of excellent companies in the late 1970s, Tom Peters and Robert Waterman included Hewlett-Packard. When Jerry Porras and James Collins wrote *Built to Last*, their celebration of long-lived companies, there was no doubt that Hewlett-Packard was worthy of inclusion. In the same vein, in 1985, *Fortune* ranked Hewlett-Packard as one of the two most highly-admired companies in the United States. The company is ranked similarly in virtually every other poll on well-managed companies or ones that would be good to work for.

"Wherever you go in the HP empire, you find people talking product quality, feeling proud of their division's achievements in that area. HP people at all levels show boundless energy and enthusiasm," observed Tom Peters and Robert Waterman in *In Search of Excellence*.

According to Louise Kehoe in the *Financial Times*, "Their legacy, and the achievement that Packard was most proud of, is a management style based on openness and respect for the individual."

For More Information

Packard, David. *The HP Way*. New York: HarperBusiness, 1995.

The Human Problems of an Industrial Civilization

by Elton Mayo

The author was part of the team conducting the Hawthorne Studies at Western Electric's Chicago plant between 1927 and 1932, early studies into motivation in the workplace. The book shows the important link between work force morale and organizational performance, and paved the way for policies and management theories based on teamwork and effective communication.

Getting Started

The Hawthorne Studies offered important insights into the motivation of workers:

- people and their motivation were critical to the success of any business;
- there was a link between morale and output—changes in working conditions led to increased output;
- it is important to restore humanity to the workplace.

Workers selected for a test felt that more attention was being paid to them. They felt chosen, and so responded positively. The feeling of belonging to a cohesive group led to an increase in productivity. Informal organizations between groups are a potentially powerful force.

Contribution

The Hawthorne Studies. According to Mayo, the studies offered important insights into the motivation of workers. It was found that changes in working conditions led to increased output, even if the changes didn't obviously improve working conditions.

Whatever the dictates of mass production and scientific management, people and their motivation were critical to the success of any business.

The Link Between Morale and Output. The researchers were interested in exploring the links between morale and output. The author documents how five women workers were removed to a test room and observed as they worked. The research was initially restricted to physical and technical variables. Sociological factors were not expected to be of any significance. The results proved otherwise.

> Mayo champions the case for teamworking and for improved communications between management and the work force.

Removed from their colleagues, the morale of the "guinea pigs" improved. By virtue of their selection, the women felt that more attention was being paid to them.

The Importance of Group Cohesion. Mayo reports that the feeling of belonging to a cohesive group led to an increase in productivity. "The desire to stand well with one's fellows, the so-called human instinct of association, easily outweighs the merely individual interest and the logic of reasoning upon which so many spurious principles of management are based," commented Mayo.

Mayo champions the case for teamworking and for improved communications between management and the work force.

The Hawthorne research revealed informal organizations between groups as a potentially powerful force, which companies could make use of or ignore at their peril.

Restoring Humanity to the Workplace. Mayo's belief that humanity needed to be restored to the workplace struck a chord at a time when the dehumanizing side of mass production was beginning to be more fully appreciated.

"So long as commerce specializes in business methods which take no account of human nature and social motives, so long may we expect strikes and sabotage to be the ordinary accompaniment of industry," Mayo notes.

The research assumed that the behavior of workers was dictated by the "logic of sentiment," while that of the bosses was driven by the "logic of cost and efficiency."

Context

The author is known for his contribution to the famous Hawthorne experiments into the motivation of workers.

The experiments were carried out in 1927–32 at the Chicago division of Western Electric. Although they were celebrated as a major event, their significance lay not so much in their results and discoveries but in the statement they made—that people and their motivation were critical to the success of any business.

The findings influenced the human relations school of thinkers, including Herzberg, McGregor, and Maslow, which emerged in the 1940s and 1950s.

The work of the Hawthorne researchers redressed the balance in management theorizing, and the scientific bias of earlier researchers was put into a new perspective.

For More Information

Mayo, Elton. *The Human Problems of an Industrial Civilization*. New York: Macmillan, 1933.

The Human Side of Enterprise
by Douglas McGregor

McGregor was a key member of the human relations school of management whose work significantly influenced management styles from the 1960s on. His most famous concept is "Theories X and Y" which describe two extreme approaches to managing people. The book highlights the potential for a more enlightened approach to human relations management and paved the way for approaches such as empowerment and the learning organization.

Getting Started

Management assumptions about controlling human resources determine an organization's character. Theory X assumes that workers are inherently lazy, needing to be supervised and motivated. Authority is the central, indispensable means of managerial control. Theory Y assumes that people want and need to work and organizations should develop employees' commitment. McGregor argues that the average human being learns, under the right conditions, not only to accept but to seek responsibility.

Contribution

The Importance of Human Resources According to the book, the assumptions management holds about controlling its human resources determine the whole character of the enterprise.

Theory X—A Traditional Management Approach. Theory X is built on the assumption that workers are inherently lazy, need to be supervised and motivated, and regard work as a necessary evil.

The Assumptions behind Theory X.

- People inherently dislike work and will avoid it if they can.
- People need to be coerced, controlled, directed, and threatened with punishment into making adequate effort toward the organization's ends.
- People lack ambition, preferring to be directed and to avoid responsibility. Above all they want security.

The Influence of Theory X. The assumption that authority is the central, indispensable means of managerial control pervades U.S. industry. In the author's view, this is a consequence not of human nature, but of management philosophy, policy, and practice. It is not people who have made organizations, but organizations that have transformed the perspectives, aspirations, and behavior of people.

Theory Y—A Humanist Approach. Theory Y is based on the principle that people want and need to work. An organization needs to develop the individual's commitment to its objectives, and then to liberate his or her abilities on behalf of those objectives.

The Assumptions behind Theory Y.

- Work is as natural as play or rest—the typical human doesn't inherently dislike work.
- External control and threat of punishment are not the only means for bringing about effort.

- Commitment to objectives is a function of the rewards associated with their achievement.
- The most important reward is the satisfaction of ego, which can be the direct product of effort directed toward an organization's purposes.
- The average human being learns not only to accept, but to seek responsibility.
- The capacity to use imagination, ingenuity, and creativity in the solution of organizational problems is widely distributed in the population.

Toward the Learning Manager. McGregor suggests that four kinds of learning are relevant for managers:

- intellectual knowledge
- manual skills
- problem-solving skills
- social interaction

Assessing Behavior. Normal teaching and learning methods ignore social skills. "We normally get little feedback of real value concerning the impact of our behavior on others. If they don't behave as we desire, it is easy to blame their stupidity, their adjustment, or their peculiarities. Above all it isn't considered good taste to give this kind of feedback in most social settings. Instead, it is discussed by our colleagues when we are not present to learn about it," says McGregor.

Context

Despite publishing little in his short life, McGregor's work remains significant. His classic study of work and motivation reflected the concerns of the middle and late 1960s, when the monolithic corporation was at its most dominant and the world at its most questioning. The common complaint against Theories X and Y is that they are mutually exclusive. To counter this McGregor was developing "Theory Z" when he died in 1964: a theory that synthesized the organizational and personal imperatives. William Ouchi later seized on the concept of Theory Z. In his book of the same name, he analyzed Japanese working methods. Here he found fertile ground for many of the ideas McGregor was proposing:

- lifetime employment;
- concern for employees including their social life;
- informal control;
- decisions made by consensus;
- slow promotion;
- excellent transmittal of information with the help of middle management;
- commitment to the firm;
- high concern for quality.

Leading author Gary Hamel commented: "Over the last forty years, we have been slowly abandoning a view of human beings as nothing more than warm-blooded cogs in the industrial machine. People can be trusted; people want to do the right thing; people are capable of imagination and ingenuity—these were McGregor's fundamental premises, and they underlie the work of modern management thinkers from Drucker to Deming to Peters, and the employment practices of the world's most progressive and successful companies."

For More Information

McGregor, Douglas. *The Human Side of Enterprise.* New York: McGraw-Hill, 1960.

In Search of Excellence

by Tom Peters and Robert Waterman

In Search of Excellence is the most popular management book of recent times. Appearing when Japanese competition had brought Western business low, it gave managers new heart and a new direction, reminding them, in Gary Hamel's words, "that success often comes from doing common things uncommonly well."

Getting Started

The book emerged from research conducted by Peters and Waterman with the consulting firm, McKinsey. They identified excellent companies, then sought to distill lessons from their behavior and performance.

The sample was eventually whittled down to 62 (which were not intended to be perfectly representative). The choices were largely unsurprising, including the likes of IBM, Hewlett-Packard, Wal-Mart, and General Electric. The emphasis was exclusively on big companies.

There is a certain irony here. Although it celebrated big manufacturing businesses, the book condemned the excesses of dispassionate modern management practice and advocated a return to simpler virtues. The authors later came to feel that their ideas were better embodied in smaller companies.

Contribution

Success Builds on First Principles. The book attacks the excesses of the rational model and the business strategy paradigm that had come to dominate Western management thinking.

It counsels a return to first principles:

- attention to customers;
- an abiding concern for people (productivity through people);
- the celebration of trial and error (a bias for action).

"The excellent companies really are close to their customers. That's it. Other companies talk about it; the excellent companies do it."

Achieve Productivity through People. The authors quote a General Motors worker laid off after 16 years making Pontiacs: "I guess I was laid off because I make poor quality cars. But in 16 years, not once was I ever asked for a suggestion as to how to do my job better. Not once."

Excellent companies encourage and nurture an entrepreneurial spirit among all employees.

The Management Role. The real role of the chief executive is to manage the values of the organization. Executives nurture and sustain corporate values. Rather than being distant figureheads, they should be there making things happen.

The word "manager" in lip-service institutions often has come to mean not someone who rolls up his or her sleeves to get the job done right alongside the worker, but someone who hires assistants to do it.

Keep Things Simple. Excellent companies "stick to the knitting." They remain fixated on what they know they are good at and are not easily distracted.

One of their key attributes is that they have realized the importance of keeping things simple, despite overwhelming pressures to complicate things.

The authors explain what they call the "smart–dumb rule" as follows.

"Many of today's managers . . . may be a little bit too smart for their own good. The smart ones . . . shift direction all the time, based upon the latest output from the expected value equation [and] have 200-page strategic plans and 500-page market requirement documents that are but one step in product development exercises. Our dumber friends are different. They just don't understand why every customer can't get personalized service, even in the potato chip business."

Become Simultaneously Loose and Tight. The debate about how to become loose and tight (controlled and empowered; big yet small) has dominated much subsequent business writing. The authors recommend new concepts that should be added to the management vocabulary. Each one turns the tables on conventional wisdom, implying both the absence of clear directions and the simultaneous need for action. They include:

- temporary structures
- ad hoc groups
- fluid organizations
- internal competition
- product champions
- skunk works

Context

Peter Drucker suggested that the book's simplicity explained its appeal: "The strength of the Peters book is that it forces you to look at the fundamentals. The book's great weakness—which is a strength from the point of view of its success—is that it makes managing sound so incredibly easy."

Gary Hamel said, "The dividing line between simple truths, and simplistic prescription is always a thin one. For the most part, Peters and Waterman avoided the facile and the tautological. Indeed, the focus on operations research, elaborate planning systems, and (supposedly) rigorous financial analysis had, in many companies, robbed management of its soul—and certainly had taken the focus off the customer."

For such a trailblazing book, it is surprisingly uncontroversial. Peters and Waterman admit that what they have to say is not particularly original. They commented that the ideas they were espousing had been generally left behind, ignored, or overlooked by management theorists.

The criteria for selecting excellence were debatable, as all criteria are, and set the authors up for criticism when their excellent companies fell from grace. In 1984 *BusinessWeek* revealed that some had speedily declined into mediocrity and, in some cases, abject failure. But Peters and Waterman had already provided a warning: "We are asked how we know that the companies we have defined as culturally innovative will stay that way. The answer is we don't."

In Search of Excellence created the impetus for the subsequent deluge of business books and, in the business world, established customer service as a key form of differentiation and advantage.

For More Information

Peters, Tom, and Robert Waterman. *In Search of Excellence*. New York: Harper & Row, 1982.

Information Rules

by Carl Shapiro and Hal R. Varian

The economy is increasingly dominated by information-based products and services. There has been a tendency to believe that companies can ignore the old rules of economics and substitute new ways of marketing and doing business. The authors urge a more cautious approach, explaining that the basics of business have not changed. However, the existing rules need to be adapted to the new marketplace. They offer practical advice, backed by case studies, on ways to develop strategies for the new economy that are based on sound business principles.

Getting Started

Information, according to Shapiro and Varian, is any product or service that can be digitized. It is costly to produce but cheap to reproduce, and it has different values for different people. They believe that information has to be carefully managed to maximize its potential value. The Internet may provide the technological infrastructure needed for instant delivery to users, but there are other related technologies, such as payment mechanisms, that are essential to the profitable development of an information economy.

Contribution

Information Pricing. The cost of production, say the authors, is dominated by first-copy costs; reproduction and distribution cost very little. There are no production constraints on producing very large or very small quantities. One million copies of a software product have the same unit cost as ten million copies.

This pricing structure, they claim, leads to two business models for an information market:

- the dominant firm model;
- the differential product model, where many firms produce competing versions of the same information.

Companies in a dominant firm market must, they argue, strive for cost leadership. In a differentiated market, companies need to add value and protect their intellectual property rights. They point out that even a commodity product can be differentiated by organizing it differently for different users. Personalizing information takes this process to its logical conclusion.

They offer three approaches to information pricing:

- personalized pricing, tailored to individual users;
- version pricing, where users choose their preferred version;
- group pricing, aimed at discrete groups such as students or companies with large numbers of users.

Personalized pricing, they claim, can be refined by the information available on customer buying habits. Group pricing is particularly effective where a product, such as software, is sold in very large numbers and effectively creates a standard that locks customers in.

Versions of Information. The authors argue that producing different versions of the same information can broaden the market. Products can be differentiated by features, availability, support levels, and quality. A "high-end" version would have all the important features; other versions would have fewer. The authors recommend offering three versions, with the middle version likely to be the most popular.

"Bundling" is another method of versioning, where producers put together distinct but related products at a discount price. Bundling software products, experience indicates, produces more overall revenue.

Information Rights Management. Shapiro and Varian point out that information, or intellectual property, should be managed and protected. Free content, they say, can act as an effective method of sampling chargeable information. Many publishers, for example, provide free executive summaries and charge for access to the complete work. As most Internet users read only a few pages, free content is unlikely to reduce overall sales.

Information Lock-in. The authors explain how certain types of information can lock a customer in to a supplier. With products that require a great deal of training, the cost of switching supplier can be prohibitively high. They recommend building a large base of customers, putting a value on that base and then maximizing its value by offering a continuous stream of new products.

The Economics of Networks. The information economy is driven by the economics of networks. Positive feedback helps to build and sustain networks. Once a product gains wide acceptance, the positive feedback encourages or forces suppliers of related products to design products that are compatible. The authors call this demand-side preference. Customers like standardization.

Compatibility is the key factor in creating networks of suppliers developing products to the same standard. The authors compare openness to building standards. Openness appears to open the door for competitors, but it also encourages more suppliers to join the network and add weight to the standard.

The Importance of Cooperation. Shapiro and Varian point out that standards and the development of networks encourage cooperation between companies who would normally be regarded as competitors. They use the term "complementors" to describe companies who benefit from each other's products—computer manufacturers and software developers are an example. Cooperation is an important part of the information economy, and the objective of dominant firms in a network is to build strong alliances so that they can offer their customers total solutions.

Context

Media hype about digital companies led to the dot-com boom in the late 1990s, a boom that was based on the belief that the old rules of business had been blown away by new media companies. The subsequent dot-com collapse showed that basic principles still applied.

Information Rules is the first book to compare the economics of the new information economy with traditional economics. The authors take a classical economics approach, but include many practical examples of the new rules in action. Books such as *Being Digital* by Nicholas Negroponte (Knopf, 1995) have explained the nature of digital information, while Nalebuff and Brandenburger's *Co-opetition* (HarperCollins Business, 1996) looks at cooperation and complementary business in the information economy.

For More Information

Shapiro, Carl, and Hal R. Varian. *Information Rules: A Strategic Guide to the Network Economy.* Boston, MA: Harvard Business School Press, 1998.

Innovation in Marketing

by Theodore Levitt

Levitt's views on the importance of marketing are highly regarded. His article "Marketing Myopia" (reprinted in the book) was one of the most popular *Harvard Business Review* articles ever published. It highlights how narrow perspectives result from companies focusing on production rather than customers.

Getting Started

Historical success encouraged the belief that low-cost production was the key to success, but this inevitably leads to narrow perspectives. In the author's view, companies must broaden their view of the nature of their business, and should be marketing-led rather than production-led. The emphasis is on providing customer-creating value satisfactions.

There is no such thing as a growth industry: success comes from being perceptive enough to spot where future growth may lie. Companies fail because they assume continued growth, believe that a product cannot be improved, and concentrate on improved production techniques to deliver lower costs. Mass-production industries aim to produce all they can and marketing gets neglected.

Contribution

A Focus on Customers. Levitt argues that the central preoccupation of corporations should be with satisfying customers rather than simply producing goods. Companies should be marketing-led rather than production-led. Management must think of itself not as producing products but as providing customer-creating value satisfactions. The lead must come from the chief executive and senior management.

Problems of Production-led Companies. Henry Ford's success in mass production fueled the belief that low-cost production was the key to business success. Ford continued to believe that he knew what customers wanted, long after they had decided otherwise.

Production-led thinking inevitably leads to narrow perspectives.

Narrow Perspectives. Companies must broaden their view of the nature of their business; otherwise their customers will soon be forgotten. The railroads are in trouble today not because the need was filled by others, but because it was not filled by the railroads themselves. They let others take customers away from them because they assumed they were in the railroad business rather than in the transportation business—they were product-oriented instead of customer-oriented.

The railroad business was constrained by a lack of willingness to expand its horizons. Similarly, the movie industry failed to respond to the growth of television because it regarded itself as being in the business of making movies rather than providing entertainment.

Taking Growth for Granted. Growth can never be taken for granted, asserts the author. There is no such thing as a growth industry—growth is a matter of being perceptive enough to spot where future growth may lie.

History is filled with companies that fall undetected into decay for these reasons:

- they assume that the growth in their particular market will continue for as long as the population grows in size and wealth;
- they believe that a product cannot be surpassed;
- they tend to put faith in the ability of improved production techniques to deliver lower costs and, therefore, higher profits.

Problems of Mass-production Industries. Mass-production industries are impelled by a great drive to produce all they can. The prospect of steeply declining unit costs as output rises is more than most companies can usually resist. The profit possibilities look spectacular, so all effort focuses on production.

Concentration on the product, in Levitt's view, also lends itself to measurement and analysis. The result is that marketing gets neglected.

Distinguishing Selling and Marketing. There is a distinction between the tasks of selling and marketing. Selling concerns itself with the tricks and techniques of getting people to exchange their cash for your product—it is not concerned with the values that the exchange is all about. It does not, as marketing invariably does, view the entire business process as consisting of a tightly integrated effort to discover, create, arouse, and satisfy customer needs.

> There is a distinction between the tasks of selling and marketing.

Context

Ted Levitt's fame was secured early in his career with "Marketing Myopia"—a *Harvard Business Review* article which enjoyed unprecedented success and attention, selling over 500,000 reprints.

It has since been reproduced in virtually every collection of key marketing texts. "Marketing Myopia" is a manifesto rather than a deeply academic article. It embraces ideas that had already been explored by others (Levitt acknowledges his debt to Peter Drucker's *The Practice of Management*).

In the 1980s, when marketing underwent a resurgence, companies began to heed Levitt's view that they were too heavily oriented toward production. Levitt's article and his subsequent work pushed marketing to center stage. In some cases it led to what Levitt called marketing mania, with companies obsessively responsive to every fleeting whim of the customer.

Many of today's leading thinkers, such as Pascale and Peters, continually re-emphasize Levitt's message that there is no such thing as a growth industry.

Influential writer Gary Hamel said: "If Ted Levitt had done nothing else in his career—and he did plenty—he would have earned his keep on this planet with the article 'Marketing Myopia.' Managers get wrapped up inside their products (railroads) and lose sight of the fundamental benefits customers are seeking (transportation). Equally provocative was Ted's 1983 *Harvard Business Review* article, 'The Globalization of Markets.' While some argue that markets will never become truly global, there are few companies that are betting against the general trend."

For More Information

Levitt, Theodore. *Innovation in Marketing*. New York: McGraw-Hill, 1962.

The Innovator's Dilemma
by Clayton M. Christensen

Christensen's book faces up to a fundamental problem facing innovative companies—how to deal with breakthrough technologies when customers may not be ready for them. It argues that normal practice—focusing investment and development on the most profitable products, those that are in demand among top customers—may ultimately be damaging. The risk is that companies may reject innovative products that do not meet this criterion. Christensen explains how to overcome this problem and manage breakthrough products successfully.

Getting Started

Christensen examines a variety of leading, well-managed companies that have failed to capitalize on innovative technologies. The dilemma is that it is often sound decisions by good managers that lead to failure. The author distinguishes between sustaining technologies, which foster improved performance, and disruptive technologies, which represent a breakthrough, but may initially lead to poorer performance. Examples of disruptive technologies include cell phones, digital photography, and online retailing.

Part of the problem, according to Christensen, is that the market may not be ready for the new technology. In other cases, leading customers may not be willing to risk a new product. Companies therefore focus on the safe bets, but may subsequently be overtaken by innovation.

Contribution

Control by Customers. The disk drive industry shows the dilemma in action. The author explains how the major players in the industry used sustaining technologies to offer their customers improved performance.

New entrants introduced disruptive technologies, such as smaller floppy discs that required new computer architecture. These innovations were, however, initially rejected by customers until they became a proven technology. The author concludes that, to a degree, the larger companies were controlled by their customers.

Value Networks. Christensen offers a possible explanation for failure in these cases—the concept of the "value network." This is a technique companies can use to assess the value of a new technology in relation to their current business and customer base. It asks what rewards the company would obtain from reallocating resources away from mainstream products.

The author believes that the problem is compounded by the scope of the company's suppliers and subcontractors. Each may have its own value network based on the needs of its own customers. Innovative ideas that come up from subcontractors may be stifled in the same way as internal ideas.

The author explains how the cost and profit structures in a value network can limit the attractiveness of an innovation. If profit margins are low, the emphasis will be on cost cutting across proven technologies. Innovation would be too risky. The other response from established companies is to move upmarket where they can earn more from existing products.

Avoiding Risk. Christensen points out that new entrants have frequently forced the pace of innovation with disruptive technologies. Established companies only moved in when there was a definite market. Disruptive technologies do not initially represent large, high-margin opportunities for established companies, and the decision-making structure can rule out innovative ideas.

The author cites five reasons why successful companies fail to capitalize on disruptive technologies:

- customers control the pattern of resource allocation;
- small markets do not solve the growth needs of large companies;
- it can be difficult to identify applications in advance;
- larger organizations rely on their core competencies and values;
- technology supply may not equal market demand.

The Importance of Spinoffs. Christensen explains how companies who did harness disruptive technologies used a number of management techniques:

- projects were handled within another "spinoff organization" that had customers who needed the new technology;
- those same project organizations could get excited about small markets and small wins;
- failure was an acceptable part of the process as companies proceeded by trial and error to the right solution;
- companies looked for new markets and developed the market where the disruptive technology offered value.

The author gives examples of large corporations that have established spinoff companies to exploit new technology. Frequently, the corporation pulls the spinoff back into the core business when it proves successful.

Context

The book claims that overdependence on customer needs can affect a company's success. This argument runs counter to the marketing and customer service books that put customer focus at the top of the corporate agenda.

Books such as *When Giants Learn to Dance* by Rosabeth Moss Kanter (Touchstone, 1990) have pointed out the problems faced by larger corporations that compete in fast-moving technology markets. Christensen's book is unusual in highlighting the problems inherent in what appears to be sound decision making.

For More Information

Christensen, Clayton M. *The Innovator's Dilemma: When New Technologies Cause Great Firms to Fail.* Boston: Harvard Business School Press, 1997.

Intellectual Capital

by Thomas Stewart

The author is widely regarded as the world's leading authority on knowledge management, and his views are valuable to any organization that wants to improve the return on its "intellectual capital." The book is a useful guide to the strategic and practical issues of identifying, capturing, and using knowledge to improve competitive advantage.

Getting Started

Traditional capital had financial or physical characteristics. In the author's view, however, the emphasis now is on an intangible asset, intellectual capital, consisting of human capital, customer capital, and structural capital.

Human capital resides in the heads of employees; customer capital represents the value of a company's ongoing relationships with customers; and structural capital is the knowledge retained within the organization.

The real value comes in being able to capture and deploy intellectual capital, Stewart argues. However, you cannot define and manage intellectual assets unless you know what you want to do with them. Knowledge working will change individual career patterns in the 21st century.

Contribution

The New Concept of Capital. Traditionally, capital could be viewed in purely financial or physical terms. It showed up in the buildings and equipment owned, and could be found in the corporate balance sheets.

The author suggests that in recent times, the emphasis has switched to an intangible form of asset, intellectual capital. Intellectual capital can be broken down into three areas: human capital; customer capital; and structural capital.

Human Capital. Human capital is the knowledge residing in the heads of employees that is relevant to the purpose of the organization.

Human capital is formed and deployed when more of the time and talent of employees is devoted to activities that result in innovation. It can grow in two ways: when the organization uses more of what people know; or when people know more that is useful to the organization. Unleashing it requires an organization to minimize mindless tasks, meaningless paperwork, and unproductive infighting.

Customer Capital. This represents the value of a company's ongoing relationships with the people or organizations to which it sells. Indicators of customer capital include market share, customer retention and defection rates, and profit per customer.

Customer capital is probably the worst managed of all intangible assets. Many businesses don't even know who their customers are.

Structural Capital. Structural capital is the knowledge retained within the organization. It belongs to the company as a whole and can be reproduced and shared. It includes technologies, inventions, publications, and business processes.

Managing Intellectual Capital. The real value comes in being able to capture and deploy intellectual capital. Knowledge assets exist and are worth cultivating only in the context of strategy. You cannot define and manage intellectual assets unless you know what you want to do with them.

There are ten principles for managing intellectual capital:

- Companies don't own human and customer capital. Only by recognizing the shared nature of these assets can a company manage and profit from them.
- To create usable human capital, a company needs to foster teamwork, communities of practice, and other social forms of learning.
- Organizational wealth is created around skills and talents that are proprietary and scarce. Companies view people with these talents as assets to invest in.
- Structural assets are the easiest to manage but those that customers care least about.
- Move from amassing knowledge "just in case" to having readily available information that customers need.
- Information and knowledge can and should substitute for expensive physical and financial assets.
- Knowledge work is custom work.
- Every company should reanalyze its own industry to see what information is most crucial.
- Focus on the flow of information not the flow of materials.
- Human, structural, and customer capital work together. It is not enough to invest in people, systems, and customers separately.

Knowledge Working and Individual Careers. Stewart argues that careers in the 21st century will have a number of characteristics:

- A career is a series of gigs, not a series of steps.
- Project management is the furnace in which successful careers are made.
- Power flows from expertise, not from position.
- Most roles in an organization can be performed by either insiders or outsiders.
- Careers are made in markets not hierarchies.
- The fundamental career choice is not between one company and another, but between specializing and generalizing.

Context

Thomas Stewart pioneered the field of intellectual capital in a series of articles that earned him an international reputation, and *Intellectual Capital* has proved itself as the definitive guide to understanding and managing intangible assets. It not only explains why intellectual capital will be the foundation of corporate success in the new century, but also offers practical guidance to companies about how to make best use of their intangible assets. Since it first appeared, there have been a flood of books on knowledge management.

The term "knowledge worker" is not a new one. In 1994, Peter Drucker wrote that, "the true investment in the knowledge society is not in machines and tools but in the knowledge of the knowledge worker. In the knowledge society the most probable assumption for organizations . . . is that they need knowledge workers far more than knowledge workers need them."

For More Information

Stewart, Thomas. *Intellectual Capital: The New Wealth of Organizations*. New York: Doubleday, 1997.

The Knowledge-Creating Company
by Ikujiro Nonaka and Hirotaka Takeuchi

The book focuses on the development of organizational knowledge in Japanese companies. The authors explain how this knowledge forms the basis of innovations that have enabled Japanese companies to become leaders in many different market sectors. They show that the ability to acquire and apply knowledge is becoming a key factor for success in the transition from an industrial economy to an information economy.

Getting Started
Nonaka and Takeuchi believe that historical adversity has forced Japanese companies to pursue a policy of continuous innovation. Organizational knowledge, according to them, is the ability of a company to create new knowledge, disseminate it throughout the organization, and embody it in innovative products, services, and systems. They distinguish between explicit knowledge, such as rules or formulas, and tacit knowledge, which is gained from experience and can rarely be learned. The Japanese, they claim, are very effective at turning tacit knowledge into explicit knowledge that can be shared throughout an organization.

Contribution
Characteristics of Knowledge Creation. According to the authors, there are three key characteristics of knowledge creation:
- metaphor and analogy
- the transition from personal to organizational knowledge
- ambiguity and redundancy

The use of metaphor and analogy helps companies to visualize difficult concepts and explain them to other people within an organization. The transition from personal to organizational knowledge depends on the successful implementation of teamwork so that individuals can interact with each other. The acceptance of ambiguity and redundancy means that Japanese companies are happy to take a number of different approaches to innovation, some of which are bound to fail. They use redundancy to encourage creativity and identify what does not work in practical terms.

Knowledge Management. The authors review theories of knowledge from ancient times onward. They analyze recent management writing to identify attitudes toward the question of knowledge. They cite Peter Drucker's "knowledge worker" and Peter Senge's "learning organization" as important concepts in knowledge creation. They also discuss the concept of core competencies and argue that this can distract companies. Core competencies, they argue, suggest that knowledge is an existing, finite resource within a company. Knowledge creation, on the other hand, emphasizes the importance of acquiring and developing knowledge from as many internal and external sources as possible.

How Knowledge Creation Works. The authors claim that there are four key processes in knowledge conversion:
- socialization
- externalization

- combination
- internalization

An example of socialization is the brainstorming camps established by Honda to solve difficult production problems. Externalization is the process of using metaphors or analogies to communicate difficult concepts in product development. Combination is the process of sorting, adding, combining, and synthesizing different types of knowledge to create new knowledge. Internalization is like relearning other people's experiences or learning by doing.

The Environment for Knowledge Creation. To create a suitable environment for knowledge creation, the authors stress the importance of vision to guide overall direction and autonomy to allow everyone in the organization to get involved in the process.

They describe a structure called "middle-up-down management" that underpins knowledge creation. This structure contrasts with the bottom-up or top-down management styles found in Western companies. The Japanese model puts middle managers at the heart of the process, acting between front-line workers and a visionary senior management team. The authors believe that this type of structure creates dialog and builds relationships between the individual specialists who contribute to a development project.

Hypertext Organizations. Nonaka and Takeuchi refer to the concept of a "knowledge crew," consisting of knowledge engineers and knowledge practitioners. Underpinning this is what they call a "hypertext organization." This is an organization with multiple layers:

- a business system layer;
- a project team layer;
- a knowledge base layer.

The business system layer and project team layer generate different types of knowledge, which are brought together in the knowledge base which can be shared throughout the organization.

Context

A number of books have looked at the process of innovation, trying to identify the factors that distinguish a successful innovator. The authors offer both theoretical and practical insight into the way that Japanese companies use knowledge as the basis for innovation. Their findings are in contrast with the widespread Western view that Japanese success is based on access to cheap capital, lifetime employment, culture, or quality.

The authors draw on a wide variety of Western management sources to highlight the differences between Japanese and Western practice. Amongst others, they quote Peter Drucker and Alvin Toffler on the importance of knowledge, and Peter Senge on the concept of the "learning organization."

For More Information

Nonaka, Ikujiro and Hirotaka Takeuchi. *The Knowledge-Creating Company: How Japanese Companies Create the Dynamics of Innovation.* New York: Oxford University Press, 1995.

Leaders: Strategies for Taking Charge

by Warren Bennis and Burt Nanus

Warren Bennis is an academic and regular presidential adviser who brought leadership to a new, mass audience. He is regarded as one of the most important contemporary thinkers.

Burt Nanus is the founder and director of the Center of Futures Research at the University of Southern California.

In this book, the authors use an eclectic selection of America's leaders to offer the readers key lessons on how to become successful. Their message is that leadership is open to all.

Getting Started

Leaders commit people to action and convert followers into leaders. They are usually ordinary people rather than particularly charismatic, as leadership is all-encompassing and open to all.

Successful leaders also have a vision that other people believe in, and communicate it effectively. Instead of being individual problem solvers, they achieve greatness through working with groups. Devising and maintaining an atmosphere in which others can succeed in the leader's creative act.

Contribution

The Ordinary Leader. In the authors' view, the new leader is one who commits people to action, who converts followers into leaders, and who may convert leaders into agents of change. Leadership is not a rare skill—leaders are made rather than born. They are usually ordinary people, or apparently ordinary, rather than charismatic. Leadership is not solely the preserve of those at the top of an organization—it is relevant at all levels. Leadership is not about control, direction, and manipulation.

Common Abilities of Leaders. From a survey of 90 U.S. leaders (including astronaut Neil Armstrong, the coach of the LA Rams, orchestral conductors, and business-people such as Ray Kroc of McDonald's), Bennis and Nanus identified four common abilities:

- management of attention
- management of meaning
- management of trust
- management of self

Management of Attention. This is a question of vision. Leadership is the capacity to create a compelling vision, translate it into action, and sustain it. Successful leaders have a vision that other people believe in and treat as their own.

Management of Meaning. A vision is of limited practical use if it is encased in 400 pages of wordy text or mumbled from behind a paper-packed desk. Effective communication relies on use of analogy, metaphor, and vivid illustration as well as emotion, trust, optimism, and hope.

Management of Trust. Trust is the emotional glue that binds followers and leaders together. Leaders have to be seen to be consistent.

Management of Self. Leaders do not glibly present charisma or time management as the essence of their success. Instead, the emphasis is on persistence and self-knowledge, commitment and challenge, taking risks and, above all, learning. The learning person looks forward to failure or mistakes, which means that the worst problem in leadership is basically early success. There's no opportunity to learn from adversity and problems.

A Positive Self-regard. Leaders have a positive self-regard, known as emotional wisdom. This is characterized by an ability to accept people as they are. They also have a capacity to approach things in terms of only the present, and an ability to treat everyone, even close contacts, with courteous attention. They need an ability to trust others, and to do without constant approval and recognition.

Leaders and Group Working. Greatness starts with superb people. Great groups don't exist without great leaders, but they give the lie to the persistent notion that successful institutions are the lengthened shadow of a great woman or man. It's not clear that life was ever so simple that individuals, acting alone, solved most significant problems. Instead of the individual problem solver, we have a new model for creative achievement.

> **Greatness starts with superb people.**

Changing Leadership Qualities. The leader is a pragmatic dreamer, a person with an original but attainable vision. He or she knows that this dream can only be realized if others are free to do exceptional work. Typically, the leader is the one who recruits the others, by making the vision so seductive that they see it too, and eagerly sign up.

Inevitably, the leader has to invent a leadership style that suits the group. The standard models, especially command and control, simply don't work. The heads of groups have to act decisively, not arbitrarily. They have to make decisions without limiting the autonomy of other participants.

The Idealistic Leader. Most organizations are dull and working life is mundane, so groups can be an inspiration. Individual leaders can create a human community that will, in the long run, lead to the best organizations. "A Great Group is more than a collection of first-rate minds. It's a miracle," say the authors. Every person has to make a genuine contribution in their lives and the institution of work is one of the main vehicles for achieving this.

Context

With the torrent of publications and executive programs on the subject, it is easy to forget that leadership had been largely overlooked as a topic worthy of serious academic interest until it was revived by Bennis and others in the 1980s. Since then, leadership has become a heavy industry. Concern and interest about leadership development are no longer an American phenomenon: they are truly global. The book stands as a humane counter to much of the military-based hero worship which dogs the subject.

For More Information

Bennis, Warren, and Burt Nanus. *Leaders: Strategies for Taking Charge*. New York: Harper & Row, 1985.

Leadership

by James MacGregor Burns

In his book *Leadership*, Burns makes an important contribution to management literature by refocusing interest on the nature of leadership. He brings practical insights from both business and politics and has used those insights to identify two key strands—transactional and transformational leadership.

Getting Started

Burns believes we know too much about our leaders, but too little about leadership. It is a structure for action. It is not the preserve of the few or the tyranny of the masses.

Burns identifies two vital strands of leadership—transformational and transactional leadership. Transactional leadership is built on reciprocity—the relationship between the leader and their followers develops from the exchange of some reward. The secret of effective leadership appears to lie in combining the two elements so that targets, results, and procedures are developed and shared.

Contribution

Problems in Defining Leadership. If we know all too much about our leaders, we know far too little about leadership. There are literally hundreds of definitions of leadership and, as a result, the concept "has dissolved into small and discrete meanings," Burns claims.

Leadership As a Structure for Action. Leadership is exercised when people with certain motives and purposes mobilize—in competition or conflict with others—institutional, political, psychological, and other resources so as to arouse, engage, and satisfy the motives of followers. Leadership is not the preserve of the few or the tyranny of the masses. The leadership approach tends often unconsciously to be elitist; it projects heroic figures against the shadowy background of drab, powerless masses. The followership approach tends to be populist or antielitist in ideology, perceiving the masses, even in democratic societies, as linked with small, overlapping circles of conservative politicians, military officers, hierocrats, and businessmen.

> Leadership is a structure for action that engages people, to varying degrees, throughout the levels and among the interstices of society.

Leadership is a structure for action that engages people, to varying degrees, throughout the levels and among the interstices of society. Only the inert, the alienated, and the powerless are unengaged. It is also intrinsically linked to morality—moral leadership emerges from, and always returns to, the fundamental wants and needs, aspirations, and values of the followers.

Transformational Leadership. Burns identifies two vital strands of leadership—transformational and transactional leadership.

Transformational leadership occurs when one or more persons engage with others in such a way that leaders and followers raise one another to higher levels of motivation and morality. Their purposes, which might have started out separate but related, become fused. Power bases are linked, not as counterweights, but as mutual support for common purpose. Various names are used for such leadership: elevating, mobilizing, inspiring, exalting, uplifting, exhorting, evangelizing.

Transformational leadership becomes moral in that it raises the level of human conduct and ethical aspiration of both the leader and the led, thus having a transforming effect on both. It is also dynamic, in the sense that the leaders throw themselves into a relationship with followers who will feel elevated by it and often become more active themselves, thereby creating new cadres of leaders.

Transformational leadership is concerned with engaging the hearts and minds of others. It works to help all parties achieve greater motivation, satisfaction, and sense of achievement. It is driven by trust, concern, and facilitation rather than direct control. The skills required are concerned with establishing a long-term vision, empowering people to control themselves, coaching and developing others, and challenging the culture to change. In transformational leadership, the power of the leader comes from creating understanding and trust.

Transactional Leadership. Transactional leadership is built on reciprocity. The relationship between the leader and his or her followers develops from the exchange of some reward, such as performance ratings, pay, recognition, and praise. It involves leaders in clarifying goals and objectives, communicating well in order to plan tasks and activities with the cooperation of their employees, so that wider organizational goals are met.

The relationship depends on hierarchy and the ability to work through the mode of exchange. It requires leadership skills such as the ability to obtain results, to control through structures and processes, to solve problems, to plan and organize, and to work within the structures and boundaries of the organization.

Combining Transformational and Transactional Leadership. In their apparent mutual exclusiveness, transformational and transactional leadership are akin to Douglas McGregor's Theories X and Y. The secret of effective leadership appears to lie in combining the two elements so that targets, results, and procedures are developed and shared.

Context

Burns's book provides an important link between leadership in the political and business worlds. For all the books on leadership, the two have usually been regarded as mutually exclusive. His examination of transformational and transactional leadership also stimulated further debate on leadership at a time when it was somewhat neglected. In the 1980s, it returned to prominence in management literature as a subject worthy of study.

Business guru Gary Hamel commented, "There is no theme in management literature which is more enduring than leadership. Among the many contributions which Burns makes to our understanding of leadership, two seem central: leadership must have a moral foundation; and the responsibility for leadership must be widely distributed. Self-interested autocrats, whether political or corporate, ignore these truths at their peril."

For More Information

Burns, James MacGregor. *Leadership*. New York: Harper & Row, 1978.

Leading Change
by John P. Kotter

Kotter is regarded as one of the world's leading figures in change management. His article, "Leading Change," published in the March–April 1995 *Harvard Business Review*, quickly became the *Review*'s best-selling reprint. Readers commented that its analysis defined the real problem of change management and found the 8-stage change framework "compelling." The book builds on the success of the article and includes dozens of examples of effective change management.

Getting Started
Kotter believes that successful change takes place when organizations operate an 8-stage process. The stages are:
1. establishing a sense of urgency;
2. creating the guiding coalition;
3. developing a vision and strategy;
4. communicating the change vision;
5. empowering employees for broad-based action;
6. generating short-term wins;
7. consolidating gains and producing more change;
8. anchoring new approaches in the culture.

Contribution
Why Change Fails. Kotter opines that most business transformations fail because they do not meet the criteria set out in his 8-point plan. These omissions would not be important in a slower-moving world, but the volatile forces of competition mean companies must change to survive and prosper. The pace of change is driven by forces such as technological development, international economic integration, the maturation of markets, and the globalization of markets and competition.

The result is that there are either more opportunities or more hazards, depending on whether an organization can adapt or not. Successful change, the sort that enables companies to grasp opportunities, goes through the 8-stage process. Kotter adds, however, that it is essential to go through all the stages in sequence. He also believes that change must be led, rather than managed.

A Sense of Urgency. Establishing a sense of urgency helps to get the cooperation needed for change. A committed group, Kotter argues, can drive change through. He suggests a number of approaches for increasing the urgency level:
- creating a vision;
- setting targets so high they cannot be achieved through business as usual;
- getting staff to talk to disgruntled customers;
- showing people that great opportunities cannot be achieved by the present organization.

Building the Guiding Coalition. Kotter's second stage is the "guiding coalition." He believes that an isolated chief executive or a weak committee cannot cope with the pace of change. The coalition must comprise people with power, expertise, credibility, and leadership. Leadership is key, because change must be led not managed. He explains why the coalition must be built on trust and a common goal, noting that team-building exercises can be an important part of that process.

Developing a Vision. According to Kotter, a vision clarifies the direction of change. Other decisions must be in line with the vision. Vision also helps to align individuals and motivate them in an efficient way. He believes that a vision should be imaginable, desirable, feasible, focused, flexible, and communicable.

Communicating Change. Kotter argues that a vision has real power only when it is communicated effectively. Effective communication is vital because employees receive vast amounts of information, and communications about change can easily get lost. Kotter's advice is to keep it simple, use metaphors, keep repeating the message, listen, and lead by example.

Empowering Employees. Turning the vision into action means removing structural barriers to change so that employees are empowered, says Kotter. That may require training, reorganization, aligning information and systems to the vision, and confronting people who try to restrict change.

Short-term Wins. According to Kotter, short-term wins are essential. They are visible and show that change is producing results. They also help to fine-tune the change process, build momentum, and reward the people who are delivering change. Pressure and challenging targets can help to deliver the gains.

Consolidating Gains. Kotter believes that all gains need to be consolidated to keep the process moving, particularly in companies where there is a high level of interdependence. Maintaining momentum also requires strong leadership, effective project management, and support for the people who are effecting change.

Anchoring Change in the Culture. The final stage in Kotter's process is anchoring the new approaches in the corporate culture. He argues that the new behavior should become the norm. Ideally, everyone in the organization should have shared values. Kotter believes that achieving this level of acceptance depends on results. It may even require changing key people.

Context

The study of change has gained importance as competition has intensified and other structural factors impact on the business environment.

Kotter's work demonstrates the positive aspects of effective change. It also shows that strong leadership is essential if change is to succeed. Rosabeth Moss Kanter's book *The Change Masters* (Touchstone, 1990) puts a similar emphasis on the importance of strategic leadership.

William Bridges, on the other hand, in *Managing Transitions* (Perseus, 1991), puts more emphasis on management of the personal consequences of change, highlighting the need to reduce anxiety and manage the process he calls "transition."

Hammer and Champy's book *Reengineering the Corporation* (HarperBusiness, 1993) took change to a logical conclusion and showed how companies would have to transform themselves to compete effectively. Unfortunately, reengineering has been widely associated with downsizing, and this has given change management negative connotations.

For More Information

Kotter, John P. *Leading Change.* Boston, MA: Harvard Business School Press, 1996.

The Living Company: Habits for Survival in a Turbulent Business Environment
by Arie de Geus

The book looks at the problem of corporate failure, presenting alarming statistics on the relatively short life of European and Japanese enterprises. The author argues that short-term focus on profits, rather than nurturing people, is a key factor in failure. *The Living Company* is the testimony of someone who practiced the human side of enterprise and who believes that companies must be fundamentally humane to prosper.

Getting Started

The author argues that corporations should last as long as two or three centuries, but the reality is that companies usually die young. And focus on profits rather than on human issues lies behind the high failure rate. However, like all organisms, the living company exists primarily for its own survival and improvement.

A successful company is one that can learn effectively, and senior executives must dedicate a great deal of time to nurturing their people.

Contribution

The Problem of Corporate Morality. Companies may be legal entities, but they are disturbingly mortal. The natural average lifespan of a corporation should be as long as two or three centuries—for example, the Sumitomo Group and the Scandinavian company, Stora.

The reality is that companies usually die young. A Dutch survey indicated 12.5 years as the average life expectancy of all Japanese and European firms. The average life expectancy of a multinational corporation—Fortune 500 or its equivalent—is between 40 and 50 years.

Reasons for Longevity. The high company failure rate is attributed to the focus of managers on profits, rather than on the human community that makes up their organization.

In an attempt to get to the bottom of this mystery, de Geus and a number of his Shell colleagues carried out some research to identify the characteristics of corporate longevity. As you would expect, the onus is on keeping excitement to a minimum. The average human centenarian advocates a life of abstinence, caution, and moderation; and so it is with companies.

The research team identified four key characteristics. The long-lived companies were:

- sensitive to their environment;
- cohesive, with a strong sense of identity;
- tolerant;
- conservative in financing.

The Importance of People. There is more to a company and to its longevity than mere money making. The skills, capabilities, and knowledge of people are paramount; capital is no longer king.

The Learning Company. A successful company is one that can learn effectively. Learning means being prepared to accept continuous change, and a company can only change if its community of people changes.

> Individuals change through learning—requiring senior executives to dedicate a great deal of time to nurturing their people.

Individuals change through learning—requiring senior executives to dedicate a great deal of time to nurturing their people. The author recalls spending around a quarter of his time on the development and placement of people; while C.E.O. of GE, Jack Welch claimed to spend half of his time on such issues.

According to de Geus, all corporate activities are grounded in two hypotheses:

- the company is a living being;
- the decisions for action made by this living being result from a learning process.

Like all organisms, the living company exists primarily for its own survival and improvement. It aims to fulfill its potential and to become as great as it can be.

Context

With its faith in learning, *The Living Company* represents a careful and powerful riposte to corporate nihilism.

The book proposes that the wisdom of the past be appreciated and used, rather than cast out in the manner of a cultural revolution.

Contrast this with reengineering, which sought to dismiss the past so that the future could begin with a blank piece of paper. De Geus suggests that the piece of paper already exists, and notes are constantly being scrawled in the margins as new insights are added.

De Geus's arguments are probably at their weakest when he contemplates why companies deserve to live long lives. The average entrepreneur would probably accept a corporate life expectancy of 12.5 years.

The Living Company is the testimony of someone who practiced the human side of enterprise, and who believes that companies must be fundamentally humane to prosper—whatever the century.

For More Information

de Geus, Arie. *The Living Company: Habits for Survival in a Turbulent Business Environment.* Boston, MA: Harvard Business School Press, 1997.

The Machine That Changed the World

by James P. Womack, Daniel T. Jones, and Daniel Roos

Lean production was Japan's secret weapon in the trade war, and it went on to conquer the world. In 1984 a team of researchers at the Massachusetts Institute of Technology (MIT) undertook a study of the phenomenon. Within the framework of an analysis of the situation and problems of car manufacturers worldwide, Womack, Jones, and Roos examined the differences between mass production and lean production. This widely read and wisely praised book presents their findings.

Getting Started

A new form of manufacturing—lean production—is about to supersede the mass production of goods, the authors announce. Lean production can simultaneously double productivity, improve quality, and keep costs low. The book recounts the history of the rise of lean production, describes its essential elements, and presents the prospects for the spread of this revolutionary management initiative.

Contribution

The Beginnings of Lean Production. In 1950 Eiji Toyoda, a Japanese engineer whose family had founded the Toyota Motor Company, and Toyota's production manager, Taiichi Ohno, visited the Ford motor works in Detroit, then the biggest and most efficient production plant in the world. The basis of the Ford system was a complete division of labor among a wide variety of specialist operatives. The conveyor belt could never be halted; faults were dealt with in postproduction.

Toyoda and Ohno felt that there was waste throughout this system: wasted labor, wasted materials, wasted time. Apart from the assemblers, none of the specialists created any value for the car.

On his return, Ohno grouped his workers in teams, to whom he delegated more tasks and who were to work together on improvements. Each worker had a duty to halt the production line if a problem arose that he or she could not deal with. The whole team would then trace the fault back to its ultimate cause and then think up a solution that would ensure it never happened again. The remedial work required before dispatch was thus reduced to zero, and lean production, the authors say, was born.

The Elements of Lean Production. The first element in lean production is the organization of the assembly works. A lean factory, the authors report, has two main organizational characteristics. First, it allots a maximum number of tasks and responsibilities to those workers who create actual value in the product on the line. Secondly, it has a fault detection system installed that quickly traces each fault back to its source.

The second element in lean production is product development. Lean production, the authors say, is quicker than mass production. The reason lies in basic differences in construction methods.

- Project leadership works on the *susha* system. The *susha* is the team leader, a position of great power in Japanese businesses. In mass-production companies the system is very different. The position of the development manager is too weak to push projects through. Top management often overrides his or her decisions.

- The *susha* creates a small, close-knit team, whose members are drawn from various specialist departments and who remain in contact with them. For the duration of the development project, however, they remain wholly under the control of the *susha*. In mass-production business, development teams consist of individuals on short-term loan from specialist departments.
- Communication too is different, say the authors. In Western mass production, it is only at a late stage in the project that there is any coordination of different interests. In Japan team members sign formal undertakings to do exactly what the team as a whole has decided. Any conflicts therefore show up at the very beginning of the crisis.

The third element in lean production highlighted by Womack and his coauthors is coordination of the supply chain. In the lean, *susha*-led product development process, all the necessary suppliers are carefully selected not on the basis of their bids, but on the basis of earlier relationships and proven performance.

Customer relations form the fourth element. Japanese car manufacturers, the authors point out, have comparatively few sales channels. These are differentiated in terms of their appealing to different types of purchaser. The objective is to establish a direct link between the production system and the customer. Employees in the sales channels are loaned to the development teams, and the dealers have a close and long-lasting relationship with the manufacturer.

The fifth major element in lean production, according to the authors, is the way the lean company is managed. Various framework conditions have to exist:

- there must be money available to finance development projects that last several years;
- career ladders must be available for qualified and motivated employees;
- decentralized activities must be coordinated worldwide.

Context

The MIT investigation was at the time the most comprehensive study of a single industry ever conducted.

While it showed the undoubted successes of lean production, it also claimed to have uncovered certain deficiencies in the concept. Lean production, it suggests, overemphasizes the aspects of savings and mechanization and neglects categories such as know-how and innovation. Lean management brings about a short-term improvement in efficiency, but not a long-term increase in productivity. In addition, the authors argue, it is unsuited to dismantling complexity. Anyone, for example, who wishes to reduce the complexity of serialized production steps through individualized manufacture must understand ever more expansive processes in their entirety. In theory, the highly innovative and flexible business organization with no hierarchy may count as the company of the future, but in everyday practice the weaknesses of lean production are clearly apparent.

For More Information

Womack, James P., Daniel T. Jones, and Daniel Roos. *The Machine That Changed the World: The Story of Lean Production.* New York: HarperCollins, 1991.

Made in Japan
by Akio Morita

Made in Japan is the story of Sony and reflects the changes that took place in postwar business history. Morita and Sony's story parallels the rebirth of Japan as an industrial power. When Sony was first attempting to make inroads into Western markets, Japanese products were sneered at as being of the lowest quality. Surmounting that obstacle was a substantial business achievement.

Getting Started

This book charts the reemergence of Japan as an industrial heavyweight. It helped change the image of "Made in Japan" from one of shoddy goods to high quality. Sony invented new markets with a pioneering spirit by bringing out product after product, innovation after innovation. Its most famous success was the Walkman, the development of which was based on instinct, not research. Analysis and education do not necessarily help you to reach the best business decisions; sometimes understanding must come before logic. "Japanese people tend to be much better adjusted to the notion of work, any kind of work, as honorable," says Morita. Recruitment is "management's risk and management's responsibility."

Contribution

The Japanese Renaissance. Morita and Sony's story parallels the rebirth of Japan as a major industrial power.

They helped change the image of "Made in Japan" from something shoddy to something reputable and desirable.

At the time when Sony first tried to break into the Western electronics market, Japanese products were considered fifth-rate. Morita helped Sony not only to overcome this prejudice, but to reverse it.

Inventing New Markets. Morita and Sony's gift was to invent new markets with a pioneering spirit. "Sony is a pioneer and never intends to follow others," says Morita.

"Through progress, Sony wants to serve the whole world. It will always seek the unknown. Sony has a principle of respecting and encouraging one's ability . . . and always tries to bring out the best in a person. This is the vital force of Sony."

> Sony's most famous success was the Walkman, the brainchild of Morita.

The Power of Innovation. While companies such as Matsushita were inspired followers, Sony set the pace with product after product, innovation after innovation.

Sony brought the world the handheld video camera, the first home video recorder, and the floppy disk.

The blemishes on its record were the Betamax video format, which it failed to license, and color television systems.

Instinct and Research. Sony's most famous success was the Walkman, the brainchild of Morita. Morita noticed that young people liked listening to music wherever they went. He put two and two together and made—a Walkman.

He did not believe that any amount of market research could have told the company that this would be successful.

"The public does not know what is possible, we do," he has famously said.

Analysis Doesn't Always Pay. Brilliant marketing by instinct was no mere accident.

Morita believes that, if you go through life convinced that your way is always best, all the new ideas in the world will pass you by.

Analysis and education do not necessarily help you to reach the best business decisions. You can be totally rational with a machine but if you work with people, sometimes understanding has to come before logic.

Japanese Culture Encourages the Work Ethic. Morita has emphasized the cultural differences in Japanese attitudes toward work. The Japanese tend to have a much stronger work ethic, and see work as an honorable occupation.

Morita believes that management has ultimate responsibility for its staff. If a recession is looming, profit should be sacrificed rather than employees laid off.

Context

The book tells the story of the rise of Sony, and it reflects the rise of Japan as a postwar industrial power. It looks at the role of quality and innovation as key factors in the success of Japanese companies. Many Western authors have focused on the role of quality in Japan, particularly the influence of people like Deming and Juran.

Richard Pascale and Anthony Athos look at the phenomenon in *The Art of Japanese Management*.

Morita and Sony took the attitude that global markets were important from the outset. Kenichi Ohmae writes on that subject from the Japanese perspective in *The Borderless World*.

For More Information

Morita, Akio. *Made in Japan*. New York: Dutton, 1986.

Management Teams: Why They Succeed or Fail

by R. Meredith Belbin

Effective teamworking is now seen as key to the success of all types of organization. Meredith Belbin identified the characteristics of people needed to make a successful team. His recommendations are still used, and the book can therefore help anyone who needs to develop a team.

Getting Started

Corporations have been preoccupied with the qualifications, experience, and achievement of individuals—but it is not the individual but the team that is the instrument of sustained and enduring success in management.

Team performance is influenced by the kinds of people making up a group, and testing indicates that certain combinations of personality types perform more successfully than others. Nine archetypal functions make up an ideal team—plant, coordinator, shaper, teamworker, completer, implementer, resource investigator, specialist, and monitor evaluator. Unsuccessful teams can be improved by analyzing their composition and making appropriate changes.

> **Unsuccessful teams can be improved by analyzing their composition and making appropriate changes.**

Contribution

The Preoccupation with Individuals. Corporations have been preoccupied with the qualifications, experience, and achievement of individuals, and have applied themselves to their selection, development, training, motivation, and promotion. However, commentators believe that the ideal individual for a given job cannot be found, because he or she cannot exist. It is not the individual but the team that is the instrument of sustained and enduring success in management.

The Contribution of Individuals in Teams. Belbin was interested in group performance and how it might be influenced by the kinds of people making up a group. He asked members engaged in a business school exercise to undertake a personality and critical-thinking test and, based on the test results, discovered that certain combinations of personality types performed more successfully than others.

Belbin realized that given adequate knowledge of the personal characteristics and abilities of team members through psychometric testing, he could forecast the likely success or failure of particular teams. Unsuccessful teams can be improved by analyzing their team design shortcomings and making appropriate changes.

Identifying Team Characteristics. A questionnaire completed by team members was analyzed to show the functional roles the managers thought they performed in a team. From this research, Belbin identified nine archetypal functions which go to make up an ideal team.

Successful Team Composition.

- Plant—creative, imaginative, unorthodox; solves difficult problems. Allowable weakness: bad at dealing with ordinary people.

- Coordinator—mature, confident, trusting; a good chairman; clarifies goals, promotes decision making. Not necessarily the smartest.
- Shaper—dynamic, outgoing, highly strung; challenges, pressurizes, finds ways around obstacles. Prone to bursts of temper.
- Teamworker—social, mild, perceptive, accommodating; listens, builds, averts friction. Indecisive in crunch situations.
- Completer—painstaking, conscientious, anxious; searches out errors; delivers on time. May worry unduly; reluctant to delegate.
- Implementer—disciplined, reliable, conservative, efficient; turns ideas into actions. Somewhat inflexible.
- Resource investigator—extrovert, enthusiastic, communicative; explores opportunities. Loses interest after initial enthusiasm.
- Specialist—single-minded, self-starting, dedicated; brings knowledge or skills in rare supply. Contributes only on narrow front.
- Monitor evaluator—sober, strategic, discerning. Sees all options, makes judgments. Lacks drive and ability to inspire others.

Context

The explosion of interest in teamworking during the last decade has prompted greater interest in Belbin's work. The teamworking categories he identified have proved robust and are still used in a variety of organizations. Gary Hamel commented, "High-performing companies increasingly believe that teams, rather than business units or individuals, are the basic building blocks of a successful organization. Belbin deserves much credit for helping us understand the basic building blocks of successful teams."

Antony Jay commented, "Corporations have been preoccupied with the qualifications, experience, and achievement of individuals . . . it is not the individual but the team that is the instrument of sustained and enduring success in management."

For More Information

Belbin, R. Meredith. *Management Teams: Why They Succeed or Fail.* Woburn, MA: Butterworth-Heinemann, 1984.

The Managerial Grid

by Robert Blake and Jane Mouton

The book made an important contribution to the measurement of management performance. It challenged existing theories and provided organizations with a grid for assessing the types of manager they needed for different positions.

Getting Started

In the early 1960s there was a sizeable gap in management theorizing, especially in terms of leadership and motivation. Douglas McGregor's Theories X and Y had a number of shortcomings in reality, and Blake and Mouton found that a management performance model with three axes was a more accurate representation of reality. The important axes were concern for productivity, concern for people, and motivation. Accurate measurement is important because of managers' capacity for self-deception.

Contribution

Challenging Management Performance Theories. During consulting work for Exxon, Blake and Mouton concluded that there was a sizeable gap in management theorizing, especially in terms of leadership and motivation. Popular among theories of the time was that of Douglas McGregor and his motivational extremes of X and Y. However, Blake and Mouton believed that many behaviors and motivations fell in the middle of these extremes. Theories X and Y were only a part of the overall picture of organizational behavior.

A New Model of Management Performance. Blake and Mouton's conclusion was that a model with three axes was a more accurate representation of reality. The three crucial axes they determined were concern for productivity, concern for people, and motivation.

Concern for production and people were both measured on a scale of one to nine, with nine being high. The reason a people axis was necessary is that managers achieve things indirectly. They don't produce nuts and bolts themselves, rather they organize others so that the production line can be efficient.

Motivation was measured on a scale from negative (driven by fear) to positive (driven by desire).

Flaws in Performance Measurement. Blake and Mouton found that, when left to rank themselves, some 80% of people give themselves a 9.9 rating. Once this is discussed and considered, this figure is routinely reduced to 20%. Given the capacity for self-deception, it is little wonder that change programs fail.

Key Management Styles. From the grid emerge five key manager styles:

- 1 (production); 1 (people): Do-nothing manager. The leader exerts a minimum of effort to get the work done, with very little concern for people or production;
- 1 (production); 9 (people): Labeled the Country Club Manager. This manager pays a lot of attention to people, but little to production. Can be seen in small firms that have cornered the market and in some public sector organizations;
- 9 (production); 1(people): This manager emphasizes production and minimizes the influence of human factors;

- 5 (production); 5 (people): Organization man who diligently fosters mundanity;
- 9 (production); 9 (people): Managerial nirvana. The ultimate, with an emphasis on team working and team building. Personal and organizational goals are in alignment; motivation high.

Context

When Blake and Mouton examined the behavior of people at Exxon, they concluded that there was a sizeable gap in management theorizing, especially in terms of leadership and motivation. They found that many behaviors and motivations fell in the middle of Douglas McGregor's X and Y extremes. They observed that Theories X and Y were only a part of the overall picture of organizational behavior.

Blake and Mouton's conclusion was that a model with three axes—concern for productivity, concern for people, and motivation—was a more accurate representation of reality.

For More Information

Blake, Robert, and Jane Mouton. *The Managerial Grid*. Houston, Texas: Gulf Publishing, 1964.

Managing

by Harold Geneen

Geneen joined the board of ITT in 1959 and set about turning the company into the world's greatest conglomerate. Along the way he became, according to *BusinessWeek*, the legendary conglomerateur. The book relates the management style and culture that helped ITT to achieve that success. In particular, it highlights the importance of knowing the numbers in minute detail.

Getting Started

Geneen's success was based on knowing every single figure possible. He did not invent the conglomerate, but he had an obsessive belief that it could be made to work. ITT bought 350 companies and appeared to be a managerial nightmare—Geneen made the nightmare work by fanatical attention to detail.

He only micromanaged the numbers; the people were generally overlooked. However, his success meant that people followed his methods without question. Over 200 days a year were devoted to management meetings held throughout the world.

Success was based on amassing all the facts so that decisions became self-evident—Geneen wanted no surprises.

Contribution

A Rigorous Management Style Geneen was the archetypal workaholic. His style was unforgiving, built on a degree of intellectual rigor that bordered on ruthlessness. He pinned his managerial faith on hard work and knowing every single figure possible. For Geneen, detail was everything. Once an accountant, always an accountant.

Making Conglomerates Work. The conglomerate was not Geneen's invention. But he brought an obsessive belief that it could be made to work. He believed that ITT could manage any business in any industry if it knew the figures.

His career with ITT, described in *Managing*, is a pageant of acquisition and diversification. Under Geneen, ITT bought companies as casually as a billionaire buys trinkets. One acquisition funded another. ITT bought 350 companies, including Avis Rent-A-Car, Sheraton Hotels, Continental Baking, and Levitt & Sons, among many others. By 1970, ITT was composed of 400 separate companies operating in 70 countries. With such huge numbers of companies in such vastly different fields, ITT was hopelessly diversified. To contemporary eyes, the company was a managerial nightmare. Yet Geneen made the nightmare work by fanatical attention to detail.

Managing the Numbers. Geneen concentrated on managing the numbers; the people were generally overlooked.

"The very fact that you go over the progression of those numbers week after week, month after month, means that you have strengthened your memory and your familiarity with them so that you retain in your mind a vivid composite picture of what is going on in your company," he wrote.

Management Culture. Geneen inculcated a remarkable culture within ITT. His success meant that people followed his methods with the unquestioning faith of true believers.

Between 1959 and 1977, ITT's sales went from $765 million to nearly $28 billion. Earnings went from $29 million to $562 million, and earnings per share rose from $1 to $4.20.

As part of Geneen's formula, over 50 executives flew every month to Brussels to spend four days poring over the figures. It was calculated that over 200 days a year were devoted to management meetings held throughout the world.

> "The highest art of professional management requires the literal ability to smell a real fact from all others," Geneen believed.

Success Based on Facts. The point was to amass all the facts available so that the decisions became self-evident. If you knew everything, you would then know exactly what to do. Facts were the lifeblood of the expanding ITT.

"The highest art of professional management requires the literal ability to smell a real fact from all others," Geneen believed. "Managers should have the temerity, intellectual curiosity, guts and/or plain impoliteness, if necessary, to be sure that what they do have is indeed what we will call an unshakable fact."

Geneen wanted no surprises. He also hoped to make people as predictable and controllable as the capital resources they must manage.

Context

Much of Geneen's managerial philosophy and practice would appear to be anathema to the contemporary executive.

However, his fundamentalist style of management remains. Management consultants, for example, continue to apply their rational models—pour in all the figures you can find and the right decision will emerge. There is still a temptation to manage by numbers rather than through and with people.

On the positive side, Geneen can be said to have elevated management to a new level. His system required a team of highly numerate, professional managers who had to take responsibility.

The Geneen legacy is most notably evident in the conglomerates that continue to survive. General Electric, first under Jack Welch and now Jeff Immelt, may be the most lauded corporation of our age, but it is also a conglomerate with interests in everything from financial services to nuclear reactors and washing machines. Harold Geneen would have regarded the survival of such companies as vindication of his methods.

Others point to the decline of ITT on his departure as a true measure of the long-term validity of Geneen's approach to management.

For More Information

Geneen, Harold. *Managing.* New York: Doubleday, 1985.

Managing Across Borders

by Christopher Bartlett and Sumantra Ghoshal

Bartlett and Ghoshal map out the new business reality of globalization and the kinds of organizations a "borderless" business world requires. The book is regarded as a classic, and has helped many companies to focus on the type of organization they need for global success.

Getting Started

According to the authors, changing patterns of international management have led to a new global model in which enabling innovation and disseminating knowledge in globally dispersed organizations is a major challenge.

A number of organizational forms are now prevalent among global companies: multinational firms offer a high degree of local responsiveness; global firms offer scale efficiencies and cost advantages; international firms have the ability to transfer knowledge and expertise to overseas environments that are less developed; and the transnational firm combines local responsiveness with global efficiency and the ability to transfer know-how better, cheaper, and faster.

Integration and the creation of coherent systems for value delivery are the new drivers of organizational structure.

Contribution

Changing Patterns of International Management. The traditional international management model was simply to export your own way of doing things elsewhere, and companies believed that global operations were simply a means of achieving economies of scale. Local nuances were overlooked in the quest for global standardization: global and local were mutually exclusive. In general, organizations either gave local operations autonomy or controlled them rigidly from a distance.

A New Global Model. Global presence with local responsiveness is now key. Companies face the challenge of enabling innovation and disseminating knowledge in globally dispersed organizations. Bartlett and Ghoshal identify a number of organizational forms prevalent among global companies.

> **Global presence with local responsiveness is now key.**

Multinational Companies. The multinational or multidomestic organization offers a very high degree of local responsiveness. It is a decentralized federation of local businesses, linked together through personal control by expatriates who occupy key positions abroad.

Global Companies. Global organizations offer scale efficiencies and cost advantages. With global scale facilities, the global organization seeks to produce standardized products. It is often centralized in its home country, with overseas operations considered as delivery pipelines to tap into global market opportunities. There is tight control of strategic decisions, resources, and information by the global hub.

International Companies. International companies have the ability to transfer knowledge and expertise to overseas environments that are less developed. They are coordinated federations of local businesses, controlled by sophisticated management systems and corporate employees. The attitude of the parent company tends to be parochial, fostered by the superior know-how at the center of the organization.

The Transnational Companies. Global competition is forcing many businesses to shift to a fourth model, which they call the transnational. This organization combines local responsiveness with global efficiency and the ability to transfer know-how better, cheaper, and faster. The transnational company is made up of a network of specialized or differentiated units, which focus on managing integrative linkages between local businesses as well as with the center. The subsidiary becomes a distinctive asset, rather than simply an arm of the parent company. Manufacturing and technology development are located wherever it makes sense, and there is an explicit focus on leveraging local know-how in order to exploit worldwide opportunities.

The Importance of Integration. Integration and the creation of a coherent system for value delivery are the new drivers of organizational structure. Companies cannot be left to their own devices, but have to be brought within the fold—while also keeping in touch with their local business environment.

What binds the companies together is a set of explicit or implicit shared values and beliefs that can be developed and managed effectively. There are three techniques crucial to forming an organization's psychology: clear, shared understanding of the company's mission and objectives; the actions and behavior of senior managers are vital as examples and statements of commitment; corporate personnel policies must be geared up to develop a multi-dimensional and flexible organization process.

Context

Managing Across Borders is one of the few business books of recent years that deserves recognition as a classic. When it was published in 1989, understanding of globalization was in its infancy. With its emphasis on networking across the global organization and transferring learning and knowledge, the book effectively set the organizational agenda for a decade and created a new organizational model.

Bartlett and Ghoshal effectively signal the demise of the divisional organization—which gives divisions independence—first developed by Alfred P. Sloan of General Motors.

For More Information

Bartlett, Christopher, and Sumantra Ghoshal. *Managing Across Borders*. Boston, MA: Harvard Business School Press, 1989.

Managing on the Edge
by Richard Pascale

This book challenges traditional management thinking, which Pascale feels is too complacent for an environment driven by change. He sets out a new perspective for "contention management" which seeks to harness the conflicting energies in an organization to achieve positive change. The book set the management agenda for a decade after its publication.

Getting Started

U.S. managerial history is largely inward-focused and self-congratulatory. Change is a fact of business life, but complacency can cause problems. It is essential to change the management perspective. The incremental approach to change is no longer effective. The new emphasis should be on asking questions. Successful organizations undergo continual renewal by constantly asking questions.

Four factors drive stagnation and renewal in organizations: fit, split, contend and transcend.

"Contention management" is essential to orchestrate tensions that arise between these four factors. Forces locked in opposition can be used to generate inquiry and adaptation, and the manager's job is to maintain a constructive level of debate.

Contribution

The Dangers of Management Complacency. Nothing fails like success. Great strengths are inevitably the root of weakness. Of the companies listed in *Fortune 500* of 1985, 143 had been dropped by 1990. In the author's view, U.S. managerial history is largely inward-focused and self-congratulatory.

The Need for Change. According to Pascale, change is a fact of business life. We are ill-equipped to deal with it and the traditional approach to managing change is no longer applicable. The incremental approach to change is effective when the goal is to obtain more of the same thing. Historically, that has been sufficient. The United States' advantages of plentiful resources, geographical isolation, and absence of serious global competition defined a league in which Americans competed with each other and everyone played by the same rules.

Growth of Management Fads. There have been more than two dozen management fads since the 1950s; a dozen emerged in the five years prior to 1990.

Driving Stagnation and Renewal. Four factors drive stagnation and renewal in organizations:

- fit—pertains to an organization's internal consistency (unity);
- split—describes a variety of techniques for breaking a bigger organization into smaller units and providing them with a stronger sense of ownership and identity (plurality);
- contend—refers to a management process that harnesses (rather than suppresses) the contradictions that are inevitable by-products of organizations (duality);
- transcend—alerts people to the higher order of complexity that successfully managing the renewal process entails (vitality).

Changing Management Perspective. Pascale calls for a fundamental shift in perspective.

Managerial behavior is based on the assumption that people should rationally order the behavior of those they manage. That mindset needs to be challenged.

The new emphasis should be on asking questions. Strategic planning, at best, is about posing questions, more than attempting to answer them.

Successful organizations undergo a continual process of renewal. Central to achieving this is a willingness to ask questions constantly and to harness conflict for the corporate good through systems that encourage questioning.

Companies must become engines of inquiry.

Contention Management. Managers are ill-equipped to deal with the contention that arises when fundamental questions are posed. Contention management is essential to orchestrate tensions that arise. Around 50% of the time when contention arises, it is smoothed over and avoided.

The forces that we have historically regarded as locked in opposition can be viewed as apparent opposites that generate inquiry and adaptive responses. Each point of view represents a facet of reality, and these realities tend to challenge one another and raise questions.

If we redefine the manager's job as maintaining a constructive level of debate, we are, in effect, holding the organization in the question. This leads to identifying blind spots and working around obstacles. Truth—personally and organizationally—lies in the openness of vigorous debate. Organizations are, in the last analysis, interactions among people.

Context

Managing on the Edge presents a formidably researched and argued challenge to complacency and timidity.

Pascale criticizes Peters and Waterman's *In Search of Excellence* saying, "Simply identifying attributes of success is like identifying attributes of people in excellent health during the age of the bubonic plague."

Passions and obsessions frequently degenerate into simplistic formulas—for example, acronyms such as KISS (Keep it simple, stupid).

Managing on the Edge set the tone for much of the management thinking of the next decade. Its emphasis on the need for constant change has since been developed by Pascale. He now argues that the issue of managing the way we change is a competence rather than an episodic necessity. The capability to change is a core competence in its own right.

Influential critic Gary Hamel commented, "In *Managing on the Edge*, Richard Pascale provides a number of useful observations on the sources of corporate vitality. One of the things I've always admired about Richard Pascale is that he focuses not on tools and techniques, but on principles and paradigms. While management bookshelves groan with the weight of simplistic how-to books (for example, *The One Minute Manager*), Pascale challenges managers to think, and to think deeply. Pascale forces managers to deconstruct the normative models on which they base their beliefs and actions."

For More Information

Pascale, Richard. *Managing on the Edge*. New York: Viking Books, 1990.

Managing Transitions

by William Bridges

This book focuses on the human aspects of change management. Change is a situation. What the author calls "transition" is the psychological process people go through to come to terms with change. The book stresses that change involves people and that managers and leaders must help people deal with the transition. The author shows, through practical examples, how managers should make people feel comfortable during a period of change and offers advice, as well as case studies, on the best way to achieve this.

Getting Started

The author believes that many companies try to impose change, but fail to manage the transition. Transition means recognizing that things cannot be the same after an organizational change. People must get used to the new ways of doing things. They do this by going through a "neutral zone" before emerging into a new beginning.

Contribution

Letting Go. The author explains that transition begins with a process of "letting go." However, this is a process that many people in an organization find difficult. They are comfortable with familiar, proven ways of doing things and they fear the unknown.

The first stage, he suggests, is to identify who is losing what, by analyzing what is going to change and identifying the impact on different groups of people. Managers should be aware that people will react in different ways. They should acknowledge the effect of the change on people and, if necessary, make some compensation for their loss. Managers should also acknowledge what was good about the existing processes and emphasize the element of continuity in the most important aspects of the new proposals.

The Neutral Zone. Bridges believes that the "neutral zone" is the most difficult part of the transition process, because this is where people's uncertainties and anxieties about change are most acute. He advises managers to give people a clear sense of direction, as well as support to help them through this difficult stage. Moving from an existing routine to a new one can prove difficult without the right help.

Bridges argues that managers can reduce the damaging impact of the neutral zone by setting short-term targets that are achievable. He also believes that they should not expect or demand exceptional performance during a period of transition.

Communication is vital, claims Bridges, at this and every stage of transition. It is also important to encourage creativity during the neutral zone, particularly when there is less pressure on people to perform. Creativity can help to overcome the sense of loss people feel about leaving old routines behind.

> Communication is vital, claims Bridges, at this and every stage of transition.

New Beginnings. When people move to the new system, uncertainties can remain, according to Bridges. There is always a risk in new ways of doing things. It is therefore essential to set out a clear plan with timings and targets. Managers should ensure that everyone has a clear part to play in the new system.

He recommends clear, regular communications to explain the objectives and rationale for the new system. A vision of the future can help to paint a clear picture for people in the organization. To reinforce the new beginning, Bridges recommends that companies should create a new identity and celebrate success.

The book also includes advice for readers on how to take care of themselves during a period of transition.

Context

This book is one of a number that deal with the subject of managing the process of change. John Kotter's *Leading Change* (Harvard Business School Press, 1996), for example, reflects on the themes of leadership, vision, and communication.

Bridges's book looks at the human perspective of change and includes a great deal of practical advice on ways of dealing with the personal issues that people face. It also contains a number of useful studies, case histories, and exercises that could be used in workshops.

As such, the book may be more helpful to people in human resources or line management roles. Senior executives who are concerned with the strategic implications of change might find more value in an author such as Kotter.

For More Information

Bridges, William. *Managing Transitions: Making the Most of Change.* Reading, MA: Addison Wesley, 1991.

Marketing Management
by Philip Kotler

Kotler is one of the leading authorities on marketing. *Marketing Management* is the definitive marketing textbook, covering the full scope of contemporary marketing. It is the most widely used marketing book in business schools.

Getting Started
Marketing continues to evolve and expand its scope exponentially. The emphasis is shifting from transaction-oriented marketing to relationship marketing—retaining customer loyalty by continually satisfying their needs. Marketing management is the process of planning and executing functions that satisfy customer and organizational objectives. Customer-delivered value is the difference between total customer value and total customer cost.

Organizations encounter three common hurdles to marketing orientation:
- organized resistance;
- slow learning;
- fast forgetting.

Contribution
Marketing Continues to Evolve. The marketing discipline is redeveloping its assumptions, concepts, skills, tools, and systems for making sound business decisions.

Marketers must know when to:
- cultivate large markets or niche markets;
- launch new brands or extend existing brand names;
- push or pull products through distribution;
- protect the domestic market or penetrate aggressively into foreign markets;
- add more benefits to the offer or reduce the price;
- expand or contract budgets as appropriate.

The scope of marketing is expanding exponentially as is demonstrated by the size and scope of *Marketing Management*. Its contents range over:
- industry and competitor analysis;
- designing strategies for the global marketplace;
- managing product life cycle strategies;
- retailing, wholesaling, and physical-distribution systems.

The Change to Relationship Marketing. The emphasis is shifting from transaction-oriented marketing to relationship marketing. Good customers are an asset which, when well managed and served, will return a handsome lifetime income stream.

In the intensely competitive marketplace, the company must retain customer loyalty by continually satisfying their needs in a superior way.

Defining the Role of Marketing. Marketing is the social and managerial process by which individuals and groups obtain what they need and want by creating, offering, and exchanging products of value with others. A market consists of all the potential customers sharing a particular need or want, who might be willing to exchange in order to satisfy that need or want.

Marketing management is the process of planning and executing the conception, pricing, promotion, and distribution of goods, services, and ideas, to create exchanges with target groups that satisfy customer and organizational objectives.

Analyzing Products. A product is anything that can be offered to a market for attention, acquisition, use, or consumption that might satisfy a want or need.

A product has five levels:

- the core benefit (marketers must see themselves as benefit providers);
- the generic product;
- the expected product (the normal expectations the customer has of it);
- the augmented product (the additional services or benefits added to it);
- the potential product (all the augmentations and transformations that this product might undergo in the future).

Customer Value. Customer-delivered value is the difference between total customer value and total customer cost. Total customer value is the bundle of benefits customers expect from a given product or service. It consists of product value, service value, personnel value, and image value. Total customer cost consists of monetary price, time cost, energy cost, and psychic cost. Combined, the two produce customer-delivered value.

Barriers to Marketing Orientation. In order to become marketing oriented, organizations encounter three hurdles:

- organized resistance—entrenched functional behavior tends to oppose increased emphasis on marketing, as it is seen as undermining functional power bases;
- slow learning—most companies only slowly embrace the marketing concept;
- fast forgetting—companies that embrace marketing concepts tend, over time, to lose touch with the principles. Various U.S. companies have sought to establish their products in Europe with scant knowledge of different marketplaces.

Achieving Market Leadership. Good companies will meet needs; great companies will create markets. Market leadership is gained by envisioning new products, services, lifestyles, and ways to raise living standards. There is a vast difference between companies offering "me-too" products and those creating previously unimagined product and service values. Marketing at its best is about value creation and improving living standards.

Context

Marketing Management is the definitive marketing textbook. Tightly argued and all-encompassing, it has been expanded and brought up to date through various editions. The eleventh edition, published in 2002, maps out the emerging challenges to all those involved in marketing. The very size and scope of *Marketing Management* demonstrates the exponential expansion of marketing. Gary Hamel commented: "There are few MBA graduates alive who have not plowed through Kotler's encyclopedic textbook on marketing, and have not benefited enormously from doing so. I know of no other business author who covers his (or her) territory with such comprehensiveness, clarity, and authority as Phil Kotler. I can think of few other books, even within the vaunted company of this volume, whose insights would be of more practical benefit to the average company than those found in *Marketing Management*."

For More Information

Kotler, Philip. *Marketing Management: Analysis, Planning, Implementation, and Control.* 11th edn. Des Moines, Iowa: Prentice Hall, 2002.

Megatrends
by John Naisbitt

Megatrends was written in 1982, before the technology revolution took hold. It attempts to predict the key changes in business and society. Naisbitt correctly anticipated a number of factors such as globalization, empowerment, and the rise of an information economy.

Getting Started
According to the author, we have changed to an economy based on the creation and distribution of information. Speed is a competitive weapon.

We must now acknowledge that we are part of a global economy. The bigger the world economy, the more powerful its smallest player—and in small organizations, we have rediscovered the ability to act innovatively and to achieve results from the bottom up. Big bureaucratic organizations can be beaten. Economies of scale are giving way to economies of scope. The acceleration of technological progress has created an urgent need for a return to human scale.

Empowerment, with responsibility, has become more important for every individual in an organization. We are more self-reliant and less hierarchical. Society is moving toward much longer-term time frames.

Contribution
Toward the Information Economy. Although we continue to think we live in an industrial society, we have in fact changed to an economy based on the creation and distribution of information.

In the early 1980s, however, traditional issues, such as production methods, still held sway. The technological possibilities in information exchange and transfer were contemplated by a small group in West Coast laboratories.

Technology with a Human Scale. We are moving in the dual directions of high tech/ high touch, matching each new technology with a compensatory human response. Heart transplants led to new interest in family doctors and neighborhood clinics; jet aircraft resulted in more face-to-face meetings.

High touch is about getting back to a human scale. All change is local and bottom-up. If you keep track of local events, you can see the shifting patterns.

You can't stop technological progress, but by the same token, you can hardly go wrong with a high-touch response. FedEx has all the reliability and efficiency of modern electronics, but its success is built on a form of high-touch hand delivery.

The Emergence of a Global Economy. We no longer have the luxury of operating within an isolated, self-sufficient, national economic system. We must now acknowledge that we are part of a global economy.

We have begun to let go of the idea that the United States is and must remain the world's industrial leader as we move on to other tasks.

The global paradox is that the bigger the world economy, the more powerful its smallest player.

A Longer Time Frame. We are moving away from a society governed by short-term considerations and rewards to one which deals with things in much longer-term time frames.

The Growth of Empowerment. In cities and states, in small organizations and subdivisions, we have rediscovered the ability to act innovatively and to achieve results from the bottom up.

Naisbitt anticipated the fashion in the late 1980s and early 1990s for empowerment with responsibility spread more evenly throughout organizations, rather than centered on a small group of managers.

Greater Self-reliance. We are shifting from institutional help to more self-reliance in all aspects of our lives.

Trends in working patterns, such as employability, suggest that this is becoming the case for a select few professionals with marketable skills.

Changing Framework of Democracy. We are discovering that the framework of representative democracy has become obsolete in an era of instantaneously shared information.

Informal Networks Replacing Hierarchy. We are giving up our dependence on hierarchical structures in favor of informal networks. This will be especially important to the business community.

This has become one of the great trends of the last decade as networks are developed in a bewildering variety of ways—with suppliers, between competitors, internally, and globally.

Technology has enabled networks never previously anticipated, with important repercussions. When everyone hears about everything at the same time, we all know that everyone is equally well-informed.

Speed as a Competitive Weapon. Linked to this is the entire question of speed, which Naisbitt identified early on as a competitive weapon.

Economies of scale are giving way to economies of scope, finding the right size for synergy, market flexibility, and above all, speed.

More Choice for Society. From a narrow "either/or" society with a limited range of personal choices, we are exploding into a free-wheeling, multiple-option society.

The Power of Small Businesses. Naisbitt championed the role of small business in generating the wealth of the future. Small companies, right down to the individual, can beat big bureaucratic companies every time.

Unless big companies reconstitute themselves as a collection of small companies, they will just continue to go out of business.

It's the small companies who are creating the global company.

Context

Megatrends identified ten critical restructurings. Some have proved accurate predictions of what has happened in intervening years, others have proved less accurate.

Naisbitt predicted the rise of the information economy when the technology was still a laboratory product and he identified the emergence of factors such as globalization and empowerment.

Naisbitt's predictions can be compared with those of Alvin Toffler in *The Third Wave*.

For More Information

Naisbitt, John. *Megatrends*. New York: Warner Books, 1982.

The Mind of the Strategist

by Kenichi Ohmae

The book illuminates the strategic thinking behind Japanese corporate success. The author shows how and why it differs from the Western approach to strategic thinking and explains that Western companies can adapt to this successful model.

Getting Started

The author argues that to a large extent, Japanese success can be attributed to the nature of Japanese strategic thinking. Japanese businesses tend not to have large strategic planning staffs. The customer is at the heart of the Japanese approach to strategy. There are three main players in any business strategy—the corporation itself, the customer, and the competition—collectively called the strategic triangle. Just as events in the real world do not always fit a linear model, the Japanese approach to strategy is irrational and nonlinear.

Contribution

Strategy Determines Japanese Success. Japanese success can be attributed to the nature of Japanese strategic thinking. This is basically creative and intuitive rather than rational, but the necessary creativity can be learned.

Unlike large U.S. corporations, Japanese businesses tend not to have large strategic planning staffs. Instead they often have a single, idiosyncratic, naturally talented strategist.

From the dynamic interaction of the company, customers, and competition, a comprehensive set of objectives and plans eventually emerges.

The Customer at the Center. In contrast to the West, the customer is at the heart of the Japanese approach to strategy and the key to corporate values.

Strategic Triangle. In the construction of any business strategy, three main players must be taken into account: the corporation itself, the customer, and the competition. Collectively they are called the strategic triangle.

The job of the strategist is to achieve superior performance. At the same time, the strategist must be sure that the strategy matches the strengths of the corporation with the needs of a clearly defined market. Otherwise, the corporation's long-term viability may be at stake.

Strategy is Irrational. The central thrust of the book is that strategy as epitomized by the Japanese approach is irrational and nonlinear.

In strategic thinking, one first seeks a clear understanding of each element of a situation, and then makes the fullest use of human brain power to restructure the elements in the most advantageous way.

Events in the real world do not always fit a linear model. Hence the most reliable means of dissecting a situation into its constituent parts and reassembling them in the desired pattern, is not a step-by-step methodology, but the ultimate nonlinear thinking tool, the human brain.

True strategic thinking thus not only contrasts sharply with the conventional mechanical systems approach, but also with the purely intuitive approach, which reaches conclusions without any breakdown or analysis.

Gaining Ground through Effective Strategy. An effective business strategy is one by which a company can gain significant ground on its competitors at an acceptable cost to itself.

There are four main ways of achieving this:

- focusing on the key factors for success (KFS);
- building on relative superiority;
- pursuing aggressive initiatives;
- utilizing strategic degrees of freedom.

The principal concern is to avoid doing the same thing, on the same battleground, as the competition.

Focusing on Key Factors for Success. Certain functional or operating areas within every business are more critical for success in that particular business environment than others.

If you concentrate effort into these areas and your competitors do not, this is a source of competitive advantage, asserts Ohmae. The problem lies in identifying these key factors for success.

Today's industry leaders, without exception, began by bold deployment of strategies based on KFS.

Building on Relative Superiority. When all competitors are seeking to compete on the KFS, a company can exploit any differences in competitive conditions. For example, it can make use of technology or sales networks not in direct competition with its rivals.

Pursuing Aggressive Initiatives. Frequently, the only way to win against a much larger, entrenched competitor is to upset the competitive environment, by undermining the value of its KFS.

That means changing the rules of the game by introducing new KFS.

Utilizing Strategic Degrees of Freedom. This means that the company should focus upon innovation in areas that are untouched by competitors.

Context

The author is Japan's only successful management guru. The book was published in the West at the height of interest in Japanese management methods.

Ohmae challenged the simplistic belief that Japanese management was a matter of company songs and lifetime employment. Instead, Japanese success could be attributed to the nature of Japanese strategic thinking.

Bestselling author Gary Hamel commented, "I loved this book! At a time when most strategy savants were focused either on the process of planning (Ansoff and his followers) or on the determinants of successful, that is, profitable, strategies (Michael Porter), Kenichi Ohmae challenged managers to think in new ways. Strategy doesn't come from a calendar-driven process; it isn't the product of a systematic search for ways of earning above-average profits; strategy comes from viewing the world in new ways. Strategy starts with an ability to think in new and unconventional ways."

For More Information

Ohmae, Kenichi. *The Mind of the Strategist: The Art of Japanese Business.* New York: McGraw-Hill, 1982.

Moments of Truth

by Jan Carlzon

Jan Carlzon is a Swedish businessman who shot to international prominence by leading a turnaround at the Scandinavian airline, SAS. The turnaround was based on excellence in customer service, and the book contains many practical examples of the way this can be applied. The SAS story is one of the most frequently used case studies in customer service training and literature.

Getting Started

Carlzon used customer service as a vehicle for turning SAS around. He held that quality service is built around moments of truth—the critical transactions at each stage of the ownership or use cycle. These critical transactions occur at initial contact; first use; problem solving; ongoing support; further purchases; and recommendations to others. Customer satisfaction and value are affected at different points in the cycle. They also vary by customer type.

This approach owes much to the Scandinavian management style—humane and people-centered. Scandinavian companies embraced team working and employee participation before they became fashionable: their leaders are anti-authoritarian; they make very effective use of coaching and mentoring, and they also communicate consistently and continually

Contribution

Making Customer Service Work. Carlzon actually made customer service work and used it as a vehicle for turning SAS—formerly an indifferent performer—into a world class organization.

Carlzon came up with the phrase "moments of truth"—the sequence of critical transactions across each stage of the ownership or use cycle. Any time a customer comes into contact with any aspect of a business, however remote, is an opportunity to form an impression.

Identifying Moments of Truth. The critical transactions are broken down into:

- initial contact;
- first use;
- problem solving;
- on-going support;
- further purchases;
- recommendations to others.

The key to understanding customer behavior is to: 1) evaluate the degree to which satisfaction and value are affected at these different points in the cycle; 2) understand how they vary by customer type. Carlzon decided dramatically to prove the company's dedication to moments of truth by sending tens of thousands of SAS managers on training programs.

The Success of the Scandinavian Approach. Like most stereotypes, the image of highly motivated, well-rewarded, hard-working, and contented Scandinavians is only partly true. However, Scandinavian companies have a track record of managing their human resources in innovative ways. Their management style tends to be humane and people-centered, and they were champions of team working and employee participation long before they became the height of managerial fashion.

Scandinavia has a very stable political system and a fairly homogeneous society, and problems typically are solved through negotiation. Historically there has been little unrest—but the counter to this is that often, without a crisis, advancement is not achieved. The Scandinavian business culture shares some characteristics with that of the Japanese. Saving face is important and, rather than direct frontal attack, Scandinavians prefer a more obtuse and subtle approach.

A Scandinavian Leadership Style. Old-fashioned virtues are in. In one survey, American executives rated honesty as the prime business virtue. Swedish executives did not include honesty at all—it was assumed.

> Old-fashioned virtues are in.

The Scandinavian leader tends to be decidedly anti-authoritarian. Highly personal and practical theories, such as coaching and mentoring, find fertile ground; being up-front and communicating openly is expected. With Carlzon and others there is a certain amount of showmanship—they play their roles to perfection. They stand in the middle of their strategy. They don't preach the strategy; they are the strategy. They communicate consistently and continually. They repeat the same messages again and again. But they never grow tired of saying them—there is no sign of boredom, no cynicism, no sarcasm. They give words real meaning. This appetite for communication is clearly linked to a more humane style of management.

Context

Carlzon set in train SAS's revival, which became a benchmark for international best practice in customer service. The achievement was celebrated, among many others, by Tom Peters in *A Passion for Excellence*.

After Carlzon left SAS, the company's halo slipped a little and Scandinavian role models were thin on the ground for a number of years. During the 1990s, however, there was a steady stream of corporate benchmarks. The new Scandinavian role models—IKEA, Skandia, Oticon, and ABB—remain indebted to Carlzon's example.

For More Information

Carlzon, Jan. *Moments of Truth*. New York: HarperBusiness, 1987.

Motion Study: A Method for Increasing the Efficiency of the Workman

by Frank Gilbreth

Frank and Lillian Gilbreth made an art of measuring motion and, in doing so, helped to bring down further the borders between measurement and management. The book is written by genuine enthusiasts for measurement. The Gilbreths, and Frank in particular, were committed to the principles of scientific management, and were among the first to find practical applications of the key theories behind the movement. Frank was an advocate of the work of F. W. Taylor, and founded the Society to Promote the Science of Management in the 1890s. After Taylor's death in 1915, the Society was renamed as the Taylor Society.

Getting Started

Analysis and measurement of work can identify inefficient practices. Through analysis of motion, the Gilbreths concluded there were 16 units of movement. They asserted that "Fatigue elimination must increase Happiness Minutes."

Contribution

Analysis of Motion. One of Frank Gilbreth's key concerns was integrating efficiency into everyday working life, benefiting at one stroke the employer (who saw an increase in productivity) and the employee (whose levels of fatigue were decreased and the risk of injury therefore lessened). Fatigue elimination, starting as it does from a desire to conserve human life and to eliminate enormous waste, must increase what Gilbreth termed "Happiness Minutes," at the very least, or would be seen to have failed in its fundamental objective.

As a practical example of this concern, Frank Gilbreth examined bricklayers at work and found them to be inefficient. In response, he designed and patented scaffolding that reduced bending and reaching, and increased output by over 100 percent.

Their analysis of motion was aided by photography, and to help in the analysis of their photographs, they developed the microchronometer, a device still used today. This was a clock that could record time to 1/2000 of a second and which was placed in the area being photographed.

As a result of their analysis, the Gilbreths concluded there were 16 units of movement. These units they named therbligs (Gilbreth backward and slightly altered for ease of pronunciation).

Measurement Tools. Henry Gantt developed the idea of what became known as a Gantt chart at around the time that the Gilbreths were conducting their research, and they made use of this new measurement tool. They also incorporated flow diagrams and process charts into their studies, which enabled them to see exactly which constituent subtasks were involved in the completion of one major task.

Context

The Gilbreths put scientific management to the test. They made an art of measurement and, in doing so, helped further blur the borders between measurement and management.

> The Gilbreths put scientific management to the test. They made an art of measurement and, in doing so, helped further blur the borders between measurement and management.

Though their methods were sometimes viewed as eccentric and their blind enthusiasm took them down some unusual avenues, the Gilbreths had a powerful effect on management thinking. They elevated measurement to an all-embracing credo and helped establish it as one of the central tasks of management.

Even though the influence of the concept of scientific management began to wane from the 1960s onward, the work of the Gilbreths should not be underestimated. They brought together the disciplines of motion study and industrial psychology and made a lasting contribution to both management thought and the ways in which we work today.

For More Information

Gilbreth, Frank. *Motion Study: A Method for Increasing the Efficiency of the Workman.* New York: D. Van Nostrand, 1911.

Motivation and Personality
by Abraham Maslow

Maslow introduced the concept of a hierarchy of needs which has formed an integral part of marketing, human resource, motivational, and management literature ever since. The book makes an important contribution to the emergence of human relations as a professional discipline.

Getting Started

There is an ascending scale of needs that provides the basis for motivation. Basic physiological needs come first; once these are met, other needs dominate. At the top of the scale is self-actualization, where individuals achieve their personal potential. Also high up are social or love needs and ego or self-esteem needs. The hierarchy of needs provides a rational framework for motivation, and human nature determines that motivation is intrinsically linked to rewards.

Contribution

The Hierarchy of Needs. There is an ascending scale of needs, which must be understood if people are to be motivated. First are the fundamental physiological needs of warmth, shelter, and food. It is quite true that man lives by bread alone—when there is no bread.

But what happens when there is plenty of bread?

Emerging Needs. Once basic physiological needs are met, others emerge to dominate. These can be categorized roughly as the safety needs. If a person's state is sufficiently extreme and chronic, he or she may be characterized as living almost for safety alone.

Next on the hierarchy are social or love needs, and ego or self-esteem needs.

Self-actualization. As each need is satisfied, eventually comes self-actualization—the individual achieves his or her own potential.

> Ostensibly a rational framework for motivation, the hierarchy of needs is undermined by people.

From Motivation to Reward. Ostensibly a rational framework for motivation, the hierarchy of needs is undermined by people. People always want more. When asked what salary they would be comfortable with, people routinely—no matter what their income—name a figure that is around twice their current income.

Instead of being driven by punishment and deprivation, motivation became intrinsically linked to reward in Maslow's system.

Context

Abraham Maslow was a member of the human relations school of the late 1950s, which also included McGregor and Herzberg.

Motivation and Personality is best known for its hierarchy of needs—a concept that was first published by Maslow in 1943. He argues that there is an ascending scale of needs, which must be understood if people are to be motivated. While the hierarchy of needs provides a rational framework for motivation, its flaw lies in the nature of humanity.

Maslow's hierarchy of needs contributed to the emergence of human relations as a discipline, and to a sea-change in the perception of motivation.

Gary Hamel commented: "However subtle and variegated the original theory, time tends to reduce it to its most communicable essence: hence Maslow's hierarchy of needs, Pascale's seven Ss, Michael Porter's five forces, and the Boston Consulting Group's growth/share matrix. Yet there is no framework that has so broadly infiltrated organizational life as Maslow's hierarchy of needs. Perhaps this is because it speaks so directly to the aspirations each of us holds for ourself."

For More Information

Maslow, Abraham. *Motivation and Personality*. 3rd ed. New York: Harper & Row, 1987.

The Motivation to Work
by Frederick Herzberg, Bernard Mausner, and
Barbara Bloch Snyderman

Herzberg's work has had a lasting influence on human resource management. Concepts such as job enrichment, self-development, and job satisfaction have evolved from his insight that motivation comes from within the individual rather than from a policy imposed by the company. It has also influenced organizations' rewards and remuneration packages.

Getting Started

Employee motivation can be improved through greater emphasis on human relations.

Research indicates that motivation at work takes two forms—hygiene factors and motivation factors. Hygiene factors, which cover basic needs at work, include working conditions, benefits, and job security. Motivation factors, which meet uniquely human needs, include achievement, personal development, job satisfaction, and recognition. Improvements in hygiene factors remove the barriers to positive attitudes in the workplace, although hygiene factors alone are not sufficient to provide true motivation to work.

Employers should aim to motivate people by means of job satisfaction rather than reward or pressure.

Contribution

The Importance of Employee Attitudes. "People are our greatest assets" has become one of the most overused clichés in business. However, before Herzberg, "people issues" took a low priority in management literature. Management thinkers rarely sought the opinions of employees, or considered them worthy of study. Herzberg and his colleagues, Mausner and Snyderman, highlighted the importance of employee attitudes in a study of 203 Pittsburgh engineers and accountants. By asking what pleased and displeased people about their jobs, he raised the wider question: "How do you motivate employees?"

Identifying Factors That Motivate Employees. Herzberg made a critical distinction between factors that cause unhappiness at work and factors that contribute to job satisfaction. This distinction was based on his earlier work in public health, where he had concluded that mental health was not the opposite of mental illness. Transferring that concept to the workplace, he suggested that the reverse of the factors that make people happy did not make them unhappy. His research indicated that motivation at work takes two forms—hygiene factors and motivation factors.

Hygiene Factors. Hygiene factors cover basic needs at work. They include working conditions, supervision levels, company policies, benefits, and job security. If these are poor or deteriorate, they lead to poor job attitudes and dissatisfaction with work. Conversely, improvements in hygiene factors remove the barriers to positive attitudes in the workplace. However, improvement in hygiene factors alone is not sufficient to provide true job satisfaction.

Motivation Factors. Herzberg discovered that the factors that lead to dissatisfaction are completely different from those that provide satisfaction. He called the positive factors "motivation factors." These meet uniquely human needs and include achievement, personal development, job satisfaction, and recognition. Improving these factors can make people satisfied with work.

Challenging the Reward Process. Herzberg concluded that organizations should aim to motivate people through job satisfaction, rather than reward or pressure.

This led to the concept of job enrichment, which would enable organizations to liberate people from the tyranny of numbers and expand the creative role of an individual within the organization.

Context

Herzberg was one of the humanist school of management thinking, emphasizing the human aspects of organizations, in contrast to the mechanistic views of scientific thinkers. The humanist tradition includes Mary Parker Follett, Elton Mayo, Douglas McGregor, Abraham Maslow, Charles Handy, and Tom Peters.

Maslow's hierarchy of needs, formulated in 1943, influenced industrial psychologists like Herzberg by showing that work can be made more satisfying by giving greater emphasis to affection, ego, and self-actualization needs.

Herzberg's breakthrough was to identify hygiene and motivation factors. His work has had a lasting influence on human resource management: concepts such as job enrichment, self-development, and job satisfaction have evolved from his insight that motivation comes from within the individual rather than from a policy imposed by the company. It has also influenced organizations' rewards and remuneration packages.

The trend toward "cafeteria benefits" reflects Herzberg's belief that people choose the form of motivation that is most important to them. Many organizations believe that money is the sole motivation for workers; Herzberg's work offers a more subtle approach. There has been much subsequent academic debate on the extent to which pay or other factors are the most important motivators.

Guru Gary Hamel commented: "Too many organizations believe that the only motivation to work is an economic one. Treating knowledge assets like Skinnerian rats is hardly the way to get the best out of people. Herzberg offers a substantially more subtle approach—one that still has much to recommend it."

Critics of Herzberg argue that pay plays an important part in the motivational equation, and can be used to reinforce other motivational levers. Others point out that people frequently describe good work experiences in terms that reflect credit on themselves—success, greater responsibility, or recognition. Conversely, they will blame bad work experiences on factors that are outside their control, such as poor working conditions or a difficult boss.

Recent commentators believe that the main application of Herzberg's theories has been to nonmanual workers, where the hygiene factors are normally well satisfied. They believe that employees who were reasonably well rewarded would tend to emphasize motivational factors as more important.

For More Information

Herzberg, Frederick, Bernard Mausner, and Barbara Bloch Snyderman. *The Motivation to Work*. New York: John Wiley, 1959.

My Life and Work
by Henry Ford

My Life and Work is an account of Henry Ford's life and business philosophy. It provides unique insights into the man who took mass production to new levels and opened up mass markets through consistently low pricing and standardization. It also highlights the risk of a single-product strategy and the problems of autocratic control.

Getting Started

Ford's policy was to reduce the price, extend the operations, and improve the article. He did not bother about the costs. Price forces the costs down. Ford reduced prices by 58% at a time when demand was such that he could easily have raised them. Mass production was the result, not the cause, of his low prices.

Management and managers were dismissed by Ford as largely unnecessary—but his lack of faith in management, along with Ford's total reliance on the Model T, later proved the undoing of the company.

Contribution

Pricing and Costs. Ford stated his policy as being "to reduce the price, extend the operations, and improve the article. The reduction of price comes first. We have never considered any costs as fixed. Therefore we first reduce the price to the point where we believe more sales will result. Then we go ahead and try to make the prices. We do not bother about the costs. The new price forces the costs down. The more usual way is to take the costs and then determine the price, and although that method may be scientific in the narrow sense, it is not scientific in the broad sense. What use is it to know the cost, if it tells you that you cannot manufacture at a price at which the article can be sold?"

> In a sense Ford was both the most brilliant and the most senseless marketer in American history.

Ford's commitment to lowering prices cannot be doubted. Between 1908 and 1916 he reduced prices by 58% at a time when demand was such that he could easily have raised them.

Marketing. In a sense Ford was both the most brilliant and the most senseless marketer in American history. He was senseless because he refused to give the customer anything but a black car. He was brilliant because he fashioned a production system designed to fit market needs.

We habitually celebrate him for the wrong reason, his production genius. His real genius was marketing.

Standardization. Ford realized that the mass car market existed—it just remained for him to provide the products the market wanted.

Model Ts were black, straightforward, and affordable. At the center of Ford's thinking was the aim of standardization—something continually emphasized by the car makers of today.

Problems of a Single Product. The problem was that when other manufacturers added extras, Ford kept it simple and dramatically lost ground.

Henry Ford is reputed to have kicked a slightly modified Model T to pieces, such was his commitment to the unadulterated version. But the company's reliance on the Model T nearly drove it to self-destruction. The man with a genius for marketing lost touch with the aspirations of customers.

Mass Production. Ford is celebrated for his transformation of the production line into a means of previously unimagined mass production.

He calculated that the production of a Model T required 7,882 different operations. Production was based around strict functional divides or demarcations. Ford believed in people getting on with their jobs and not raising their heads above functional parapets. He didn't want engineers talking to salespeople, or people making decisions without his say-so.

Authoritarian Control. Management and managers were dismissed by Ford as largely unnecessary, and he made a systematic, deliberate and conscious attempt to run the billion-dollar business without managers.

Ford's lack of faith in management proved the undoing of the huge corporate empire he assembled. Without his autocratic belligerence to drive the company forward, it quickly ground to a halt.

Innovation in Business. In some respects Ford remains a good role model. He was an improviser and innovator who borrowed ideas and then adapted and synthesized them. He developed flow lines that involved people; now, we have flow lines without people, but no one questions their relevance or importance.

Though he is seen as having dehumanized work, Ford provided a level of wealth for workers and products for consumers which weren't previously available. He introduced the $5 wage for his workers which, at that time, was around twice the average for the industry.

He had an international perspective that was ahead of his time. His plant at Highland Park, Detroit, produced. But the world, not just the United States, bought.

Ford was acutely aware that time was an important competitive weapon. "Time waste differs from material waste in that there can be no salvage," he wrote.

Context

My Life and Work is a robust account of Ford's life and business philosophy, although it is notable for the dominance of the former and the lack of the latter. Ford's business achievements and contribution to the development of industrialization are likely to be remembered long after his theories on politics, history, motivation, or humanity are forgotten.

Leading author Gary Hamel said, "Henry Ford may have been autocratic and paranoid, but he brought to men and women everywhere a stunningly precious gift—mobility. Whatever his faults, Henry Ford was driven by the dream of every great entrepreneur—to make a real difference in people's lives—and to do it globally."

For More Information

Ford, Henry. *My Life and Work*. New York: Doubleday, Page & Co, 1923.

My Years with General Motors
by Alfred P. Sloan, Jr.

Alfred P. Sloan, Jr. is one of the very few figures who undoubtedly changed the world of management. He was also one of the first managers to write an important theoretical book. *My Years with General Motors* is an account of his remarkable career and the creation of a new organizational form, the multidivisional form, that spawned a host of imitators.

Getting Started

Alfred P. Sloan, Jr., a leading figure at General Motors from 1917, became its chief executive in 1946 and honorary chairman from 1956 until his death in 1966.

When he joined, the automobile market was dominated by Ford, and GM's market share was a mere 12%. GM was then an unwieldy combination of companies with eight models that competed against each other as well as against Ford. Sloan cut the eight models down to five and targeted each at a particular segment of the market. The five ranges were updated regularly and came in more than one color—unlike Ford's Model T. He also reshaped the organization so that it was better suited to deliver his aspirations.

> The book reveals that Sloan was committed to what at the time would have been regarded as progressive human resource management.

He created eight divisions—five car and three component divisions. In the jargon of 50 years later, these were strategic business units. Each had responsibility for its own commercial operations and its own engineering, production, and sales department. The divisions were supervised by a central staff responsible for overall policy and finance.

The main interest of *My Years with General Motors* for modern management thinkers lies in how Sloan managed to coordinate the semiautonomous divisions with the center and balance flexibility with control.

Contribution

Balancing Flexibility with Control. The policy that Sloan labeled "federal decentralization" marked the invention of the decentralized, divisionalized organization.

The multidivisional form enabled Sloan to utilize the company's size without making it cumbersome. Executives had more time to concentrate on strategic issues and operational decisions were made by people in the front line rather than at a distant headquarters.

By 1925, with its new organization and commitment to annual changes in its models, GM had overtaken Ford. More than that, however, Sloan's segmentation of the company changed the structure of the car industry and provided a model for how firms could do the same in other industries.

Commitment to Employees. The book reveals that Sloan was committed to what at the time would have been regarded as progressive human resource management. In 1947 he established GM's employee-research section to look at employee attitudes, and he invested a large amount of his own time in selecting the right people for the job.

Problems in Decentralization. The decentralized structure built up by Sloan revolved around a reporting and committee infrastructure that eventually became unwieldy.

As time went by, more and more committees were established. Stringent targets and narrow measures of success stultified initiative. The organization proved quite incapable of creating and developing new businesses internally. This inability to manage organic expansion into new areas was caused by many factors:

- operating responsibilities and measurement systems focused on profit and market share in existing markets;
- business unit managers were not expected to look for new opportunities;
- the boxes in the organization chart defined their product or geographic scope;
- small new ventures could not absorb the large central overheads and return the profits needed to justify the financial and human investments.

As Sloan himself put it: "In practically all our activities we seem to suffer from the inertia resulting from our great size. There are so many people involved and it requires such a tremendous effort to put something new into effect that a new idea is likely to be considered insignificant in comparison with the effort that it takes to put it across."

Context

Sloan established GM as a benchmark of corporate might, a symbol of American strength and success. "What's good for GM is good for America," ran the popular mythology. Peter Drucker and Alfred Chandler celebrated his approach, but the deficiencies of the model, apparent to Sloan himself, have become more so since the publication of his book, and are most obviously manifested in the decline of GM.

By the end of the 1960s the delicate balance which he had brilliantly maintained between centralization and decentralization was lost. Finance emerged as the dominant function, and GM became paralyzed by what had once made it great.

Gary Hamel commented: "Can you be big and nimble? The question is as timely today as it was when Sloan took over General Motors. Despite divisionalization and decentralization, Sloan's organizational inventions, GM still fell victim to its size . . . [T]he corporate superstructure that emerged to manage GM's independent divisions was more successful in creating bureaucracy than in exploiting cross-divisional synergies. The challenge of achieving divisional autonomy and flexibility on one hand, while reaping the benefits of scale and coordination on the other, is one that has eluded not only GM, but many other large companies as well."

One thing that should not be forgotten is that Sloan believed in managers and management in a way that his great rival Henry Ford did not. Nevertheless, as *The Economist* said: "Alfred Sloan did for the upper layers of management what Henry Ford did for the shopfloor: he turned it into a reliable, efficient, machine-like process."

Of the book as a whole, Peter Drucker remarked: "It is perhaps the most impersonal book of memoirs ever written. And this was clearly intentional. Sloan's book knows only one dimension: that of managing a business so that it can produce effectively, provide jobs, create markets and sales, and generate profits."

For More Information

Sloan, Alfred P, Jr. *My Years with General Motors*. New York: Doubleday, 1963.

Natural Capitalism

by Paul Hawken, Amory B. Lovins, and L. Hunter Lovins

The book offers an environmental perspective on economic activities. It includes practical advice on ways to transform business so that the Earth's resources are protected.

Getting Started

Natural Capitalism recognizes the critical relationship between the traditional creation of financial capital and the maintenance of the natural resources that are fundamental to any form of economic activity. The book suggests an approach for reconciling ecological and economic priorities, one that not only protects the Earth's environment, but also improves profits and competitiveness. The authors point out that environmental and economic priorities are normally considered contradictory, so that any state of balance requires tradeoffs. However, they believe that the best solutions may be based on design integration at all levels of economic activity, an approach they call "natural capitalism."

Contribution

The Concept of Natural Capital. "Natural capital," according to the authors, comprises the world's resources, living systems, and ecosystem services. These, they feel, are being depleted at a dangerous rate. They explain how increased resource productivity would enable business and consumers to obtain the same amount of utility from a product or process while using less material or energy. These natural efficiencies, they argue, go way beyond industry's current marginal performance gains. They believe that, if natural capitalism became widely accepted, resource productivity could grow at least fourfold, allowing people to live twice as well, yet use half as much.

The Stages of Natural Capitalism. The authors divide natural capitalism into four key strategies:

- radical resource productivity
- biologically inspired production models
- a solutions-based business model
- reinvesting in natural capital

These strategies, they say, offer benefits and opportunities in markets, finance, materials, distribution, and employment.

Radical Resource Productivity. According to the authors, radical resource productivity is the cornerstone of natural capitalism. It means obtaining the same amount of utility or work from a product while using fewer materials and less energy. In simple terms, this means doing more with less. The authors believe that fundamental changes in production design and technology offer the opportunity to develop ways to make natural resources such as energy, minerals, water, and forests stretch 5, 10, even 100 times further than they do today.

In manufacturing, transportation, forestry, construction, energy, and other industrial sectors, their evidence suggests that radical improvements in resource productivity are both practical and cost-effective. Designers, they believe, are already developing ways to make natural resources work much harder. These efficiencies transcend the marginal gains in performance that industry constantly seeks as part of its evolution. According to the authors, these revolutionary leaps in design and technology will alter industry itself.

Biologically Inspired Production Models. Taking examples from the natural world, the authors show how living organisms can produce complex "products" from recycled materials using minimal amounts of sustainable resources. Some of these products, such as the spider's silk or the cellulose produced by trees, have qualities that outperform their human-made equivalents. They argue that industry should learn from these natural techniques, a process they call "bio-mimicry." This approach seeks not only to reduce waste, but to eliminate the very concept of waste.

They demonstrate how every output, in closed-loop production systems modeled on nature's designs, is returned harmlessly to the ecosystem as a nutrient, like compost, or becomes an input for manufacturing another product. They point out how this compares with the inefficiency of many production processes where as little as 6% of the materials consumed actually end up in the product.

A Solutions-based Business Model. The business model of traditional manufacturing rests on the sale of goods: a consumer uses the product for a limited period and disposes of it at the end of its useful life. This process, the authors argue, is extremely wasteful. They offer an alternative model, where a physical product owned by a consumer is replaced by a flow of services.

A simple example might be a washing machine that is owned, maintained, and upgraded by the manufacturer. When its useful life is finished, the manufacturer is responsible for recycling the product. Another example would be providing access to the entire catalogs of music companies by subscription rather than the purchase of individual CDs. This shift of responsibility, they claim, would reduce consumption, but improve consumer choice.

Reinvesting in Natural Capital. According to the authors, sustaining, restoring, and expanding natural stocks of capital would work toward reversing worldwide planetary destruction, and governments are already recognizing the importance of using resource productivity to achieve this. They use terms such as "Factor Four," which means that resource productivity can and should grow fourfold, in other words, the amount of wealth extracted from one unit of natural resources can quadruple. On that basis, people could live twice as well, yet use half as much.

Context

Natural Capitalism is one of the increasing number of books that argue for a more ecologically sound approach to business. Unlike many more confrontational books that attack industry and offer no solution, *Natural Capitalism* shows how industry can adapt by learning from the natural world. While most commentators believe that environmental and economic priorities are contradictory, this book attempts to reconcile them. Above all, it indicates opportunities that could lead to nothing less than a transformation of commerce and all societal institutions.

For More Information

Hawken, Paul, Amory B. Lovins, and L. Hunter Lovins. *Natural Capitalism: The Next Industrial Revolution.* Boston: Little, Brown and Co., 1999.

The Nature of Managerial Work

by Henry Mintzberg

Mintzberg is regarded by many as a leading contemporary management thinker, and this book was the first to explore what managers actually do at work. It goes behind the myths and the self-perceptions to describe the day-to-day work of a manager.

Getting Started

What managers actually do, how they do it, and why, are fundamental questions. Managers believe they deal with big strategic issues—in reality they move from task to task dogged by diversions. Managerial work is marked by variety, brevity, and fragmentation.

Managers have three key roles, and the prominence of each role varies in different managerial jobs.

Contribution

What Managers Do—The Myth. What managers actually do, how they do it, and why they do it, are fundamental questions. There are a number of generally accepted answers.

Managers believe:

- that they sit in solitude contemplating the great strategic issues of the day;
- that they make time to reach the best decisions;
- that their meetings are high-powered, concentrating on the metanarrative rather than the nitty-gritty.

The reality largely went unexplored until Henry Mintzberg's book.

What Managers Do—The Reality. Mintzberg went in search of the reality. He simply observed what a number of managers actually did. The resulting book blew away the managerial mystique.

> What managers actually do, how they do it, and why, are fundamental questions.

Managers did not spend time contemplating the long term. They were slaves to the moment, moving from task to task with every move dogged by another diversion, another call. The median time spent by a manager on any one issue was a mere nine minutes.

The Characteristics of the Manager at Work. Mintzberg observed that the typical manager:

- performs a great quantity of work at an unrelenting pace;
- undertakes activities marked by variety, brevity, and fragmentation;
- has a preference for issues that are current, specific, and nonroutine;
- prefers verbal rather than written means of communication;
- acts within a web of internal and external contacts;
- is subject to heavy constraints but can exert some control over the work.

Managers' Key Roles. From these observations, Mintzberg identified the manager's work roles as:

- interpersonal
- informational
- decisional

Interpersonal Roles.
- Figurehead: representing the organization/unit to outsiders.
- Leader: motivating subordinates, unifying effort.
- Liaiser: maintaining lateral contacts.

Informational Roles.
- Monitor: overseeing information flows.
- Disseminator: providing information to subordinates.
- Spokesperson: transmitting information to outsiders.

Decisional Roles.
- Entrepreneur: initiating and designing change.
- Disturbance handler: handling nonroutine events.
- Resource allocator: deciding who gets what and who will do what.
- Negotiator: negotiating.

All managerial work encompasses these roles, but the prominence of each role varies in different managerial jobs.

Context

Henry Mintzberg is perhaps the world's premier management thinker, according to Tom Peters. His reputation has been made not by popularizing new techniques, but by rethinking the fundamentals of strategy and structure, management, and planning.

His work on strategy—in particular his ideas of emergent strategy and grass-roots strategy making—has been highly influential.

Influential author Gary Hamel commented: "Five reasons I like Henry Mintzberg: he is a world class iconoclast. He loves the messy world of real companies. He is a master storyteller. He is conceptual and pragmatic. He doesn't believe in easy answers."

The Nature of Managerial Work has produced few worthwhile imitators, but Mintzberg's rigor and originality have given his ideas staying power.

For More Information

Mintzberg, Henry. *The Nature of Managerial Work*. New York: Harper & Row, 1973.

The New Corporate Cultures

by Terrence Deal and Allan Kennedy

Deal and Kennedy wrote the first significant book on corporate culture, *Corporate Cultures: Rites and Rituals of Corporate Life*, in 1982. Their later book, *The New Corporate Cultures*, reexamines its role in the light of accelerating changes in the business environment. They set out to demonstrate how organizations with a strong culture have survived and succeeded, despite the impact of globalization, information technology, mergers, and downsizing, and how an understanding of corporate cultures, coupled with strong leadership, can prove an effective model for business.

Getting Started

The authors argue that corporate culture is a unifying factor that enables people to cooperate to achieve a common goal. However, a number of factors have militated against the development and maintenance of an effective culture—the demand for short-term results, the impact of downsizing and mergers, the introduction of outsourcing, and the effect of computers on business relationships. Organizations wishing to regain lost ground must now rebuild their cultures from the bottom up through strong leadership and high performance.

Contribution

Culture Breeds Financial Success The authors demonstrate the value of corporate culture by analyzing financial performance. The companies they identified as top performers in 1982 outperformed average stock market growth by nearly 50%.

The Impact of Short-term Needs. They also explain, however, how the rise of stockholder value played a key role in reducing the importance of corporate culture. The emphasis on short-term results, coupled with a growth in institutional ownership, meant that long-term actions proved unattractive to many organizations.

Short-termism, they believe, had a significant impact on employee loyalty and productivity, initiating a vicious circle that produced more and more short-term responses. Cutting costs to achieve short-term results led to a wave of downsizing and reengineering. This, in turn, ended the concept of lifetime employment and destroyed trust within organizations.

Outsourcing, Downsizing, Mergers, and IT. Downsizing damages corporate culture by destroying trust and breaking the link between leaders and employees.

Outsourcing, the authors claim, has a similarly damaging effect, since when organizations focus on their core activities and outsource everything else, employees may be transferred to other organizations, losing benefits and severing their links with the original employer.

The rapid increase in mergers has likewise tested corporate cultures. Mergers create a climate of uncertainty for employees, because there are always winners and losers.

Information technology too has, in their view, had a significant adverse effect. Although personal computers empower the people who use them, they can also isolate people from each other and break the informal links that are an important part of corporate culture.

The Effect of Globalization. Globalization, according to Deal and Kennedy, has accelerated the outsourcing and downsizing trends by enabling companies to source from around the world. Management is also affected by globalization, as multinational managers struggle to operate in different cultures.

The Need for Cultural Leadership. The authors believe that cultural leadership is key to overcoming the problems that have emerged. Managers must find out what employees really believe about the company and translate that into a statement that represents the company's position. Finding the common ground and turning it into a set of shared beliefs helps to shape the overall corporate vision.

Challenge People. It is important, the authors suggest, to measure the progress of cultural revitalization in financial terms. Celebrating victories can bring people together. However, as they explain, performance standards should not necessarily be based on financial targets. Setting people other challenges can help to create a strong culture.

Companies must rebuild trust by emphasizing the importance of employees to the business. Transparency is an important part of that process. To ensure a high standard of performance, the authors recommend hiring and rewarding the right people. However, they point out that the organizational structure must be right to get the most from people. A rigid divisional structure tends to isolate people, so transferring them can help to redress the balance.

Building Teamwork. The authors recommend the introduction of cultural revitalization teams with access to senior management. The team should try to identify subcultures, small informal groups who work together and can form the basis of strong teams. Encouraging formal and informal meetings also helps to rebuild the connections inside a company.

Rebuilding the social context of work helps give people a sense of belonging. The authors explain how factors such as job security, job satisfaction, and a socially rewarding environment create a more attractive culture.

Context

When Deal and Kennedy introduced the term "corporate cultures" in 1982, it received a mixed reaction. Supporters believed it gave a valuable insight into the inner workings of an organization. Critics felt that it was a superficial application of the discipline of anthropology to management.

The term has now become an accepted part of business language and often forms a key element of corporate strategy. For example, Edgar Schein, writing in *Organization, Culture, and Leadership*, believes that the only important thing leaders do is create and manage corporate culture. John Kotter and James Hesketh, in *Corporate Culture and Performance*, analyze the performance of companies with a strong cultures, and in *Built to Last* James Collins and Jerry Porras look at companies with a long history of success and compares their performance with companies lacking a strong corporate culture.

In 1995, *Fortune* magazine published a survey on corporate reputation and introduced the feature with a comment that robust culture appeared to be the factor that set the top-ranking companies apart.

For More Information

Deal, Terrence, and Allan Kennedy. *The New Corporate Cultures.* Reading, MA: Perseus Publishing, 1999.

New Patterns of Management
by Rensis Likert

The author was a pioneer of attitude surveys and introduced an attitude scale that is now widely used in business research. The book explains how he used his research tools to identify patterns of participative management and organization that would bring success in an increasingly competitive environment.

Getting Started

Rensis Likert was a pioneer of attitude surveys and poll design, as well as social research as a whole. According to Likert, there are four types of management style:

- exploitative and authoritarian
- benevolent autocracy
- consultative
- participative

Participative management is the best option, as increased participation and individualism are essential to meet increased competition. Participative groups can improve management and performance. The greater the loyalty of a group, the greater the motivation to achieve its goals.

An organization's style can be linked directly to its performance. The route to understanding managerial performance is improved measurement.

Contribution

Measuring Attitudes. In his doctoral thesis, written in 1932 while Likert was at Columbia University, and entitled *A Technique for the Measurement of Attitudes*, he introduced a straightforward five-point scale by which attitudes could be measured. The now well-known scale ranges from "strongly agree" to "strongly disagree" and is known as the Likert Scale.

The Contribution of Participative Groups. Likert's business research focused on the ways in which participative groups could improve management and performance. It also examined the human systems that exist in organizations.

> Likert identified four types of management style, each of which tends to mold people in its own image.

The greater the loyalty of a group, the greater is the motivation among members to achieve the goals of the group, and the greater the probability that the group will achieve its goals.

Management Styles. Likert identified four types of management style, each of which tends to mold people in its own image. Authoritarian organizations tend to develop dependent people and few leaders. Participative management was seen by Likert as the best option, both in a business and a personal sense. Participative organizations tend to develop emotionally and socially mature people capable of effective interaction, initiative, and leadership.

Organization Style and Performance. "Managers with the best records of performance in American business and government are in the process of pointing the way to an appreciably more effective system of management than now exists," Likert wrote in the book's opening. With the assistance of social science research, it is now possible to state a generalized theory of organization based on the management practices of these highest producers.

The Importance of Participation. Increased participation in the workplace and individualism are necessary consequences of increased competition and fast-accelerating technological improvement. There is much greater need for co-operation and participation in managing the enterprise than there was when technologies were simple and the chief possessed all the technical knowledge needed.

The Importance of Measurement. Management can make a difference, and the route to understanding managerial performance is improved measurement. An organization should be outstanding in its performance:

- if it has competent personnel;
- if it has leadership which develops highly effective groups and uses the overlapping group form of structure;
- if it achieves effective communication and influence, decentralized and coordinated decision making, and high performance goals coupled with high motivation.

Context

Likert's research highlights the importance of participative styles of management. This book bids farewell to the world of blind obedience and corporate coercion. Likert picks up the mood of individualism which was to sweep the world later in the 1960s. The book provides a blueprint for the ideal organization which has largely stood the test of time.

For More Information

Likert, Rensis. *New Patterns of Management*. New York: McGraw-Hill, 1961.

On Becoming a Leader

by Warren Bennis

Warren Bennis is widely respected as one of the foremost thinkers on leadership, and this book is regarded as a classic. It explains how people become leaders, how they lead, and how organizations respond to leadership. It is not based on academic theory, but offers practical advice based on interviews with a mix of leaders from many different fields.

Getting Started

Bennis believes that there is no exact science of leadership. Leaders vary in background, education, and experience. However, he identifies certain characteristics as essential for success. According to Bennis, leaders should know what they want and should be able to communicate what they want to others in order to gain their support. Leaders should also understand their own strengths and weaknesses and use them to achieve their goals. Bennis explains the phenomenon of leadership by defining its distinctive qualities—especially those that set a leader apart from a boss or manager, by highlighting the experiences that were vital to the development of leaders, by identifying the turning points, and by examining the role of failure.

Contribution

The Importance of Leadership. Bennis explains that leaders are important for three reasons:
- they are responsible for the effectiveness of organizations;
- they provide a focal point;
- they provide a recognizable constant in the midst of rapid change.

Leading and Managing. According to Bennis, the ingredients of leadership are wide-ranging and they include guiding vision, passion, integrity, self knowledge, trust, and daring. Leaders, he argues, can be highly competent, but fail to win the hearts and minds of the people they are leading.

> Leaders, according to Bennis, are their own best teachers.

Bennis believes that there is a significant difference between a leader and a boss, especially a boss who comes up from a results-driven management role. The drive for short-term results can run counter to the effectiveness of a visionary leader.

There are also many important differences between managers and leaders, he argues. The former have short-term rather than long-term perspectives, focus on systems rather than people, accept the status quo rather than challenging it, and exercise control instead of inspiring trust.

Leaders and Learning. Leaders, according to Bennis, are their own best teachers. They accept responsibility and gain from their own experience and that of others.

He distinguishes between maintenance learning and shock learning, both of which are familiar to managers, and what he calls innovative learning, which involves listening to others. This type of learning, he explains, means that people are free to express themselves, rather than just explain themselves. True intellect, he believes, is being able to see how things can be different.

The Value of Failure. Bennis suggests that leaders also learn from adversity. Making mistakes should not be punished. Leaders must operate on instinct, a process based on the use of the left- and right-hand sides of the brain. Managers, in contrast, rely on tried and tested processes.

According to Bennis, leaders should try everything, even in the face of failure. Few people venture into uncharted waters because of the risk of failure.

Achieving Goals. Leaders should be able to shift perspective so that they can see what is most important.

Bennis argues that leadership, unlike any other skill, cannot be broken down into a series of repeatable maneuvers. The creative process involved in reaching a goal is infinitely complex. As he explains, leaders have to be able to move through chaos and synthesize all the elements needed for success.

Gaining Support. Bennis argues that leaders must get people on their side to effect change. Empathy is therefore an important characteristic of leadership. This, he explains, is in contrast to theories of leadership by force.

Leadership, he believes, requires persuasion, not giving orders. This requires an understanding of the needs of other people and the ability to communicate a vision.

Context

Leadership is now one of the most popular topics in management literature and training, and Warren Bennis has made an important contribution. Leadership did not attract serious academic interest until the 1985 publication of Bennis's *Leaders: Strategies for Taking Change*, written in conjunction with Burt Nanus.

Bennis's work is based on extensive research with leaders in every field. One project involved interviews with 90 of America's leaders, including astronaut Neil Armstrong, the coach of the LA Rams, orchestral conductors, and businesspeople such as Ray Kroc of McDonald's.

Bennis argues that leadership is not a rare skill. Leaders are made rather than born; leaders are usually ordinary, or apparently ordinary, people rather than obviously charismatic figures. Leadership, moreover, is not solely the preserve of those at the top of the organization—it is relevant at all levels.

For More Information

Bennis, Warren. *On Becoming a Leader.* 2nd ed. Reading, MA: Perseus Publishing, 1994.

On the Economy of Machinery and Manufactures

by Charles Babbage

Charles Babbage was one of the great minds of the first industrial revolution. He is credited with pioneering the computer, and he wrote extensively about the importance of data and manufacturing. The book offers fascinating insights into the early development of manufacturing techniques.

Getting Started

In an age of economic theory, Babbage argued for a highly scientific approach. His emphasis on fact-finding influenced not only the practical elements of factory management in the early industrial era, but the formation of interpretive theory. Mechanical principles govern manufacturing, he said, and merchants and manufacturers are the best people to supply the data on which all the reasoning of political economists is founded. People should not fear bad deductions from good facts.

Good factory organization is important, and factories require an entire system of operation.

The most important principle of manufacture is the division of labor.

It is vital to calculate the life expectancy of capital equipment. In five years capital equipment ought to have paid for itself, and in ten it should be superseded by a better version.

Contribution

Mechanical Principles Govern Manufacturing. Babbage's fundamental approach was highly scientific. He held that mechanical principles regulate the application of machinery to arts and manufacture.

First, he said, it's essential to gather the evidence. Babbage did so by touring factories exhaustively in the United Kingdom and Europe. The book provides helpful hints and a checklist of questions on how to find the best information when touring a factory.

Make Use of Facts. Political economists have been reproached with too small a use of facts, and too large an employment of theory. "If facts are wanting, the closet-philosopher is unfortunately too little acquainted with the admirable arrangements of the factory," Babbage wrote. "The merchant and manufacturer are the best people to supply readily, and with so little sacrifice of time, the data on which all the reasoning of political economists are founded."

Collecting Data Is Essential. People should not fear that erroneous deductions may be made from recorded facts. The errors which arise from the absence of facts are far more numerous and more durable than those which result from unsound reasoning based on true data.

Babbage encourages managers to follow his example and gather their own data. Collecting data is essential for the manufacturer who wants to know how many additional customers he will acquire by a given reduction in the price of the article he makes.

Good Factory Organization Is Important. The arrangements that should regulate the interior economy of a factory are founded on deeply-rooted principles. Babbage recognized that the factory requires an entire system of operation. It needs to be organized in a vastly different way than the conventional means of production.

Babbage provides insights in two central areas. First, economies of scale and second, the division of labor.

Calculating the Right Division of Labor. Perhaps the most important principle on which the economy of manufacture depends is the division of labor among the people who perform the work." The number of operations performed in a given time may frequently be counted when the workman is quite unconscious that any person is observing him," Babbage said. "For example, the sound made by the motion of a loom may enable the observer to count the number of strokes per minute, even though he is outside the building in which it is contained."

> Perhaps the most important principle on which the economy of manufacture depends is the division of labor among the people who perform the work.

Life Expectancy of Capital Equipment. Machinery for producing any commodity in great demand seldom actually wears out. New improvements, by which the same operations can be executed either more quickly or better, generally supersede it long before that time arrives. To make such an improved machine profitable, it is usually reckoned that in five years it ought to have paid for itself, and in ten to be superseded by a better one.

Context

The book was a bestseller in its day. It was one of the first to recognize the importance of factories, economically and socially. In that sense, it is like the first book on the potential of the Internet.

Babbage was a pioneer of modern management. His approach bears more than a passing resemblance to that later adopted by that champion of scientific management, Frederick Winslow Taylor. He beckoned in the industrial era and, in doing so, laid the intellectual groundwork for Marx, Engels, and John Stuart Mill. Contrasts can be made with Adam Smith, whose economic viewpoint remained stuck in the agricultural era.

Joseph Schumpeter called the book "a remarkable performance of a remarkable man."

For More Information

Babbage, Charles. *On the Economy of Machinery and Manufactures*. London: Frank Cass & Co., 1835.

On War

by Carl von Clausewitz

Business is a form of human competition resembling war. Military theory and practice frequently mirror management thinking in such areas as strategy, leadership, logistics, and human resources. Von Clausewitz provides a valuable insight into issues such as motivation, setting objectives, and achieving results with the most efficient use of resources.

Getting Started

According to von Clausewitz, a war is an important and continuing element of overall strategy. Decisions about war should be rational and based on estimated gains and losses. Any war, he argues, should have a clear objective, and all tactics should be focused on the single objective of winning. There is no such thing as a limited victory. Although theory plays an important part in developing strategy, plans should take account of practicalities such as the enemy's strengths and weaknesses. They should also be flexible enough to meet changing circumstances. The most effective leaders achieve their results by the most efficient use of their resources. Creative leaders who can motivate their people effectively can win, even with fewer resources.

Contribution

War Is a Constant Element in Strategy. No one, according to von Clausewitz, should wage a war simply for its own sake. War, which he defines as an act of force or violence designed to compel opponents to fulfill the other party's will, should be part of an overall strategy to achieve certain goals. It is a continuation of that strategy using other means. It should only be used when politics has failed.

War Is Used to Achieve Rational Goals. He also suggests that we see war as a rational instrument of policy: in other words, it must have a clear goal based on an assessment of potential costs and benefits. The only true test of a war is victory, so all strategy and tactics must be directed toward winning.

Strategy and Tactics Are Different. Strategy, according to von Clausewitz, is the overall plan for winning the war. Tactics are just part of that overall plan. Strategy does not change throughout the war. Tactics, on the other hand, can be changed on a day-to-day basis to deal with changing conditions and challenges. In changing the tactics, a leader should never lose sight of the

> Strategy, according to von Clausewitz, is the overall plan for winning the war.

overall strategy. He also points out that decisions about strategy appear, at first sight, to be simple but that that does not necessarily make them easy to achieve. Decisions about tactics, on the other hand, are made in the heat of the moment in response to an event.

Information Is Important. Von Clausewitz believes that a leader should have a good understanding of all elements that could influence the outcome of a war. Part of that understanding is based on theoretical knowledge, part on knowledge of the terrain and the enemy. However, von Clausewitz also believes that the qualities of leadership supersede theoretical and local knowledge, and those qualities cannot be taught.

Concentrate on One Objective at a Time. He points out that it is essential to concentrate on one battle at a time. However, a leader should understand how each battle contributes to the achievement of the overall objective.

Leaders Must Be Flexible. Plans must take into account the strengths and weaknesses of the enemy. A leader must be alert to those and be willing to adopt different tactics if circumstances change.

Achieve Results with the Least Effort. Von Clausewitz argues that a leader should use the equivalent of cost-benefit analysis in planning for war. The most effective result uses the least possible resources to achieve the objective.

Context

Colonel F. N. Maude, in his editor's introduction to the 1908 edition of *On War*, pointed out that business is a form of human competition greatly resembling war. Von Clausewitz himself felt that comparisons between war and commerce were useful and valid. Commerce, he believed, was a conflict of interests and activities.

He was also one of the first to note the difference between strategy and tactics, although the debate on the difference still continues in management literature. The thinking behind the theory of "management by objectives" can be seen in von Clausewitz's view that leaders should concentrate on one battle at a time, but consider each battle as part of a series that leads to the final goal of victory.

The military thinking of historical figures such as Sun Tzu, Hadrian, the Duke of Wellington, and Napoleon continues to play an important role in the development of management thinking. Sun Tzu, for example, is considered to be the first person to develop the concept of strategy. Hadrian believed a leader should stay close to the troops and share their conditions. Wellington demonstrated the importance of flexibility in resolving crises during the Napoleonic Wars. He too kept close to his troops and the action during a campaign. With that degree of involvement, he was able to deal with any crisis as it occurred and adjust his tactics to suit the circumstances.

More contemporary figures such as Basil Liddell Hart, Colin Powell, and Norman Schwarzkopf have also influenced both thinking and practice. Business guru Richard Pascale has also considered the views of military leaders and thinkers on current issues such as leadership, training, motivation, and strategy. In the November/December 1996 issue of *Human Resources*, he examines the role of training on motivation in the U.S. Army.

For More Information

von Clausewitz, Carl. *On War.* eds. Peter Paret and Michael Howard. New York: Alfred A. Knopf, 1993. First published in English, London: N. Trubner, 1873.

Onward Industry

by James Mooney and Alan Reiley

The book provides insights into early thinking about the nature of organizations and their impact on the performance of industry. The authors argue that organization is a universal phenomenon and benefits the overall standard of living.

Getting Started

Organization is a universal phenomenon that has occurred throughout history. The organization of businesses is crucial to prosperity and living standards.

Production without distribution is worthless; the emphasis must be on finding and exploiting markets. Industry should encourage participation in business so that purchasing capacity can be created and extended. Organizational size is less important than knowing what to do with the organization.

Contribution

Organization Is a Universal Phenomenon. People love to organize, and organization is as old as human society itself. Consider the scalar organization of the Catholic Church, governmental organization, and the evolution of different forms of organization from Roman times to medieval times, through to the company of the early 20th century.

Organization Is Crucial to Standards of Living. The organization of businesses is crucial to overall standards of living. There is a direct link between industrial prosperity, built on modern management techniques, and the affluence of society as a whole.

> The organization of businesses is crucial to overall standards of living.

"The highest development of the techniques both of production and distribution will be futile to supply the material wants of those who, because of poverty, are unable to acquire through purchase," they write. The final task of industry, therefore, is to organize participation in these activities, even in the poorest communities and countries, through which purchasing capacity can be created and extended.

Production Without Distribution Is Worthless. Before the 1930s, production was the overarching driving force. Later the emphasis shifted to finding new markets and enhancing and expanding distribution to make inroads into those markets.

The Value of Size. Size isn't everything. Modern business leadership has been generally characterized by the capacity to create large organizations, but by failure in knowing exactly what to do with them.

Key Organizational Principles. Mooney and Reiley's theory of organizations identified three central organizational principles:

- the coordinative principle, leading to effective coordination;
- the scalar process, resulting in functional definition;
- the functional effect, leading to interpretative functionalism.

Context

The book provides an organizational model that is firmly of its time. It applies the reasoned science of Frederick W. Taylor to the broader organizational canvas.

The argument that production without distribution is worthless marks something of a watershed. Before the 1930s, production was the overarching driving force. From World War II, the emphasis shifted to finding new markets and enhancing and expanding distribution to make inroads into these markets.

For More Information

Mooney, James, and Alan Reiley. *Onward Industry*. New York: Harper & Bros., 1931.

The Organization Man
by William Whyte

From the point of view of the age of uncertainty, the age of downsizing, reengineering, and "discontinuous change," the 1950s and 1960s can easily seem like a golden age. The careers enjoyed by corporate executives were built on solid foundations, workers had jobs for life, suburbia was heaven, and everything seemed set to go on and on and on. William Whyte showed the downside to this corporate utopia. Read his brilliant, witty, and often poignant analysis to get both the postwar past and the present in perspective.

Getting Started

William Whyte joined the staff of *Fortune* magazine in 1946 after graduating from Princeton and serving in the U.S. Marines during World War II. *The Organization Man* is based on articles he wrote for the magazine. He subsequently left *Fortune* and, in his later years, wrote mainly on the subject of urban sprawl, urban planning, and human behavior in urban spaces.

1950s America still publicly and privately subscribed to the idea that rugged individualism was the hallmark of the American character and the foundation stone of the nation's success. According to Whyte, this was a delusion. Average Americans in fact subscribed to a collectivist social ethic that was turning them into organization people—and they needed to realize the fact and do something about it.

Contribution

The Social Ethic. Whyte believed that the condition he was analyzing did not affect America alone: he referred to "a bureaucratization that has affected every country."

The bureaucratic or collectivist ethic rested on three major principles:

- a belief in the group as the source of creativity;
- a belief in "belongingness" as the ultimate need of every individual;
- a belief in the application of science to achieve belongingness.

And above all he believed that "the fundamental principle of the new model executive is . . . that the goals of the individual and the goals of the organization will work out to be one and the same."

The Importance of Loyalty. Gray-suited and obedient, corporate man was unstintingly loyal to his employer. He spent his life with a single company and rose slowly, but quietly, up the hierarchy.

Loyalty and solid performance brought job security. This was mutually beneficial.

The executive gained a respectable income and a high degree of security. The company gained loyal, hardworking executives.

But while loyalty is a positive quality, it can easily become blind. What if the corporate strategy is wrong or the company is engaged in unlawful or immoral acts? The corporation becomes a self-contained and self-perpetuating world supported by a complex array of checks, systems, and hierarchies. The company is right.

In a remark reminiscent of George Orwell's *1984*, Whyte suggested that the organization man "must not only accept control, he must accept it as if he liked it."

> **Customers, who exist outside the organization, are often regarded as peripheral.**

Low-risk Environment. Customers, who exist outside the organization, are often regarded as peripheral.

In the 1950s, 1960s, and 1970s, it sometimes seems, no executive ever lost his job by delivering poor quality or indifferent service. In some organizations, executives only lost their jobs by defrauding their employer or insulting their boss. Jobs for life was the refrain and, to a large extent for executives, the reality.

Clearly, such an environment was hardly conducive to the fostering of dynamic risk-takers. It rewarded the steady foot soldier, the safe pair of hands, the organization man living with his organization wife.

Context

Reviewing the book in the *New York Times*, C. Wright Mills wrote: "Whyte understands that the work-and-thrift ethic of success has grievously declined, except in the rhetoric of top executives; that the entrepreneurial scramble to success has been largely replaced by the organizational crawl."

Chester Barnard noted in *The Functions of the Executive*: "The most important single contribution required of an executive, certainly the most universal qualification, is loyalty [allowing] domination by the organization personality."

Twenty years after the publication of Whyte's book, things had not changed very much. When she came to examine corporate life for the first time in her 1977 book, *Men and Women of the Corporation*, Rosabeth Moss Kanter found that the central characteristic expected of a manager was dependability.

Fortune founder Henry Luce commented: "It was *Fortune*'s William H. Whyte, Jr. who made the 'organization man' a household word, and the organization wife too. His was a fine achievement in sociological reporting. In it he related the phenomenon of the business organization to questions of human personality and values. The kind of people who are eager to hear the worst about American society assumed that Mr. Whyte was predicting the destruction of individualism by the organization."

Whyte was uneasy about corporate life, which seemed to stifle creativity and individualism. He was uneasy about the subtle pressures in the office and at home that called for smooth performance rather than daring creativity. However, he did not urge the organization men to leave their secure environment. Instead he urged them to fight the organization when necessary, and he was optimistic that the battle could be successful.

For More Information

Whyte, William. *The Organization Man*. New York: Simon & Schuster, 1956.

Organizational Culture and Leadership
by Edgar H. Schein

> *Organizational Culture and Leadership* clarified the entire area of corporate culture in a way no previous book had. It brought culture into the management debate and paved the way for a plethora of further studies. Even today, its perspectives on culture as a constantly changing force in corporate life remain as disconcerting as they are valuable.

Getting Started

Schein is sometimes seen as the inventor of the term "corporate culture;" he is, at the very least, one of its originators. After a long and distinguished academic career, he is currently the Sloan Fellows' Professor of Management Emeritus at the MIT Sloan School of Management.

In this book, he not only provides a sophisticated definition of culture, but he turns the abstract concept into a tool to assist managers in understanding the dynamics of organizations. In addition, he tackles the vital question of how an existing culture can be changed—one of the toughest challenges for leadership.

Contribution

The Basis of Corporate Culture. Culture is a pattern of basic assumptions invented, discovered, or developed by a given group as it learns to cope with its problems of external adaptation and internal integration. These assumptions have worked well enough to be considered valid and, therefore, to be taught to new members as the correct way to perceive, think, and feel in relation to those problems.

They can be categorized into five dimensions.

- humanity's relationship to nature—while some companies regard themselves as masters of their own destiny, others are submissive, willing to accept the domination of their external environment;
- the nature of reality and truth—organizations and managers adopt a wide variety of methods to reach what becomes accepted as the organizational truth;
- the nature of human nature—organizations differ in their views of human nature. Some follow McGregor's Theory X and work on the principle that people will not do the job if they can avoid it. Others regard people in a more positive light and attempt to enable them to fulfill their potential for the benefit of both sides;
- the nature of human activity—the West has traditionally emphasized tasks and their completion rather than the more philosophical side of work. Achievement is all. Schein suggests an alternative approach—"being-in-becoming"—emphasizing self-fulfillment and development;
- the nature of human relationships—organizations make a variety of assumptions about how people interact with each other. Some facilitate social interaction, while others regard it as an unnecessary distraction.

These five categories are not mutually exclusive, but are in a constant state of development and flux. Culture does not stand still.

Shaping Organizational Values. Key to the creation and development of corporate culture are the values embraced by the organization. A single person can shape these values and, as a result, an entire corporate culture. The heroic creators of corporate cultures include such people as Henry Ford and IBM's Thomas Watson, Sr.

Development of Corporate Culture. There are three stages in the development of a corporate culture:

- birth and early growth—the culture may be dominated by the business founder. It is regarded as a source of the company's identity, a bonding agent protecting it against outside forces;

- organizational mid-life—the original culture is likely to be diluted and undermined as new cultures emerge and there is a loss of the original sense of identity. At this stage, there is an opportunity for the fundamental culture to be realigned and changed;

- organizational maturity—culture, at this stage, is regarded sentimentally. People are hopelessly addicted to how things used to be done and unwilling to contemplate change. Here the organization is at its weakest, as the culture has been transformed from a source of competitive advantage and distinctiveness to a hindrance in the marketplace. Only through aggressive measures will it survive.

Changing Corporate Culture. Each stage of the culture's growth requires a different method of change.

If culture is to work in support of a company's strategy, there has to be a level of consensus covering five areas:

- the core mission or primary task;
- goals;
- the means to accomplish the goals;
- the means to measure progress;
- remedial or repair strategies.

Achieving cultural change is a formidable challenge, one that well-established executives in strong cultures often find beyond them. The exceptional executives who achieve cultural change from within a culture they are closely identified with (such as GE's Jack Welch) are rarities, and are known as cultural hybrids.

Context

Schein's findings gave rise to a host of other studies of the subject. His basic assumptions are rephrased and reinterpreted elsewhere in a variety of ways. Perhaps Chris Argyris comes closest to him when discussing "theories-in-use."

Gary Hamel says: "It is impossible to change a large organization without first understanding that organization's culture. Ed Schein gave us an ability to look deeply into what makes an organization what it is, thus providing the foundation of any successful effort at transformation or change. *Organizational Culture and Leadership* remains essential reading for all aspiring change agents."

For More Information

Schein, Edgar H. *Organizational Culture and Leadership*. 2nd ed. San Francisco, CA: Jossey-Bass, 1997.

Organizational Learning
by Chris Argyris and Donald Schön

This book shows why organizational learning is the ultimate competitive advantage. It also explains two of the central paradoxes of business life—how individual initiative and creativity can work in an organizational environment where rules will always exist, and how teamworking and individual working can coexist fruitfully.

Getting Started

Learning is a key business activity. Many organizational models only achieve single-loop learning, which—while this permits a company to carry on its present policies and achieve its current objectives—is limited to detection and correction of organizational error.

Double-loop learning, however, enables organizations to detect and correct errors in ways that involve the modification of underlying norms, policies, and objectives. With double-loop learning, managers can act on information and learn from others. Most organizations do quite well in single-loop learning, but have great difficulties with double-loop learning.

Deutero-learning is the process of inquiring into the learning system by which an organization detects and corrects its errors. It underpins the concept of the learning organization.

Increasingly, the art of management is managing knowledge—and effective leadership means creating the conditions that enable people to produce valid knowledge. Success in the marketplace increasingly depends on learning, yet most people don't know how to learn.

Contribution

The Weakness of Single-loop Learning. The authors investigate two basic organizational models.

Model 1 is based on the premise that we seek to manipulate and form the world in accordance with our individual aspirations and wishes. In Model 1, managers concentrate on establishing individual goals. They keep to themselves and don't voice concerns or disagreements. The onus is on creating a conspiracy of silence in which everyone dutifully keeps their head down. Defense is the prime activity in a Model 1 organization, though occasionally the best means of defense is attack. Model 1 managers are prepared to inflict change on others, but resist any attempt to change their own thinking and working practices.

Model 1 organizations are characterized by single-loop learning—the detection and correction of organizational error that permits the organization to carry on its present policies and achieve its current objectives.

The Importance of Double-loop Learning. Model 2 organizations emphasize double-loop learning—where organizational error is detected and corrected in ways that involve the modification of underlying norms, policies, and objectives.

In Model 2 organizations, managers act on information. They debate issues and respond to change—as well as being prepared to change themselves. They learn from others. A virtuous circle emerges of learning and understanding.

Most organizations do quite well at single-loop learning, but have great difficulties with double-loop learning.

The Challenge of Deutero-learning. Deutero-learning offers even greater challenges. This is the process of inquiring into the learning system by which an organization detects and corrects its errors. The examination of learning systems is central to the contemporary concept of the learning organization.

The Importance of Managing Knowledge. Learning is powerfully practical, and increasingly the art of management is managing knowledge. Organizations should not manage people per se, but rather the knowledge that they carry.

Leadership means creating the conditions that enable people to produce valid knowledge in ways that encourage personal responsibility. Knowledge must relate to action, not simply understanding and exploring.

The Learning Imperative. There is a natural temptation for organizations and individuals to limit themselves to single-loop learning rather than its more demanding alternatives. However, the need better to understand learning in all its dimensions is now imperative. Any company that aspires to success in the tougher business environment of the 1990s and beyond must embrace learning—yet most people don't know how to learn. Those members of an organization who are assumed by many to be the best at learning are, in fact, not very good at it.

Context

If you wished to trace the roots of the learning organization, you would invariably find yourself reading *Organizational Learning*. *Organizational Learning* grew out of Argyris and Schön's 1974 book, *Theory in Practice*. Chris Argyris was part of the human relations school of the late 1950s and involved in the work of the National Training Laboratories. He was drawn to the riddles of human nature—in particular, why do people fail to live up to their own professed ideals? Why is so much human behavior so self-frustrating, particularly within organizations?

Argyris's ideas have become increasingly fashionable. This is most apparent in the upsurge of interest in the concept of the learning organization. *Organizational Learning* appeared in 1978, but it took Peter Senge's 1990 bestseller, *The Fifth Discipline*, to propel the learning organization from an academic concept to mainstream acceptance.

Charles Hampden-Turner of the U.K. Judge Institute of Management says, "There is an urgent need for alternative visions of science and Schön's work, along with that of Argyris, provides some of the best ideas and answers. Few have gone so far in reconciling the vigor of relevance and in building a bridge between the isolated academic fortresses of the sciences and the humanities." Gary Hamel concurs, "If your organization has not yet mastered double-loop learning, it is already a dinosaur. No one can doubt that organizational learning is the ultimate competitive advantage. We owe much to Argyris and Schön for helping us learn about learning."

For More Information

Argyris, Chris, and Donald Schön. *Organizational Learning*. New York: Addison-Wesley, 1978.

Out of the Crisis

by W. Edwards Deming

This book is regarded as a classic of literature on quality management. It reflects Deming's experience in introducing quality management to Japan, and its goal was to transform the style of U.S. management. Deming is regarded as the leading figure on quality and this book sets out the methods that taught industry the power of quality.

Getting Started

Deming argues that profit comes from repeat customers who respond to good quality. Statistical quality control produces spectacular results, so senior managers must take charge of quality, and quality training should begin at the top of the organization. Quality is a way of living, Deming says: it is not the preserve of the few but the responsibility of all. In his view, factory workers already understood the importance of quality but were stymied by managers focused on increasing productivity regardless of quality. Japanese culture is uniquely receptive to the quality message.

Contribution

The Importance of Quality. Profit in business comes from repeat customers, customers who boast about your product and service, and who bring friends with them.

Quality is more than statistical control, though this is important. Statistical quality control produces spectacular results by using tools to improve processes in ways that minimize defects and eliminate rejects, rework, and recalls.

Deming's work bridges the gap between science-based application and humanistic philosophy.

The Quality Gospel. The book's quality gospel embodies a number of basic precepts:

- if consistent quality is to be achieved senior managers must take charge of it;
- implementation requires a cascade, with training beginning at the top of the organization before moving downward through the hierarchy;
- the use of statistical methods of quality control is necessary so that, finally, business plans can be expanded to include clear quality goals,
- quality is a way of living, the meaning of industrial life and, in particular, the meaning of management.

Deming's Fourteen Points.

- Create constancy of purpose for improvement of product and service.
- Adopt the new philosophy.
- Cease dependence on inspection to achieve quality.
- End the practice of awarding business on the basis of price tag alone. Instead, minimize total cost by working with a single supplier.
- Improve constantly and forever every process for planning, production, and service.
- Institute training on the job.
- Adopt and institute leadership.

- Drive out fear.
- Break down barriers between staff areas.
- Eliminate slogans, exhortations, and targets for the work force.
- Eliminate numerical quotas for the work force and numerical goals for management.
- Remove barriers that rob people of pride of workmanship. Eliminate the annual rating or merit system.
- Institute a vigorous program of education and self-improvement for everyone.
- Put everybody in the company to work to accomplish the transformation.

The Importance of Empowerment. The simplicity of the Fourteen Points disguises the immensity of the challenge, particularly to management: quality is everyone's responsibility. In arguing this case Deming was anticipating the fashion for empowerment.

Workers are not the problem. "Ever since there has been anything such as industry, the factory worker has known that quality is what will protect his job. He knows that poor quality in the hands of the customer will lose the market and cost him his job. He knows it and lives with that fear every day. Yet he cannot do a good job. He is not allowed to do it because the management wants figures, more products, and never mind the quality."

The Problem of Management. Management is 90% of the problem, a problem caused in part by the Western enthusiasm for annual performance appraisals. Japanese managers receive feedback every day of their working lives. The basic cause of sickness in American industry and resulting unemployment is failure of top management to manage.

The Japanese culture was uniquely receptive to Deming's message for a number of reasons. Its emphasis on group rather than individual achievement enables the Japanese to share ideas and responsibility. It also promotes collective ownership in a way that the West often finds difficult to contemplate, let alone understand.

Context

W. Edwards Deming has a unique place among management theorists. He had an impact on industrial history that others only dream of. Deming visited Japan after World War II on the invitation of General MacArthur, and played a key role in the rebuilding of Japanese industry. During the 1950s, Deming and the other U.S. standard bearer of quality, Joseph Juran, conducted seminars and courses throughout Japan. Deming, and Japanese management, was eventually discovered by the West in the 1980s.

British management journalist Robert Heller says, "Deming didn't invent quality but his sermons had a uniquely powerful effect because of this first pulpit and congregation: Japan and Japanese managers. Had his fellow Americans responded with the same intense application, post-war industrial history would have differed enormously."

For More Information

Deming, W. Edwards. *Out of the Crisis.* Bambridge, MA: MIT Center for Advanced Engineering Study, 1982.

Parkinson's Law
by C. Northcote Parkinson

Parkinson's Law, like *The Dilbert Principle*, takes a cynical look at business. The book treats the growth of bureaucracy in a humorous way, but the findings reflect real life situations, particularly in government organizations.

Getting Started

Companies grow without thinking of how much they are producing and without making any more money. The time to complete a task depends on the person doing the job and his or her unique situation. Work expands to fill the time available for its completion and officials make work for each other.

Contribution

How Organizations Grow. Parkinson's Law is simply that work expands to fill the time available for its completion. As a result, companies grow without thinking of how much they are producing.

Even if growth in numbers doesn't make them more money, companies grow and people become busier and busier.

> **Parkinson's Law is simply that work expands to fill the time available for its completion.**

The author contends that an official wants to multiply subordinates, not rivals, and that officials make work for each other.

Work Expands to Fill the Time. The notion of a particular task having an optimum time for completion is wrong. There are no rules—it depends on the person doing the job and his or her unique situation.

For example, an elderly lady of leisure can spend an entire day in writing and dispatching a postcard to her niece.

The total effort which would occupy a busy man for three minutes may, in this fashion, leave another person prostrate after a day of doubt, anxiety, and toil.

Administration Expands. Faced with the decreasing energy of age and a feeling of being overworked, administrators face three options:

- resign;
- halve the work with a colleague;
- ask for two more subordinates.

There is probably no instance in civil service history of choosing any but the third alternative.

The number of admiralty officials in the British Navy increased by 78% between 1914 and 1928 while the number of ships fell by 67% and the number of officers and enlisted personnel by 31%.

The expansion of administrators tends to take on a life of its own, says Parkinson, and the conclusion drawn is that officials would have multiplied at the same rate had there been no actual seamen at all.

Context

Parkinson's Law is an amusing interlude in management literature.

It is a kind of *Catch-22* of the business world, by turns irreverent and humorous, but with a darker underside of acute observation.

The book was written in the late 1950s when the human relations school in the United States was beginning to flower and thinkers were actively questioning the bureaucracy that had grown up alongside mass production.

Max Weber's model of a paper-producing bureaucratic machine appeared to have been brought to fruition as the arteries of major organizations became clogged with layer upon layer of managerial administrators.

Gary Hamel had this to say: "Yes, I know that bureaucracy is dead. We're not managers any more, we're leaders. We're not slaves to our work, we've been liberated. And all those layers of paper-shuffling administrators between the C.E.O. and the order-takers—they're all gone, right? Well then, why does a re-reading of *Parkinson's Law*, written in 1958, at the apex of corporate bureaucracy, still ring true? *Parkinson's Law* was to the fifties what *The Dilbert Principle* is to the 1990s."

For More Information

Parkinson, C. Northcote. *Parkinson's Law*. London: John Murray, 1958.

The Peter Principle

by Laurence Peter

This book is one of the most enduring books to take a cynical view of management. It is a humorous book that sets the tone for later works like *The Dilbert Principle*.

Getting Started

According to the author, in a hierarchy, every employee tends to rise to his or her level of incompetence. There are no exceptions to the Peter Principle. In time, every post tends to be occupied by an employee who is incompetent to perform his or her duties. If at first you don't succeed, you may be at your level of incompetence. There are two kinds of failures: those who thought and never did, and those who did and never thought. There are two sorts of losers—the good loser, and the other one who can't act.

Contribution

Finding a Level of Incompetence. In a hierarchy every employee tends to rise to his or her level of incompetence.

A position of incompetence is the apotheosis of a corporate career—or, indeed, of any career in any profession in which there is a hierarchy

No one is exempt from the Peter Principle.

The author contends that for each individual, the final promotion is from a level of competence to a level of incompetence. So, given enough time—and assuming the existence of enough ranks in the hierarchy—each employee rises to, and remains at, his level of incompetence.

In time, every post tends to be occupied by an employee who is incompetent to carry out his duties.

Dealing with Failure. If at first you don't succeed, you may be at your level of incompetence.

> A position of incompetence is the apotheosis of a corporate career—or, indeed, of any career in any profession in which there is a hierarchy.

If you don't know where you are going, you will probably end up somewhere else.

An economist is an expert who will know tomorrow why the things he predicted yesterday didn't happen.

Human inadequacy is universal, as is the human capacity to build vacuous power structures. In our supposedly leaner and fitter times, there are still hierarchies aplenty. The difference is, perhaps, that we have simply become more adept at disguising them.

There are two kinds of failures: those who thought and never did, and those who did and never thought.

There are two sorts of losers—the good loser, and the other one who can't act.

Fortune knocks once, but misfortune has much more patience.

Computerized Incompetence. Computerized incompetence is the incompetent application of computer techniques or the inherent incompetence of a computer.

Context

Cynicism about the way businesses and managers operate is nothing new. For example, *The Dilbert Principle* is simply an accurate and amusing portrayal of corporate cynicism, 1990s-style.

From *Murphy's Law* to *Parkinson's Law*, from Pudd'nhead Wilson to Stanley Bing, a steady infusion of comic skepticism has been injected into the corporate canon.

The Peter Principle is perhaps the most enduring, cynical classic.

The book carries many echoes of that other humorous classic of the 1960s, *Catch-22*.

The Peter Principle remains a poignant antidote to the blind optimism and sugary reality of most business books. It is a reminder that corporate reality is not usually about grand designs and great decisions. It is more mundane and frustrating. Too mundane and too frustrating to be taken seriously.

> **The Peter Principle remains a poignant antidote to the blind optimism and sugary reality of most business books.**

Dilbert creator Scott Adams commented, "Now, apparently, the incompetent workers are promoted directly to management without ever passing through the temporary competence stage. When I entered the workforce in 1979, *The Peter Principle* described management pretty well. Now I think we'd all like to return to those Golden Years when you had a boss who was once good at something."

The book remains relevant today. When Peter refers to codophilia (defined as speaking in letters and numbers instead of words), he could be talking of today's consultants.

Microsoft's Bill Gates echoes Peter, saying, "The art of management is to promote people without making them managers."

For More Information

Peter, Laurence. *The Peter Principle*. New York: William Morrow & Co, 1969.

Planning for Quality

by Joseph M. Juran

Juran, like W. Edwards Deming, was one of the key figures in the quality revolution. In this book he stresses that the human aspect of quality management is as important as statistical control. The book underscores the contribution that quality teams and empowerment give to the quality process.

Getting Started

Unlike the West, the Japanese have made quality a priority at the top of the organization.

The key elements in a quality philosophy are:

- quality planning;
- quality management;
- quality implementation.

Juran contends that quality is nothing new, but it has become ignored in the West where it is treated as an operational issue. There is more to quality than specification and rigorous testing: it cannot be delegated and has to be the goal of each employee, individually and in teams. Quality can be seen as an invariable sequence of steps. Planning consists of developing processes to meet customers' needs; the human side is just as important.

Contribution

National Attitudes to Quality Matter. Talking to Japanese audiences in the 1950s, Joseph Juran's message was enthusiastically absorbed by groups of senior managers—the Japanese have made quality a priority at the top of the organization. In the West, Juran's audiences were made up of engineers and quality inspectors. Quality was delegated downward—an operational rather than a managerial issue.

In the post war years, U.S. businesses were caught unaware for two reasons:

- they assumed their Asian adversaries were copycats rather than innovators;
- chief executives were too obsessed with financial indicators to notice any danger signs.

The Quality Trilogy. Juran's quality philosophy is built around a "quality trilogy" based on "Company-Wide Quality Management" (CWQM), which aims to create a means of disseminating quality to all. Juran insisted that quality cannot be delegated, and he was an early exponent of what has become known as empowerment.

Quality has to be the goal of each employee, individually and in teams, through self-supervision.

> Juran insisted that quality cannot be delegated, and he was an early exponent of what has become known as empowerment.

The Historical Context of Quality. Manufacturing products to design specifications and then inspecting them for defects to protect the buyer was something the Egyptians had mastered 5,000 years previously when building the pyramids. The ancient Chinese established a separate department of the central government to establish quality standards and maintain them.

Juran's message is therefore that quality is nothing new. But if it is so elemental and elementary, why had it become ignored in the West?

The Human Side of Quality. There is more to quality than specification and rigorous testing for defects; Juran regarded the human side of quality as critical. He developed all-embracing theories of what quality should entail.

The Quality Planning Process. Quality planning consists of developing the products and processes required to meet customers' needs. Quality planning includes the following activities:

- identifying the customers and their needs;
- developing a product that responds to those needs;
- developing a process able to produce that product.

Quality planning can be produced through an invariable sequence of steps:

- identify the customers;
- determine their needs;
- translate those needs into our language;
- develop a product that can respond to those needs;
- optimize the product features to meet our needs as well as customers' needs;
- develop a process which is able to produce the product;
- optimize the process;
- prove that the process can produce the product under operating conditions;
- transfer the process to the operating forces.

Context

Juran is critical of Deming's *Out of the Crisis* as being over-reliant on statistics. Juran's approach is less mechanistic than Deming's and places greater stress on human relations. It is based on Company-Wide Quality Management (CWQM), a means of disseminating quality to all. Juran was an early exponent of what has become known as empowerment and believed that quality should be the goal of each employee.

Gary Hamel commented: "The impact of Juran, and of Deming as well, went far beyond quality. By drawing the attention of Western managers to the successes of Japan, they forced Western managers to challenge some of their most basic beliefs about the capabilities of their employees and the expectations of their customers."

For More Information

Juran, Joseph M. *Planning for Quality*. New York: Free Press, 1988.

The Practice of Management
by Peter F. Drucker

Peter Drucker is regarded as the major management and business thinker of the century. *The Practice of Management* is a book of huge range, encyclopedic in its scope and historical perspectives. It laid the groundwork for many of today's accepted management practices and is an excellent primer in management thinking.

Getting Started

Drucker asserts that management will remain a basic and dominant institution, with managers being at the epicenter of economic activity.

A business's purpose is to create a customer; and the two essential functions of business are marketing and innovation. Organization is a means to achieving business performance and results.

There are five basics of the managerial role—to set objectives; organize; motivate and communicate; measure; and develop people. Management has a moral responsibility, and must be driven by objectives.

Contribution

The Importance of Management. Management will remain a basic and dominant institution perhaps as long as Western civilization itself survives. Drucker places management and managers at the epicenter of economic activity.

Rarely has a new basic institution emerged as fast as has management since 1900, and never before has a new institution proved indispensable so quickly.

A Marketing Attitude Is Critical. There is only one valid definition of business purpose: to create a customer.

Markets are created by businesspeople. The want they satisfy may have been felt previously by the customer, but it was theoretical. Only when the action of businesspeople provides a means to satisfy that want is there a customer, a market.

Since the role of business is to create customers, its only two essential functions are marketing and innovation. Marketing is not an isolated function, it is the whole business seen from the customer's point of view.

The Nature of Organizations. Though indispensable, organization is not an end in itself, but a means to achieving performance and results. The wrong structure will seriously impair performance and may even destroy the business.

The first question in discussing structure must be: what is our business and what should it be? Organization structure must be designed in such a way that it's possible to achieve business objectives for 5, 10, 15 years hence.

The Managerial Role. There are five basics of the managerial role. These are to: set objectives; organize; motivate and communicate; measure; and develop people. The function that distinguishes the manager above all others is educational. The unique contribution he or she must make is to give others vision and ability to perform.

The Importance of Moral Responsibility. It is vision and moral responsibility that, in the last analysis, define the manager. This morality is reflected in five areas.

- There must be high performance requirements, no condoning of poor or mediocre performance, and rewards must be based on performance.
- Each management job must be rewarding in itself, rather than just a step on the ladder.
- There must be a rational and just promotion system.
- There must be clear rules on who has the power to make life-and-death decisions affecting a manager; and some way to appeal to a higher court.
- In its appointments, management must realize that integrity is the one quality that a manager has to bring to the job and cannot be expected to acquire later on.

Management by Objectives. A manager's job should be based on tasks which will help attain the company's objectives. The manager should be directed and controlled solely by the objectives of performance.

The manager must understand what the business goals demand in terms of performance, and be judged accordingly.

Tasks for the Manager of the Future. Drucker identified seven new tasks for the manager of the future. Given that these were laid down over 40 years ago, their prescience is astounding. Tomorrow's managers must:

- manage by objectives;
- take more risks and for a longer period ahead;
- be able to make strategic decisions;
- be able to build an integrated team, each member of which is capable of managing his or her own performance in relation to the common objectives;
- be able to communicate information fast and clearly;
- be able to see the business, and the industry, as a whole and to integrate his or her function with it.

Context

The Practice of Management laid the groundwork for many of the developments in management thinking during the 1960s, and is notable for its ideas concerning the tools and techniques of management. The book is also important for the central role it argues management has in 20th-century society.

Drucker coined phrases such as "privatization" and "knowledge worker," and championed concepts such as management by objectives. Many of his innovations have become accepted facts of managerial life.

The Economist commented, "In a field packed with egomaniacs and snake-oil merchants, he remains a genuinely original thinker."

Influential author Gary Hamel says, "No other writer has contributed as much to the professionalization of management as Peter Drucker. Drucker's commitment to the discipline of management grew out of his belief that industrial organizations would become . . . the world's most important social organizations—more influential, more encompassing, and often more intrusive than either church or state. Professor Drucker bridges the theoretical and the practical, the analytical and the emotive, the private and the social more perfectly than any other management writer."

For More Information

Drucker, Peter F. *The Practice of Management*. New York: Harper & Row, 1954.

The Prince

by Niccolò Machiavelli

Although written over 400 years ago, Machiavelli's advice to leaders remains relevant to managers today, and covers many popular topics such as motivation, dealing with change, and leadership qualities.

Getting Started

Change management, leadership style, motivation, and international management were just as relevant in the 16th century as they are today. Executives continue to see themselves as natural rulers of an organization, and to the leader, presentation is as important as ability.

Introducing change is extremely difficult. It's essential to keep motivation high—success is not the result of luck or genius, but happy shrewdness. Leaders who rise rapidly often fall just as quickly, and people ruling foreign countries should be on the spot to prevent trouble. Sometimes leaders have to practice evil when necessary.

Contribution

Executives Have Not Changed. Machiavelli covers topics as apparently contemporary as change management, leadership style, motivation, and international management. Like the leaders Machiavelli sought to defend, some executives tend to see themselves as the natural rulers in whose hands organizations can be safely entrusted.

Theories abound on their motivation: is it a defensive reaction against failure, or a need for predictability through complete control? The effect of the power-driven Machiavellian manager is usually plain to see.

Presenting the Right Image. According to Machiavelli, "It is unnecessary for a prince to have all the good qualities [I have] enumerated, but it is very necessary to appear to have them. It is useful to be a great pretender and dissembler."

> In the author's opinion, success is not the result of luck or genius, but happy shrewdness.

Managing Change and Motivation. "There is nothing more difficult to take in hand, more perilous to conduct, or more uncertain in its success, than to take the lead in the introduction of a new order of things. A leader ought above all things to keep his men well organized and drilled, to follow incessantly the chase."

Managing Internationally. "When states are acquired in a country with a different language, customs, or laws, there are difficulties; good fortune and great energy are needed to hold them. It would be a great help if he who acquired them should go and live there. If one is on the spot, disorders are seen as they spring up, and one can quickly remedy them; but if one is not at hand, they are heard of only when they are great, and then one can no longer remedy them."

The Qualities of Leadership. In the author's opinion, success is not the result of luck or genius, but happy shrewdness. He felt that a Prince "ought to have no other aim or thought, nor select anything else for his study, than war and its rules and discipline; for this is the sole art that belongs to him who rules."

"In addition, those who solely by good fortune become princes from being private citizens have little trouble in rising, but much in keeping atop," says the author. "They have no difficulties on the way up, because they fly, but they have many when they reach the summit."

It is all very well being good, but the leader "should know how to enter into evil when necessity commands."

Context

The Prince is the 16th-century equivalent of Dale Carnegie's *How to Win Friends and Influence People*. Many of its insights are as appropriate to today's managers and organizations as they were half a millennium ago. Antony Jay's 1970 book *Management and Machiavelli* developed the comparisons.

The book offers something for everyone. It covers topics as apparently contemporary as change management, leadership style, motivation, and international management.

Gary Hamel has said: "We occasionally need reminding that leadership and strategy are not twentieth century inventions. It's just that in previous centuries they are more often the concerns of princes than industrialists. Yet power is a constant in human affairs, and a central theme of Machiavelli's *The Prince*. It is currently out of fashion to talk about power. We are constantly reminded that in the knowledge economy, capital wears shoes and goes home every night. No place here for the blunt instrument of power politics? But would Sumner Redstone, Bill Gates, or Rupert Murdoch agree? What is interesting is that after 400 years, Machiavelli is still in print. What modern volume on leadership will be gracing bookstores in the year 2500? Does Machiavelli's longevity tell us anything about what are the deep, enduring truths of management?"

For More Information

Machiavelli, Niccolò. *The Prince*. New York: Penguin, 1967.

Principles of Political Economy

by John Stuart Mill

Can liberalization and ethics be combined? Is there a just way of distributing wealth? These are still very relevant issues in the age of globalization and neoliberalism. They also exercised the mind of John Stuart Mill (1806–73) in the middle of the 19th century. He gives lucid and humane expression to the view that the objective of economic policy must be to ensure an appropriate material livelihood for everyone. Rejecting the premises of "homo economicus," the rational maximizer of profit and consumption, and the unrestricted belief in the progress of his age, he evolved a concept of the "good" society that is ultimately a vision of cooperative socialism.

Getting Started

Mill deals with the principles of production and distribution, embedding economic issues in a broader sociopolitical context. Free competition is necessary, Mill believed, in order to liberate useful social energies. However, the state is not thereby relieved of all its responsibilities, though the scope of its interventions should be strictly limited. Mill draws the balance of a whole period of scientific research and connects economic principles with their practical applications.

Contribution

Production and Distribution. The national economy, Mill argues, has to be redefined. Production and distribution must be separated. Whereas the laws of production may be natural laws, the only laws to be investigated in the case of distribution are human-made.

Progress. Belief in progress should not, he believes, be unqualified. A "stationary" state in which economic production stagnates is not a crisis signal or catastrophe for industrialized countries, but an opportunity to develop a more just, leisured, and cultivated society. It is not an unhappy and discouraging prospect but a chance to create a harmonious social order. He confessed that he was "not charmed with the ideal of life held out by those who think that the normal state of human being is that of struggling to get on; that the trampling, crushing, elbowing, and treading on each other's heels, which form the existing type of social life are the most desirable lot of human kind or anything but the disagreeable symptoms of one of the phases of industrial progress."

Progressive economic development, Mill thought, is characterized by the continuing and unlimited growth of human control over nature and the constant increase in the security of persons and property.

Production and Prosperity. Increase in production remained of significance only for underdeveloped countries, in Mill's view. Distribution was much more important for developed countries. The objective there is not mere increase in the result of aggregate production, but prosperity for all.

Where producers join together to form cooperatives, Mill suggests, the overall productivity of industry increases. A strong impetus is given to productive energy inasmuch as the workers are placed in relation to their work as a single body. But the material benefit is nothing in comparison to the moral transformation of society that would accompany this. Cooperatives reduce the profits of capitalists.

Private Property. The principle of private property is, according to Mill, important for three reasons. First, individuals have a right vis-à-vis society, a claim to the rewards of the labor or their frugality. Second, the criterion of economic efficiency is operative in that people are motivated to perform to the best of their abilities when they can appropriate the results of their efforts to their own use. Third, private property develops as a function of individuality itself.

State Interference. In Mill's opinion, state interventions in the economy are to be rejected. For one thing, individuals know what benefits them and what harms them; for this reason state interventions are always inferior to private initiatives. For another, state interventions increase the power of the state and tend to lead to despotic and centralized rule.

The Good Society. A happy society is characterized by the following elements. In Mill's words:

- "a well-paid and affluent body of laborers"
- "no enormous fortunes, except what were earned and accumulated during a single lifetime"
- "a larger body of people than at present not only exempt from coarser toils, but with sufficient leisure . . . to cultivate freely the graces of life, and afford examples of them to the classes less favourably circumstanced for their growth"

Modern states, he says, will need to learn the lesson that the welfare of a nation must rest on the justice and the judicious self-determination of its individual citizens. Progress in the future depends on the degree to which they are educated to be able to think for themselves.

Context

The English economist, philosopher, and logician, John Stuart Mill, is one of the chief exponents of empirically oriented thought and of utilitarianism. He made his name as an advocate of radical reform in political and social life and of equality for women. He wished to unite the political economy of capital with the demands of the working class. His thoroughgoing investigation of the methodological questions relating to national economies made him the epistemologist of the liberal school. His inquiries at the interface of pure economics, social philosophy, and ethics gave liberalism a new social cast and are still relevant today. Mill's reflections have once again attracted attention in the course of the debate on "the limits of growth."

For More Information

Mill, John Stuart. *Principles of Political Economy with Some of Their Applications to Social Philosophy.* New York: Oxford University Press, 1999.

Principles of Political Economy
by David Ricardo

David Ricardo (1772–1823) is one of the most important theorists in the history of political economy. *The Principles of Political Economy and Taxation* is one of the cornerstones of the classical approach to the subject. His ideas, especially the theory of comparative cost advantage, formed the basis for the discussion of free trade and protective tariffs throughout the 19th century. His work forms a bridge between that of Adam Smith, who was Ricardo's immediate inspiration, and that of Karl Marx. He is also often said to be the inspirer of the Chicago "monetarist" school that had such a profound influence on the economics and the politics of the late 20th century. The book is still acknowledged as a masterpiece for its isolation and abstraction of basic principles, its synthesis, and its logic.

Getting Started

In this book, first published in 1817, Ricardo gets to grips with the concept of exchange value and expounds the theory of comparative cost advantage. His central argument runs as follows: the exchange of goods between two countries is worthwhile for both, even if one country can produce all the goods more cheaply than the other. He uses two trading nations, Britain and Portugal, and two types of good, cloth and wine, as examples. In addition, he sets out criteria for the objective valuation of goods. According to his doctrine, the value of any good is determined solely by how much labor is necessary for its production. He also deals with prosperity and poverty in the social classes, and the connections between the factors of production, labor, land, and capital, and develops general principles of taxation.

Contribution

On Value. Ricardo states that the value of a good depends on the relative quantity of labor required for its production. By this he means not merely the labor expended in actually creating it, but also that expended on the machines, tools, and buildings that support the immediate work of production.

On Foreign Trade. Expansion of foreign trade will not, according to Ricardo, immediately increase the sum of value in a country. As the value of all foreign goods is measured by the quantity of the products of the country's soil and labor expended in exchange for them, it will not possess greater value if, through the discovery of new markets, it receives double the quantity of foreign goods for a specific quantity of its own.

On Taxes. Taxes, says Ricardo, are a part of the product of the land and labor of a country that is put at the disposal of the government. They are always paid out of the country's capital or revenue.

Taxes on luxury goods only affect those who use luxuries. Taxes on necessities, however, are a burden on consumers not only in proportion to the quantity they consume, but often in far greater measure. This is because, argues Ricardo, anything that increases wages reduces the profit from capital; any taxes on goods consumed by workers tend to bring down rates of profit.

Income taxes likewise increase wages and reduce the rate of profit on capital. Consequently, in Ricardo's view, only those who employ workers contribute to income tax, not money capitalists, nor landowners, nor any other social class.

He also argues, however, that a tax on essential consumer goods does not entail any particular disadvantage insofar as it raises wages and lowers profits. Profits are indeed reduced, but only to the extent of the worker's contribution to the tax, which in any event must be borne either by the worker's employer or the consumers of the products of his or her labor.

On Currencies and Banks. The exchangeability of paper money for metal is not essential to ensure its value, Ricardo says. It is only necessary that its quantity should be regulated in accordance with the value of the metal that has been declared as the standard. If gold of a specific weight and fineness is the standard, then the amount of paper money in circulation can be increased whenever gold declines in value or, which is the same thing in its effect, whenever the price of goods rises.

On the Influence of Supply and Demand on Prices. Production costs, Ricardo argues, determine the prices of goods, not the relationship between supply and demand. This relationship may influence the market price of a good for a time, until it is delivered in greater or lesser quantities depending on whether demand has risen or fallen. But this will only be a temporary effect.

Context

In his thoughts on foreign trade, Ricardo went against the spirit of his age. Whereas his homeland, Great Britain, protected its own economy with customs barriers, his theorem of comparative cost advantages argued in favor of free trade. His views on foreign trade are a guiding light in the liberalization of world trade even today: his portrait adorns the Web site of the World Trade Organization (WTO).

Ricardo's arguments on the value of goods and his ideas on the division of income between workers, capitalists, and landowners influenced many later economists. In particular, his theory of added value was taken up by Karl Marx and became a weapon in the arsenal of socialism.

Before he began writing, Ricardo was one of the best-known speculators of his time. As a young man, he was a dealer in government securities and made a fortune on the stock exchange. In Ricardo's system of distribution, however, landowners come off best in the long run. He himself acted in accordance with his own principles: he sold his securities and bought an estate.

For More Information

Ricardo, David. *The Principles of Political Economy and Taxation.* Amherst, NY: Prometheus Books, 1996.

The Principles Of Scientific Management

by Frederick Winslow Taylor

At the time *The Principles of Scientific Management* was published, "business management as a discrete and identifiable activity had attracted little attention" as Lyndall Urwick, the British champion of scientific management, said. The book put management on the map, and its influence on working methods and managerial attitudes for most of the 20th century, especially in mass-production industries, was enormous. Taylor's principles have been alternately reviled, rejected, and rediscovered. They remain undeniably significant even today.

Getting Started

Frederick Winslow Taylor was a U.S. engineer and inventor whose fame rests chiefly on this book. He shares with Henry Ford the dubious distinction of founding an "-ism." Taylorism is the practice of the principles of scientific management, which emerged from Taylor's work at the Midvale Steel Works, where he was chief engineer. It involves rigorous measurement of work processes, total objectivity in the assessment of which methods work best, and the consequent mechanization of work and elimination of the human element. The objective standards arrived at, however, are as binding on managers, who have to enforce them, as on the workers who have to meet them. Like the unstoppable assembly line, scientific management imposes its discipline on everyone. Not surprisingly, to most members of the humanistic school of management it is the enemy *par excellence*.

Contribution

Measuring Work. Taylor's science consisted in the minute examination of individual tasks. Having identified every single movement and action involved in doing something, he could determine the optimum time required to complete a task.

Armed with this information, the manager could determine whether a person was doing the job well.

Putting Science Before Opinion. The most obvious consequence of scientific management is a dehumanizing reliance on measurement.

The experts, who first analyze and then accurately time the various ways of doing each piece of work, will finally know from exact knowledge, and not from anyone's opinion, which method will accomplish the results with the least effort and in the quickest time.

The exact facts will have in this way been developed and they will constitute a series of laws, which are destined to control the vast multitude of our daily personal acts which, at present, are the subjects of individual opinion.

A System with No Initiative. The Taylorist system envisages no room for individual initiative or imagination. People are labor, mechanically accomplishing a particular task and doing what they are told.

According to Robert McNamara: "those who were so important in the early stages of American manufacturing, the foremen and plant managers, were disenfranchised. Instead of being creators and innovators, as in an earlier era, now they depended on meeting production quotas. They could not stop the line and fix problems as they occurred; they lost any stake in innovation or change" (quoted in *Promise and Power* by Debora Shapley).

Taylor's programs for objectively determining best practices for every imaginable job could, on the other hand, be said to have freed front-line workers from the capricious discipline of unscientific, turn-of-the-century supervisors.

Context

While Taylor's concepts are now usually regarded in a negative light, the originality of his insights and their importance are in little doubt. He himself announced that he was ushering in a revolution, "a complete mental revolution on the part of the working man engaged in any particular establishment or industry, a complete mental revolution on the part of these men as to their duties toward their work, toward their fellow men, and toward their employees."

Peter Drucker observed in *The Practice of Management*: "Few people had ever looked at human work systematically until Frederick W. Taylor started to do so around 1885. Work was taken for granted and it is an axiom that one never sees what one takes for granted. *Scientific Management* was thus one of the great liberating, pioneering insights."

Lyndall Urwick adds: "At the time Taylor began his work, business management . . . was usually regarded as incidental to, and flowing from knowledge of . . . a particular branch of manufacturing, the technical know-how of making sausages or steel or shirts. The idea that a man needed any training or formal instruction to become a competent manager had not occurred to anyone."

The legacy of Taylor's work is most obvious in companies that tend to emphasize quantity over quality. His ideas were enthusiastically taken up by Henry Ford in the development of mass-production techniques.

Drucker goes on to identify two fundamental flaws in scientific management.

"The first of these blind spots is the belief that, because we must analyze work into its simplest constituent motions, we must also organize it as a series of individual motions, each if possible performed by an individual worker; the second that it divorces planning from doing."

Gary Hamel sums up the position thus: "The development of modern management theory is the story of two quests: to make management more scientific, and to make it more humane. It is wrong to look at the latter quest as somehow much more enlightened than the former. Indeed, they are the yin and yang of business. The unprecedented capacity of twentieth century industry to create wealth rests squarely on the work of Frederick Winslow Taylor. While some may disavow Taylor, his rational, deterministic impulses live on. Indeed, reengineering is simply late twentieth century Taylorism. Though the focus of reengineering is on the process, rather than the individual task, the motivation is the same: to simplify, to remove unnecessary effort, and to do more with less."

For More Information

Taylor, Frederick Winslow. *The Principles of Scientific Management*. New York: Harper & Row, 1911.

Quest for Prosperity

by Konosuke Matsushita

This book describes how Konosuke Matsushita built a global business—Panasonic—from nothing. It contains lessons on customer service, business ethics, and marketing that would benefit any business.

Getting Started

According to the author, customer service is critical to success—customers want goods that will benefit them. After-sales service is more important than assistance before sales.

Business with a conscience cements loyalty. We are using precious resources that could be better used elsewhere unless we make a good profit. Production efficiency and quality products are key. The mission of a manufacturer should be to overcome poverty, to relieve society as a whole from misery, and to bring it wealth.

Contribution

Building a Winning Business. The Matsushita story is one of the most impressive industrial achievements of the 20th century.

The company's first break was an order to make insulator plates. The order was delivered on time and was high quality. Matsushita began to make money. He then developed an innovative bicycle light. Initially, retailers were unimpressed. Then Matsushita had his salesmen leave a switched on light in each shop. This simple product demonstration impressed the retailers, and the business took off.

> To be out of stock is due to carelessness.

The Importance of Customer Service. The company understood customer service before anyone in the West had even thought about it:

- don't sell customers goods that they are attracted to. Sell them goods that will benefit them;
- after-sales service is more important than assistance before sales. It is through such service that one gets permanent customers.

Efficiency and Quality. Matsushita emphasized efficient production and quality products.

To be out of stock is due to carelessness. If this happens, apologize to the customers, ask for their address, and tell them that you will deliver the goods immediately.

Risk-taking Pays. Matsushita took risks and backed his beliefs at every stage.

The classic example of this is the development of the videocassette. Matsushita developed VHS video and licensed the technology. Sony developed Betamax, which was immeasurably better, but failed to license the technology. The world standard is VHS and Betamax is consigned to history.

Business with a Conscience. Matsushita advocated business with a conscience, reflected in his paternalistic employment practices. During a recession early in its life the company did not lay anyone off. This cemented loyalty.

It is not enough to work conscientiously. No matter what kind of job, you should think of yourself as being completely in charge of and responsible for your own work.

The Role of the Leader. Big things and little things are the leader's job. Middle-level arrangements can be delegated.

Matsushita also explained the role of the leader in more cryptic style: "The tail trails the head. If the head moves fast, the tail will keep up the same pace. If the head is sluggish, the tail will droop."

The Broader Obejctives of Business. Matsushita mapped out the broader spiritual aims he believed a business should have. Profit was not enough. The mission of a manufacturer should be to overcome poverty, to relieve society as a whole from misery, and bring it wealth.

He outlined his basic management objective as follows: "Recognizing our responsibilities as industrialists, we will devote ourselves to the progress and development of society and the well-being of people through our business activities, thereby enhancing the quality of life throughout the world."

Failure to make a profit was regarded as a sort of crime against society: "We take society's capital, we take their people, we take their materials, yet without a good profit, we are using precious resources that could be better used elsewhere."

Business is demanding, serious, and crucial: "Business, we know, is now so complex and difficult, the survival of firms so hazardous in an environment increasingly unpredictable, competitive, and fraught with danger, that their continued existence depends on the day-to-day mobilization of every ounce of intelligence."

Context

Matsushita created a $42-billion business from nothing. He also created Panasonic, one of the world's most successful brands, and amassed a personal fortune of $3 billion.

The book explains the principles that made his business a success.

For More Information

Matsushita, Konosuke. *Quest for Prosperity*. Kyoto, Japan: PHP Institute, 1988.

Reengineering the Corporation
by James Champy and Michael Hammer

Reengineering the Corporation is seen as the key book in the reengineering revolution. It encourages organizations to take a fresh look at inefficient and outdated processes, and to focus on dramatic improvements in cost, quality, service, and speed. Although the message has been misinterpreted, reengineering remains a powerful tool for change.

Getting Started

In the authors' view, reengineering must focus on the fundamental rethinking and radical redesign of key business processes. Dramatic improvements in cost, quality, service, and speed are the objective, and organizations must make key processes as lean and profitable as possible, discarding peripheral processes and people if necessary.

Reengineering should go far beyond altering and refining processes: the aim is "to reverse the Industrial Revolution." Organizations should start with a blank piece of paper and map out processes to identify how their business should operate. They should then attempt to translate the paper into concrete reality.

Reengineering puts a premium on the skills and potential of the people at the center of the organization, and should also tackle three key areas of management managerial roles, styles, and systems.

Contribution

Focus on Improving Core Processes. In the context of a fiercely competitive environment and the ability of IT to transform business processes, the book encourages organizations to take a fresh look at inefficient and outdated processes. Reengineering, according to the authors, is the fundamental rethinking and radical redesign of business processes.

Create a Lean Organization. The authors argue that organizations need to identify their key processes and make them as lean and profitable as possible. In some cases, peripheral processes and people need to be discarded.

> True reengineering is a recipe for a corporate revolution, and should go far beyond altering and refining processes: the past is history; the future is there to be coerced into the optimum shape.

Unfortunately, many organizations have taken this advice literally and downsized without reengineering. CSC, the consultancy founded by Champy and Hammer, surveyed more than 600 companies involved in reengineering projects in 1994. In the United States, an average 336 jobs were lost on each project. In Europe, the figure was 760 jobs per project.

Achieve a Complete Corporate Revolution. Simple business process reengineering is not enough, say the authors. True reengineering is a recipe for a corporate revolution, and should go far beyond altering and refining processes: the past is history; the future is there to be coerced into the optimum shape.

The authors believe that reengineering is concerned with rejecting conventional wisdom and received assumptions about the past. However, this can mean ignoring the experience of the past. Companies are discouraged from trying to understand why they have been successful and building on that.

Transform the Future. The authors suggest that organizations should start with a blank piece of paper. They should map out their processes to identify how their business should operate, and then attempt to translate the paper into concrete reality.

In practice, this has proved difficult to achieve. The authors now believe that companies tend not to cast the reengineering net widely; they find processes that can be reengineered quickly and stop at that point. They lack a vision for the future and the revolutionary approach to take reengineering forward.

Reengineer Management As Well. Part of the problem, they now believe, is that managers fail to impose change on themselves—they concentrate on tearing down processes, but they leave their own jobs and management styles intact. However, the old ways of management could eventually undermine the very structure of their rebuilt enterprise. The reengineering process should therefore tackle three key areas of management—managerial roles, styles, and systems.

Reengineering Should Be Built on Trust, Respect, and People. The authors believe that reengineering actually puts a premium on the people at the center of the organization. Once peripheral activities have been cut away, the new environment puts a premium on skills of the people who are left. Experience suggests that this has not happened so far: downsizing creates a difficult environment in which trust is frequently absent.

Context

Reengineering is seen by some as an old concept with a new label. Frederick W. Taylor's *Scientific Management* advocated similar change, but at an individual rather than an organizational level. Gary Hamel pointed out that reengineering followed a line from scientific management, industrial engineering, and business process improvement.

The mechanistic theme has been a key focal point for critics, who have made the point that reengineering owes more to visions of the corporation as a machine, rather than a human system. Peter Cohan, a former colleague, said the authors ignored the importance of people, describing them as objects who handle processes. Christopher Lorenz of the *Financial Times* believed that the authors failed to state whether organizations should undertake behavioral and cultural changes in parallel with reengineering.

It has also been easy to take the book's messages too literally. Reengineering has been seen as a synonym for redundancy, and the book has been blamed for a wave of downsizing.

For More Information

Champy, James, and Michael Hammer. *Reengineering the Corporation.* New York: HarperBusiness, 1993.

Relationship Marketing

by Regis McKenna

Relationship marketing has become one of the most important determinants of corporate success. Retaining customers and maximizing lifetime customer value are critical to long term revenue and profitability. Regis McKenna's book sets out the principles of building successful relationships, using technology to understand customers and communicate effectively with them.

Getting Started

The author insists that marketing is not a separate corporate function. Marketing, he says, is everything. No longer mass marketing, it is now customization and personalization. Technology enables this change, allowing companies to deal with the growing power of the customer and the accelerating pace of change.

Contribution

Integrating the Customer with the Company. McKenna believes that technology and the choices it offers are transforming the marketplace. All companies are technology companies, using technology to customize and offer unlimited choice. The knowledge and understanding available through technology are changing the nature of marketing.

Dominating Markets. A strong brand reflects a successful relationship. Owning the market, not just competing in it, is therefore a key goal. Market dominance is vital to attracting customers, business partners, and the best employees. The starting point is to define a narrow market and dominate it, before deepening and widening the relationships.

Dialog with Customers. One-way advertising is no longer valid. Companies need to have dialog with customers using trials, user groups, and other feedback mechanisms. McKenna calls this "experience-based marketing" based on a deep understanding of the customer.

Merger of Products and Services. In industries like computing, around 75% of the business consists of services such as consulting, systems integration, security, and customer support. These are all essential to customers and form part of a solution that builds relationships.

Faster Time to Market. Companies must reduce time to market as much as possible, as delay leads to lost opportunities. The marketplace is also changing rapidly so it is important to stay close to customers.

Market Creation Replaces Market Sharing. Companies must differentiate their products to dominate a market. This may mean starting with small sectors and acting like entrepreneurs. Market creation also means educating customers and listening to them. However, quantitative information can distract companies from entering small sectors. Qualitative judgment may be more important.

The Importance of Relationships. Relationships, according to McKenna, are more important with complex high-risk products. Customers need reassurance, education, support, and services to build and maintain their confidence in a company.

Dynamic Positioning. The author explains how dynamic positioning differs from traditional positioning. There are three elements:

- product positioning determines how a product fits into a competitive market;
- market positioning requires a company to understand the infrastructure, influences, and distribution channels in its market;
- corporate positioning determines whether a company is perceived as a credible and trusted supplier.

Product Positioning. Product positioning requires an understanding of the market environment, and must also focus on the intangible factors that are important to customers. Trust arises where customers have a strong relationship and continue to buy.

Product Success. McKenna cites ten characteristics of a successful product:

- appeals to a new market
- takes advantage of the best existing technologies
- depends on the market infrastructure for newly-developed technologies
- timing is right
- adapted to market requirements
- developed by small entrepreneurial teams
- customers involved in development
- adopted by early users
- generates a new language
- used in demonstrations, workshops, and user groups

Developing Relationships. Successful companies develop relationships with the whole market, not just customers. This is market infrastructure and it includes analysts, developers, retailers, journalists, suppliers, and other organizations who are mutually dependent. The leaders set the standard for their market and everyone else works with them in structural relationships. Strategic relationships with partners are important as they reduce development costs and speed up time to market. For smaller companies, the relationships provide credibility and access.

Selling to the Right Customers. McKenna breaks buyers into four categories: innovators, early adopters, majority, and laggards

It is important for companies to identify the type of customers they are aiming at.

Context

This book was one of the first to highlight the importance of relationships with customers, suppliers, distributors, and other players in the marketplace. Relationship marketing is now a mainstream marketing practice and an essential tool for companies in every field.

The book uses examples mainly from high tech companies where McKenna had a great deal of hands-on experience, but lessons from the book can be easily adapted for other markets. One of its key points is the dependent relationships that have grown within technology markets. Companies in hardware, software, and related services depend on each other for success and even competitors have been known to form strategic alliances to ensure market development. This theme is explored in *Co-opetition* by Nalebuff and Brandenburger (HarperCollins Business, 1996).

For More Information

McKenna, Regis. *Relationship Marketing: Successful Strategies for the Age of the Customer*. Cambridge, MA: Perseus, 1991.

Riding the Waves of Culture

by Fons Trompenaars and Charles Hampden-Turner

Riding the Waves of Culture is an examination of the cultural imponderables faced by managers in the global village. Based on exhaustive research, it systematically "dimensionalizes" cultural differences, identifying seven areas, such as attitude to rules and awareness of time, in which different nations have fundamentally different conceptions. Anyone whose work involves dealing with people from other cultures would benefit from reading it.

Getting Started

Fons Trompenaars studied at a top U.S. business school where he started thinking about cultural differences. "I started wondering if any of the American management techniques I was brainwashed with in eight years of the best business education money could buy would apply in the Netherlands, where I came from, or indeed in the rest of the world."

Charles Hampden-Turner is an international authority on cross-cultural communication who taught for many years in the United States and, like his coauthor, worked for Shell.

The book is based on meticulous quantitative research (over 15 years, 15,000 people from 50 countries were surveyed) and more than 900 seminars presented in 18 countries. Its main contentions are that basic to understanding other cultures is the awareness of cultural difference; that cultural difference can be systematically analyzed; that flexibility, a certain amount of humility, and a sense of humor are needed in dealing with cultures other than our own; and that the reconciliation of difference is the supreme managerial art.

Contribution

Culture. Culture is a series of rules and methods that a society has evolved to deal with the recurring problems it faces. They have become so basic that, like breathing, we no longer think about how we approach or resolve them.

People should be aware, first, that they belong to a culture and have a specific way of doing things, and they should be prepared, second, for a different response from the one they are accustomed to receiving when they do business with someone whose culture differs from theirs.

Seven Dimensions of Culture. In analyzing cultural differences, the authors identify seven dimensions in which different or contrasting attitudes are particularly crucial. They are:

- universalism vs. particularism
- individualism vs. collectivism
- neutral vs. emotional
- specific vs. diffuse
- achievement vs. ascription
- attitude toward time
- attitude toward the environment

Universalism and Particularism. There are two fundamentally distinct ways of dealing with situations that the book labels "universalism" and "particularism."

Universalists (including Americans, Canadians, Australians, and the Swiss) advocate one best way, "what is good and right can be defined and always applies." They focus on rules and procedure. Particularists (South Koreans, Chinese, and Malaysians) feel that circumstances dictate how ideas and practices should be applied. They focus on the peculiar nature of any given situation and on particular relationships.

Universalists doing business with particularists should be prepared for meandering or irrelevancies that do not seem to be going anywhere.

Particularists doing business with universalists should be prepared for rational and professional arguments and presentations and little else.

Collectivist and Individualist. The book also contrasts the collectivist mindset with the individualist one.

The United States again comes at one extreme of the spectrum, emphasizing the individual before the group. Countries such as Egypt and France are at the other end.

Individualists working with collectivists must tolerate time taken to consult and negotiators who can only agree tentatively and may withdraw an offer after consulting with superiors.

The Role of the International Manager. Given the wide range of basic differences in how different cultures perceive the world, it is evident that the international manager is moving in a world riddled with potential pitfalls. There are also profound differences between those who show their feelings (such as Italians) and those who hide them (such as the Japanese), and those who accord status on the basis of achievement and those who ascribe it on the basis of family and age.

The international manager needs to go beyond awareness of cultural differences. He or she needs to respect these differences and take advantage of diversity through reconciling cross-cultural dilemmas. The international manager reconciles cultural dilemmas. In the end, the only positive route forward is through reconciliation. Those societies that can reconcile better are better at creating wealth.

Context

Tom Peters called *Riding the Waves of Culture* a masterpiece. "What's not okay is cultural arrogance. If you come to another's turf with sensitivity and open ears . . . you're halfway home."

Gary Hamel takes the authors to task for their criticisms of U.S. cultural inflexibility: "So Americans will never understand foreign cultures? Funny how American companies are out-competing their European competitors in Asia and Latin America. . . . Where I agree with Trompenaars is that the future belongs to the cosmopolitans."

The cultural aspects of managing internationally are likely to gain in importance as the full force of globalization affects industries and individuals. In this respect the value of the book's contribution is undeniable. It has been argued, however, that its stress on cultural relativism and adaptability might become outmoded if capital markets were to enforce "global rules of the game" independent of different cultures.

For More Information

Trompenaars, Fons, and Charles Hampden-Turner. *Riding the Waves of Culture*. 2nd ed. New York: McGraw-Hill, 1997.

The Rise and Fall of Strategic Planning

by Henry Mintzberg

Mintzberg shows how over-emphasizing analysis and hard facts limits strategic planning. Planning should be something visionary and creative. The book has become an influential classic.

Getting Started

Planning is concerned with analysis; strategy making is concerned with synthesis. Strategic planners tend to make false assumptions that discontinuities can be predicted; the future will resemble the past; and strategy making can be formalized. They tend to be detached from action and the reality of the organization.

Planners typically gather hard data on their industry, markets, and competitors. Soft data—such as networks of contacts, talking with customers, suppliers, and employees—have been ignored. Strategy formulation has been dominated by logic and analysis. This narrows options. Intuition and creativity need to become part of the process.

Contribution

Strategy and Planning. Planning codifies, elaborates, and operationalizes existing company strategy. In contrast, strategy is either an emergent pattern or a deliberate perspective, and cannot be planned. While planning is concerned with analysis, strategy making is concerned with synthesis.

The Nature of Planners. Planners do have value, but only as strategy finders, analysts, and catalysts. At their most effective, they unearth strategies in unexpected pockets of the organization, whose potential can then be explored.

Problems with Planning Practices. The three main pitfalls are:

- the assumption that discontinuities can be predicted;
- planners become detached from the reality of the organization;
- the assumption that strategy making can be formalized.

The Assumption That Discontinuities Can Be Predicted. Forecasting techniques often assume that the future will resemble the past. This gives artificial reassurance, and creates strategies that disintegrate as they are overtaken by events.

Detachment from the Reality of the Organization. If the system does the thinking, strategy must be detached from operations, and thinkers from doers. This disassociation of thinking from acting lies at the root of strategic planning's problem.

Hard Data and Soft Data. Planners typically gather hard data on their industry, markets, and competitors. Soft data—networks of contacts, talking with customers, suppliers, and employees, using intuition, and using the grapevine—have all but been ignored.

Hard data are often anything but. There is the fallacy of measuring what's measurable. There is a tendency to favor cost-leadership strategies (emphasizing operating efficiencies, which are generally measurable) over product-leadership strategies (emphasizing innovative design or high quality, which tend to be less measurable).

To gain useful understanding of an organization's competitive situation, soft data need to be dynamically integrated into the planning process. They may be difficult to analyze, but they are indispensable for synthesis—the key to strategy making.

The Assumption That Strategy Making Can Be Formalized. The emphasis on logic and analysis creates a narrow range of options. Alternatives that do not fit into the predetermined structure are ignored.

The right side of the brain needs to become part of the process, with its emphasis on intuition and creativity. Planning defines and preserves categories. Creativity creates categories or rearranges established ones.

Thus strategic planning can neither provide creativity, nor deal with it when it emerges. Mold-breaking strategies grow initially like weeds—they are not cultivated and can take root anywhere.

The Nature of Strategy Making. Mintzberg defines strategy making thus:

- It is derived from synthesis.
- It is informal and visionary, rather than programmed and formalized.
- It relies on divergent thinking, intuition, and using the subconscious. This leads to outbursts of creativity as new discoveries are made.
- It is irregular, unexpected, ad hoc, and instinctive. It upsets stable patterns.
- Managers are adaptive information manipulators—opportunists, rather than aloof conductors.
- It is done in time of instability characterized by discontinuous change.
- It results from an approach that takes in broad perspectives and is, therefore, visionary, and involves a variety of actors capable of experimenting and then integrating.

Context

The book reflects a general dissatisfaction with strategic planning. Research by the U.S. Planning Forum found that only 25% of companies considered their planning was effective.

The book attracted much attention and debate. It also brought a spirited response from the defenders of strategy. Andrew Campbell, coauthor of *Corporate-level Strategy*, wrote: "Strategic planning is not futile. Research has shown that some companies—both conglomerates and more focused groups—have strategic planning processes that add real value." Campbell further argued that the corporate center must develop a value-creating, corporate-level strategy and build the management processes needed to implement it.

Management guru Gary Hamel commented: "Henry views strategic planning as a ritual, devoid of creativity and meaning. He is undoubtedly right when he argues that planning doesn't produce strategy. But rather than use the last chapter of the book to create a new charter for planners, Henry might have put his mind to the question of where strategies actually do come from!"

For More Information

Mintzberg, Henry. *The Rise and Fall of Strategic Planning*. New York: Free Press, 1994.

Small Is Beautiful

by E. F. Schumacher

Schumacher's book has become one of the most influential works ever on environmental issues and business. It looks at traditional Western economics in a radical way, arguing that big is not always best. His work has struck a chord with politicians, environmentalists, and a growing number of business leaders.

Getting Started

Schumacher argues that the relentless pursuit of profit and progress has resulted in economic inefficiency, environmental pollution, and inhumane working conditions. Instead, he proposes greater use of "intermediate technology," based on smaller work units, communal ownership, and the use of local labor and resources.

Contribution

The Problem of Production. Schumacher believes that business has not solved the problem of production. Businesses are using up the store of natural capital and he cites the spiraling demands on fossil fuels and other finite natural resources. The proposal to replace fossil fuels with human-made energy sources such as nuclear fuels creates its own problems.

The author's view is that the concept of peace through universal prosperity is also unachievable. He argues that if prosperity grew in line with population growth, the impact on fuel consumption and subsequent atmospheric pollution would be extremely damaging.

Changing the Emphasis of Economics. The solution, he claims, lies in a reorientation of science and technology. The emphasis should not be on concentrating production in larger and larger units, it should be on making technology accessible and suitable for small-scale application. He also believes that technology should leave room for human creativity, rather than replacing it.

> Traditional economic theories are driven by market forces.

Traditional economic theories are driven by market forces. Schumacher believes that they ignore humanity's dependence on the natural world. Economics, he says, is also overdependent on quantitative measures such as gross domestic product and consequently overlooks qualitative measures such as the impact of the economy on the environment.

According to Schumacher, economics looks upon human labor as a necessary "input" to wealth. Business takes every opportunity to reduce the cost, making work meaningless. An alternative point of view says that work should enable people to utilize their faculties and join in a common cause. This is in contrast to the theory that consumption is the only real end.

Toward a Smaller Scale. Schumacher points out that scale is another important element of economic thinking. The traditional theory is that economic organizations, such as businesses, should be as large as possible. He counters that they only need to be big enough to meet real needs.

Schumacher also argues for the more effective use of land. It is not simply a factor of production. He cites the flight from the land as evidence of this misunderstanding.

The Efficiency Gap. The author is critical of modern industrial efficiency. The United States, for example, has around 5% of the world's population, yet requires almost 40% of the world's primary resources to sustain its economy.

Apart from the demand on resources, Schumacher argues that this situation also creates problems between producer and consumer countries. An economy that is so dependent on other resources must in the long term suffer.

A Human Face for Technology. Schumacher believes that technology needs a human face. Technology should free people from the burdens of work. He describes how the Intermediate Technology Development Group aims to broaden the use of technology, supporting production by the masses instead of mass production. This approach, he feels, would be an effective way to support regional economic development around the world.

Despite his emphasis on small-scale regional development, Schumacher accepts that large organizations will remain an important part of the economy. He believes that setting up smaller units within a larger organization could help to overcome any inherent problems of size.

Context

Schumacher, like Paul Hawken et al. in *Natural Capitalism*, highlights the conflict between business growth and the destruction of natural resources. He proposes a system of environmentally friendly business that takes account of limited resources and offers everyone a stake in success.

He draws on a wide variety of influences and sources to develop his themes, including Buddhist economics, Adam Smith, Ghandi, and economists such as J. K. Galbraith.

Although Schumacher's work could be regarded as utopian, he proposes practical working solutions, some of which have already been put into successful practice.

For More Information

Schumacher, E. F. *Small is Beautiful: A Study of Economics As If People Mattered.* New York: HarperCollins, 1989.

Strategy and Structure
by Alfred Chandler

Chandler's book is regarded by many commentators as a masterpiece. It demonstrates the critical link between a company's strategy and its structure, and played an influential role in the profitable decentralization of many leading corporations. The book's findings remain relevant to new forms of organization such as the federated organization, the multicompany coalition, and the virtual company.

Getting Started

According to the author, structure should be driven by strategy—and if it isn't, inefficiency results. The structure of many corporations is driven by market forces: recognition that production had to be market-driven led large organizations to change to a looser divisional structure.

Increases in scale also led to business owners having to recruit a new breed of professional manager, as professional management coordinates the flow of product to customers more efficiently than market forces.

A planned economy is important to long-term organizational success.

Contribution

Structure Should Be Driven by Strategy Strategy is the determination of the long term goals and objectives of an enterprise, and the adoption of courses of action and the allocation of resources necessary for reaching these goals.

A firm's structure is dictated by its chosen strategy—and unless structure follows strategy, inefficiency results.

A company should establish a strategy and then seek to create the structure appropriate to achieving it.

Structure Driven by Market Forces. Organizational structures in companies such as Du Pont, Sears Roebuck, General Motors, and Standard Oil were driven by the changing demands and pressures of the marketplace.

The market-driven proliferation of product lines in Du Pont and General Motors led to a shift from a functional, monolithic organizational form to a more loosely coupled divisional structure.

> Organizations and their managements require a planned economy rather than a capitalist free-for-all dominated by the unpredictable whims of market forces.

The Rise of the Multidivisional Organization. The multidivisional organization removed the executives responsible for the destiny of the entire enterprise from the more routine operational responsibilities.

It gave them the time, information, and even psychological commitment for long-term planning and appraisal.

The Professionalization of Management. The managerial revolution was fueled by the rise of oil-based energy, the development of the steel, chemical, and engineering industries, and a dramatic rise in the scale of production and the size of companies.

Increases in scale led to business owners having to recruit a new breed of professional manager. The roles of the salaried manager and technician are vital, as the visible hand of management coordinates the flow of product to customers more efficiently than Adam Smith's "invisible hand" of the market.

The Importance of a Planned Economy. Organizations and their managements require a planned economy rather than a capitalist free-for-all dominated by the unpredictable whims of market forces.

Context

The book is based on Chandler's research into major U.S. corporations between 1850 and 1920. Its subtitle is "Chapters in the history of the American industrial enterprise," but its impact went far beyond that of a brilliantly researched historical text. Alfred Chandler's *Strategy and Structure* is a theoretical masterpiece which has had profound influence on both practitioners and thinkers.

Chandler was highly influential in the trend among large organizations for decentralization in the 1960s and 1970s. While in 1950 around 20% of Fortune 500 corporations were decentralized, this had increased to 80% by 1970. In the 1980s, Chandler's thinking was influential in the transformation of AT&T from what was in effect a production-based bureaucracy to a marketing organization.

Until recent times, Chandler's conclusion that structure follows strategy has largely been accepted as a fact of corporate life. Now, the debate has been rekindled.

Tom Peters said, "I think he got it exactly wrong. For it is the structure of the organization that determines, over time, the choices that it makes about the markets it attacks."

In *Managing on the Edge*, Richard Pascale said, "The underlying assumption is that organizations act in a rational, sequential manner. Yet most executives will readily agree that it is often the other way around. The way a company is organized, whether functional focused or driven by independent divisions, often plays a major role in shaping its strategy. Indeed, this accounts for the tendency of organizations to do what they best know how to do—regardless of deteriorating success against the competitive realities."

Gary Hamel, author of *Leading the Revolution*, said, "Those who dispute Chandler's thesis that structure follows strategy miss the point. Of course strategy and structure are inextricably intertwined. Chandler's point was that new challenges give rise to new structures. The challenges of size and complexity, coupled with advances in communications and techniques of management control, produced divisionalization and decentralization. These same forces, several generations on, are now driving us toward new structural solutions—the federated organization, the multi-company coalition, and the virtual company. Few historians are prescient. Chandler was."

For More Information

Chandler, Alfred. *Strategy and Structure*. New York: Doubleday, 1962.

Theory of Economic Development
by Joseph A. Schumpeter

One of Schumpeter's claims to fame—many have rated him one of the greatest economists of the 20th century— is that he was among the first to set out a clear concept of entrepreneurship and its function within an economy. The key factor is innovation. Entrepreneurs innovate. Innovations create dynamism. Schumpeter's work was for a long time overshadowed by that of Keynes, but increased interest in innovation since the 1980s has led to a renaissance of Schumpeterian economics and a renewal of interest in this book in particular.

Getting Started

The Theory of Economic Development sets out to uncover the forces within an economy that produce endogenous change. Schumpeter explains the processes of economic development by means of microtheory; he bases his study on innovative entrepreneurs and uses them to make large-scale factors, such as capital accumulation, interest, and company profits, understandable as dynamic processes.

Contribution

Static and Dynamic Phenomena. According to Schumpeter, static general concepts of the workings of national economies are inadequate to explain the periodic changes in their stationary equilibrium, that is, the fluctuations of the economic cycle, and economic progress. This is because such concepts ascribe change solely to external influences. The central element in any overall concept ought, in his view, to be economic development, which alters the existing balance endogenously, that is, from within.

It is necessary then to distinguish between static phenomena, in which no changes take place, and dynamic ones, which constitute a disturbance of the static balance and lead to changes until counteracting forces bring the economy into a new state of balance. This development is apparent in alternating phases of boom and recession, which, consequently, represent necessary manifestations accompanying economic development.

The Stationary Economy. Schumpeter's starting point is a stationary economy, that is, a system in a state of balance that periodically repeats itself. These are some of its features.

- All economic plans are aimed at achieving an optimum and need only be updated from period to period.
- In all private households and businesses the income corresponds exactly to the outgoings.
- In each period only those goods are consumed that were produced in the foregoing period and then exchanged.
- The possibilities of production are fixed in advance. This means that the production function is invariable, with the result that there are no possibilities for improvement or further investment.
- Perfect competition reduces aggregate profit to zero and consequently removes any incentive to entrepreneurial action.

But the function of capitalism is not, says Schumpeter, to administer existing structures, but to change them:

- In the static concept, there is no endogenous mechanism that could lead out of the status quo. Consequently, changes can only be brought about exogenously, that is, by external factors, social, political, and cultural influences, such as population growth, capital growth, or altered preferences and technical or organizational improvements (organic growth).
- In the dynamic concept, on the other hand, economic development originates in innovations. Here too, progress in production methods and organizational improvements play a part, but as a result of entrepreneurial action.

Innovations. Innovations are the practical implementation of knowledge, ideas, or discoveries, and rely, therefore, not on inventiveness as such, but on entrepreneurial abilities. Technological and organizational improvements could be described as new possibilities for factor combination. The innovation could, therefore, lie in the introduction of new products or production methods, in the opening up of new markets or supplies of resources, or in organizational changes.

These innovations are put into practice by dynamic entrepreneurs; they represent the microfoundation of the macrophenomenon of social development. Schumpeter posits two conditions as necessary for innovative entrepreneurs to appear as economic actors:

- Development takes place by means of individual actions and of incentives and appears as the aggregate of the consequences of individual actions. Only when profits can be realized through innovations, will the latter happen.
- Companies must have the opportunity to react to these incentives by changing the way they act. In balanced conditions, all production capacity is fully exploited. Consequently banks must make capital available so that potentially profitable investment opportunities can be realized through a change in the input of resources.

The Outcomes of Innovation. Profits from innovation make it possible to meet interest payments. As a result the rate of interest will be determined by the demand for capital and this demand, in turn, by the extent of profitable investment opportunities. Interest rates are consequently indicators of economic progress. Profit and interest can thus be explained as outcomes of economic dynamism.

Context

Joseph Schumpeter (1883–1950) was an Austrian professor of political economy who belonged to the Vienna school of national economics. He later emigrated to the United States and held a professorship at Harvard. His work is considered to be a precursor of econometrics.

Schumpeter's thoughts had Marxist roots, but since Marx's doctrine of the value of labor was in disrepute, he chose the neoclassical theory of value as the foundation for his work. This makes it difficult to assign Schumpeter a place in economic history. He proclaimed the significance of the business organization, but at the same time believed in the victory of socialism, famously answering no when asked if capitalism would survive. He realized himself that his work was likely to be overshadowed by Keynes's, and for most of the latter part of the 20th century this proved indeed to be the case.

For More Information

Schumpeter, Joseph A. *The Theory of Economic Development: An Inquiry into Profits, Capital, Credit, Interest, and the Business Cycle.* (trans. Opies). New Brunswick, NJ: Transaction Publishers, 1982.

The Theory of Social and Economic Organization

by Max Weber

It is quite easy to make Weber's book sound as if it was intended to be a source text for Franz Kafka's novels and Charlie Chaplin's film *Modern Times*, not to mention George Orwell's *1984*. Weber is often incorrectly assumed to have been an advocate of bureaucracy and a mechanistic society, rather than someone who described bureaucracy—with at least some degree of correctness—as the most efficient and rational means of organization. In fact, as R. J. Kilcullen puts it, "bureaucracy was for Weber what capitalism was for Marx, the admired enemy." No understanding of the way modern organizations work would be complete without a study of this book.

Getting Started

Max Weber was a versatile thinker who was a professor of political economy at the universities of Freiburg and Heidelberg in Germany. He is best known today as one of the founding fathers of modern sociology.

The Theory of Social and Economic Organization grew out of his philosophical inquiries into the nature of authority and how it is transmitted. Weber identified three types of authority, the "charismatic," based on the individual qualities of a leader and reverence for him or her among his or her followers, the "traditional," based on custom and usage, and the "rational-legal," based on the rule of objective law. Bureaucracy is the most efficient way of implementing the rule of law.

Contribution

How Bureaucracy Works. There are four main principles identified by Weber as characteristic of a rational-legal bureaucracy:

- The organization is structured around official functions which are bound by rules, each area having its own specified competence.
- Functions are structured into offices organized into a hierarchy that follows technical rules and norms for which training is provided.
- The administration is separated from the ownership of the means of production.
- The rules, decisions, and actions of the administration are recorded in writing.

The Impersonality of Bureaucracy. The most important feature of bureaucracy—its main strength as well as its main weakness—is its impersonality.

Impersonality is a strength in that it minimizes the abuse of power by leaders because:

- offices are ranked in hierarchical order;
- operations are conducted in accordance with impersonal rules;
- officials are allocated specific duties and areas of responsibility;
- appointments are made on the basis of qualifications and suitability for the post.

It is a weakness in that:

- their characteristic information processing and filtering to the top makes bureaucracies cumbersome and slow to react;

- their machinery makes it difficult to handle individual cases, because rules and procedures require all individuals to be treated as if they were the same;
- bureaucratization leads to depersonalization, because the roles of officials are circumscribed by written definitions of their authority, and there is a set of rules and procedures to cater for every contingency.

Toward Ultimate Efficiency. The purely bureaucratic type of administrative organization is, from a purely technical point of view, capable of attaining the highest degree of efficiency. It is, in this sense, the most rational known means of carrying out imperative control over human beings. It is superior to any other form of organization in precision, in stability, in the stringency of its discipline, and in its reliability.

Context

Bureaucratic organization as expounded by Max Weber became the model for the 20th-century organization, and was encapsulated in Alfred P. Sloan, Jr.'s General Motors and Harold Geneen's ITT. Strictly implemented, and in combination with regimented mass-production as practiced by Henry Ford, who echoed some of Weber's thoughts in his faith in strict demarcations and his fervently mechanistic approach to business, it could produce a nightmare scenario for the world of work in the 20th century.

Weber himself could see no realistic substitute for bureaucracy. He regarded its triumph with distaste, but as inevitable. Only in the latter part of the 20th century did new and more humane concepts of the organization emerge and start to win adherents. The roots of some of the latest are in biology and the new sciences of chaos and complexity, areas unknown to Weber. Today's organizations are talked of in terms of fractals and amoebas—they are imagined as elusive and ever-changing rather than efficient and static.

The regularity of the machine age has given way to the tumult, ambiguity, and complexity of the information age.

Even so, Max Weber remains important. In his book *Gods of Management*, Charles Handy chose as one of the gods Apollo, who is characterized by a Weber-like faith in rules and systems. Aspects of the bureaucratic model remain alive and well in a great many organizations where hierarchies, demarcations, and exhaustive rules dominate.

The influential author Gary Hamel notes: "Every organization wrestles with two conflicting needs: the need to optimize in the name of economic efficiency, and the need to experiment in the name of growth and renewal. Authoritarian bureaucracies, of the sort that rebuilt the Japanese economy after the war, serve well the goal of optimization. While there is experimentation here, it is tightly constrained. Anarchical networks, of the sort that predominate in Italy's fashion industry, allow for unfettered experimentation, but are always vulnerable to more disciplined competitors. Weber staked out one side of the argument; Tom Peters the other. As always, what is required is a synthesis."

For More Information

Weber, Max. *The Theory of Social and Economic Organization*. New York: Free Press, 1947.

Theory Z

by William Ouchi

The book is subtitled *How American Business Can Meet the Japanese Challenge,* and the issue is still as important as it was when *Theory Z* was published in 1981. Ouchi believes that one of the major differences between Japanese and Western companies is their respective approach to managing people. He claims that Western companies who adopt the Japanese approach and adapt it to the Western business environment will be able to transform their business.

Getting Started

Ouchi believes that Japanese success is derived from a very strong company philosophy, a distinct corporate culture, long-range staff development, and decision making based on consensus. The result, he claims, is lower staff turnover, increased job commitment, and higher productivity—all important factors in determining competitiveness. He argues that Western companies should not simply adopt Japanese practices, but adapt them. These are the firms that he calls Type Z organizations and he gives detailed insights into U.S. companies that have transformed themselves in this way.

Contribution

The Real Forces behind Productivity. Ouchi believes that productivity is not just working harder. Trust is an essential factor, enabling people to make a contribution that will be respected. Subtlety is also important, allowing teams to balance their members in line with their skills, rather than seniority. According to the author, intimacy is a feature of all aspects of Japanese life, and this enables people to cooperate effectively at work.

Lifetime Employment. The author reports that major firms hire people just once a year. Staff are guaranteed employment until their retirement at 55, and any promotion takes place from within. The employment system is mirrored in the satellite system of suppliers and subcontractors that surround a major firm and its bank. The trading relationships are permanent and stable.

Job Rotation. Ouchi points out that the Japanese employment system features nonspecialist career paths so that staff gain a broader experience of the ways of the whole company. This is a form of lifelong job rotation. The Western system, he claims, rewards specialists and there is less chance of interaction between staff.

Working to Common Objectives. According to the author, the basic mechanism of control in Japan is the corporate philosophy and objectives. All other company policy is derived from that. The company values and beliefs are also derived from the overall philosophy.

Decision Making by Consensus. Ouchi explains that, in this method of decision making, everyone gets involved. This may not result in the best decision, but it means that everybody understands the reasons for the decision and shares a commitment and responsibility for its success.

Japanese and Western Companies Compared. According to Ouchi, these are the key differences:

- lifetime employment versus short-term employment;
- slow promotion versus rapid promotion;
- nonspecialist career path versus specialist career path;
- implicit control mechanisms versus explicit;
- collective decision making versus individual decision making;
- collective responsibility versus individual responsibility.

Type Z Companies. Ouchi uses the term to describe Western companies that have adapted Japanese practices. They encourage employees to stay longer, but have a faster promotion ladder. They substitute "management by walking about" for the job rotation of Japanese firms. Type Z companies encourage collaboration, but still maintain individual responsibility for decision making.

Creating a Type Z Company. The author outlines the key stages for leaders who want to transform their company:

- understand a Type Z company and your own role in it;
- audit your company's philosophy to detect inconsistencies;
- define a suitable company philosophy;
- create structures and incentives to support the new philosophy;
- develop staff interpersonal skills;
- involve employees and unions in the transformation;
- stabilize employment;
- broaden career path development;
- encourage participation.

Context

Comparing Japanese and Western business practice has a long tradition.

W. Edwards Deming, paradoxically, took Western ideas on quality to Japan after World War II. He made an important contribution to Japanese economic recovery and the country's subsequent reputation for quality. It was only when Western observers realized the potential impact of Japan on Western economies that they took notice of Deming's writings.

William Ouchi offers a valuable insight into the human factors that make Japanese business so successful. However, Nonaka and Takeuchi in their 1994 book *The Knowledge-creating Company* caution readers about over-reliance on contributory factors such as lifetime employment. They focus on the management of innovation within Japanese companies as a key competitive weapon.

Richard Pascale's *The Art of Japanese Management*, published in 1981, argues that Japanese success is largely attributable to what he called "soft factors"— style, shared values, skills, and staff. Western companies concentrate on "hard factors" such as strategy, structure, and systems.

For More Information

Ouchi, William. *Theory Z*. Reading, MA: Addison-Wesley, 1981.

The Third Wave
by Alvin Toffler

The obvious reason for reading a work of futurology more than 20 years after its publication is to see if the futurologist got it right. In many respects Toffler did. But there is a danger there also. Toffler predicted the electronic office and its effects. Now that most people work in electronic offices and live with their effects, perhaps it seems redundant to read a book simply in order to be able to congratulate the author on his foresight. What is startling about *The Third Wave* is that it was written so recently, and yet the technological leaps made since its publication have been so immense. The intriguing thing now is whether the author's broader analysis encompassed the developments that flowed from the developments he immediately foresaw. For many people Toffler's ideas are still intriguing.

Getting Started

Alvin Toffler began his career as a journalist but shot to international fame as a futurologist with the publication of his first book *Future Shock* in 1970. *The Third Wave* appeared ten years later, and *Power Shift* ten years after that.

The "Third Wave" referred to in the title is the superindustrial society that emerged toward the end of the 20th century and is still taking shape. It succeeded the "Second Wave," the industrialized society produced by the Industrial Revolution, which itself succeeded the agricultural phase of human development, the "First Wave." Each new wave was ushered in by the development of new technology. Electronics brought in the third.

Though the various waves followed one another in time, they did not affect the whole of the human race simultaneously—many people are still living under First Wave conditions. Toffler's main concern is with the transition from the Second to the Third Wave in advanced societies, but he also deals with possible areas of friction between people coexisting at different stages of development.

Contribution

Toward Mass Customization. The Third Wave, according to Toffler, is characterized by mass customization rather than mass production.

The essence of Second Wave manufacture was the long run of millions of identical standardized products. By contrast, the essence of Third Wave manufacture is the short run of partially or completely customized products.

The Second Wave strictly separated consumer and producer. The Third Wave will see the two become almost indistinguishable, as the consumer becomes involved in the actual process of production, expressing choices and preferences.

The Growth of Flexible Working. Toffler predicted the demise of the nine-to-five working day.

Machine synchronization shackled the human to the machine's capabilities and imprisoned all of social life in a common frame. It did so in capitalist and socialist countries alike. Now, as machine synchronization grows more precise, humans, instead of being imprisoned, are progressively freed. They are freed into more flexible ways of working, whether it is flextime or working at home.

Changes in Working Relationships. A partial shift toward the electronic office will be enough to trigger an eruption of social, psychological, and economic consequences. The coming word-quake means more than just new machines. It promises to restructure all the human relationships and roles in the office.

The Third Wave will produce anxiety and conflict as well as reorganization, restructuring, and, for some, rebirth into new careers and opportunities. The new systems will challenge all the old executive turfs, the hierarchies, the sexual role divisions, the departmental barriers of the past.

The Impact on the Corporation. Instead of clinging to a sharply specialized economic function, the corporation, prodded by criticism, legislation, and its own concerned executives, is becoming a multipurpose institution.

The organization is being driven to redefinition through five forces.

- Changes in the physical environment. Companies must take greater responsibility for the effect of their operations on the environment.
- Changes in the lineup of social forces. The actions of companies now have greater impact on those of other organizations such as schools, universities, civil groups, and political lobbies.
- Changes in the role of information. As information becomes central to production, as information managers proliferate in industry, the corporation, by necessity, impacts on the informational environment exactly as it impacts on the physical and social environment.
- Changes in government organization. The profusion of government bodies means that the business and political worlds interact to a far greater degree than ever before.
- Changes in morality. The ethics and values of organizations are becoming more closely linked to those of society. Behavior once accepted as normal is suddenly reinterpreted as corrupt, immoral, or scandalous. The corporation is increasingly seen as a producer of moral effects.

The organization of the future will be concerned with ecological, moral, political, racial, sexual, and social problems, as well as traditional commercial ones.

Context

Other studies of the future of working life tend to plunge headfirst into celebrations of the miracles of technology with little attempt to understand the human implications. Toffler is aware of them.

Many of his ideas have since been developed further by others. Charles Handy, for instance, has done a lot of work on the rise of homeworking.

Gary Hamel, author of *Leading the Revolution*, commented: "The post-industrial society is here! And Alvin Toffler saw it coming in 1980 . . . One of the challenges for anyone reading Toffler, or any other seer, is that there is no proprietary data about the future. Your competitors read Toffler, Naisbitt, and Negroponte too! The real challenge is to build proprietary foresight out of public data!"

For More Information

Toffler, Alvin. *The Third Wave*. New York: Bantam, 1980.

Toyota Production System
by Taiichi Ohno

During the last 40 years, Western car-makers have lurched from one crisis to another. They have always been one step behind. The company they have been following is the Japanese giant Toyota, and the reasons for this are explained by Taiichi Ohno in his brief book *Toyota Production System: Beyond Large-scale Production*.

Getting Started
The Toyota Production System was developed to help the company catch up with the United States. U.S. car workers were producing nine times as much as their Japanese counterparts. The Toyota system differed from the Western approach, emphasizing a reduction in costs rather than an increase in selling price.

According to the author, the company should be seen as a continuous and uniform whole, including suppliers as well as customers. Asking the question "why?" five times at each stage helps identify and solve problems before moving on.

Contribution
Catching Up with the West. The roots of the Toyota Production System lie in the immediate postwar years.

Toyoda Kiichiro, president of Toyoda Motor Company, demanded that the company should catch up with the United States. He gave his company three years to do so. Otherwise, he anticipated, the Japanese car industry would cease to exist.

At that time in the car industry, an average U.S. worker produced around nine times as much as a Japanese worker.

A Different Approach to Production. The Toyota Production System evolved by Ohno was strikingly different from approaches used in the West.

In the West, selling price was regarded as the combination of actual costs plus profit.

Toyota, believing that the consumer actually sets the price, concluded that profit resulted when costs were subtracted from the selling price. Their emphasis therefore was on reducing costs rather than increasing the selling price.

The Principles of the Toyota System. Three simple principles underlie the Toyota system:

- just-in-time production;
- wider responsibility for quality;
- concept of value stream.

Just-in-time Production. There is no point in producing cars, or anything else, in blind anticipation of someone buying them; production has to be closely tied to the market's requirements.

Wider Responsibility for Quality. Responsibility for quality rests with everyone.

Any quality defects need to be rectified as soon as they are identified.

Concept of Value Stream. The company should not be seen as a series of unrelated products and processes.

It should be seen as a continuous and uniform whole, a stream including suppliers as well as customers.

The Five Whys. Another central element in Ohno's system was the process of the five whys. This suggested that by asking "why?" five times and discovering the answer at each stage, the root of any problem can be discovered and solved.

Context

These concepts were brought to mass Western audiences thanks to work conducted at MIT as part of its International Motor Vehicle Program. The MIT research took five years, covered 14 countries, and looked exclusively at the worldwide car industry.

The researchers concluded that U.S. car-makers remained fixed in the mass-production techniques of the past. In contrast, Japanese management, workers, and suppliers worked to the same goals as each other—resulting in increased production, high quality, happy customers, and lower costs.

This research was the basis for the 1990 bestseller by James Womack, Daniel Jones, and Daniel Roos, *The Machine That Changed the World*. From lean production, Womack and Jones went on to propose the lean enterprise (based on research covering 25 U.S., Japanese, and German companies) and lean management. As with most management fads, it was willfully misinterpreted. It became linked to reengineering and, more worryingly, with downsizing.

The reality is that lean production as introduced by Ohno and Toyota is a highly effective concept. It can provide the economies of scale of mass production, the sensitivity to market and customer needs usually associated with smaller companies, and job enrichment for employees.

The West continues to see lean production as a means of squeezing more production from fewer people. This is a fundamental misunderstanding. Reducing the number of employees is the end rather than the means. Western companies have tended to reduce numbers and then declare themselves as lean organizations.

Womack argues that while lean production requires fewer people, the organization should then accelerate product development to tap new markets to keep the people at work.

Inevitably, lean production has its downside. The most obvious one is that its natural home is the mass-manufacturing world of car making. It can be more difficult to apply in other industries.

The second obvious problem with lean production is that it fails to embrace innovation and product development. It is one thing to make a product efficiently, but how do you originate exciting and marketable products in the first place?

Womack and Jones suggest that the critical starting point for lean thinking is value, but this is effectively one stage beyond the initial one of generating ideas. Even so, lean production has raised awareness, provided a new benchmark, and brought operational efficiency to a wider audience.

Harvard Business School's Michael Porter argues, "Organizations did well to employ the most up-to-date equipment, information technology, and management techniques to eliminate waste, defects, and delays. They did well to operate as close as they could to the productivity frontier. But while improving operational effectiveness is necessary to achieving superior profitability, it is not sufficient."

For More Information

Ohno, Taiichi. *Toyota Production System.* Cambridge, MA: Productivity Press, 1988.

Up the Organization
by Robert Townsend

Like any good satire, *Up the Organization* is not only irreverent and wickedly humorous, it is based on shrewd insight and sound common sense. Its questioning of the ghastly stifling orthodoxies of corporate thinking, corporate behavior, and corporate society is, many commentators note regretfully, as relevant now as it was when the book was first published over 30 years ago.

Getting Started
Townsend's first concern is for the people who are trapped in rigid organizational structures and unable to realize anything like their full potential. He has no time for the adornments of executive office or indeed anything that separates a management elite off from the experiences of ordinary workers. Turning his attention to more general issues, he suggests that all major organizations are operating on the wrong assumptions.

Contribution
The Organizational Trap. According to Townsend, in the average company, the employees in the mailroom, the president, the vice presidents, and the administrative staff have three things in common: they are docile, they are hired, and they are dull.

He claims that they are trapped in the pigeonholes of organization charts and that they have been made slaves to the rules of private and public hierarchies that run mindlessly on and on because nobody can change them.

The Problems of Business Schools. Townsend's advice to companies is not to hire Harvard Business School graduates.

He believes that this so-called elite is lacking in some pretty fundamental requirements for success: humility; respect for people on the firing line; deep understanding of the nature of the business and the kind of people who can enjoy themselves making it prosper; respect from way down the line; a demonstrated record of guts, industry, loyalty, judgment, fairness, and honesty under pressure.

> All the special perquisites of executive office are anathema to Townsend.

The End of Executive Office Perks. All the special perquisites of executive office are anathema to Townsend.

His list of no-nos includes:
* reserved parking spaces;
* special-quality stationery for the boss and the elite;
* muzak;
* bells and buzzers;
* company shrinks;
* outside directorships and trusteeships for the chief executive;
* the company plane.

The Wrong Kind of Leaders. According to Townsend, those with power, or who think they have power, are dangerous beings.

He claims that there is nothing fundamentally wrong with the country except that the leaders of all our major organizations are operating on the wrong assumptions.

Townsend believes that the United States is in a mess because for the last two hundred years it has been using the Catholic Church and Caesar's legions as the patterns for creating organizations.

He argues that until 40 or 50 years ago it made sense. The average churchgoer, soldier, and factory worker was uneducated and dependent on orders from above. And authority carried considerable weight because disobedience brought the death penalty or its equivalent.

Context

Townsend's genius lies in debunking the modern organization for its excess, stupidity, and absurdity. He collected his material in the course of his successful career as a director of American Express and president of Avis Rent-a-Car, then transformed himself into a witty commentator on the excesses of corporate life.

His bestseller *Up the Organization* is subtitled *How to Stop the Corporation from Stifling People and Strangling Profits*. Robert Heller called the book the first pop bestseller on business management. It is in the tradition of humorous bestsellers debunking managerial mythology and the high-minded seriousness of the theorists. In the 1950s there was *Parkinson's Law*, at the end of the 1960s came Townsend, more recently the Dilbert series has followed in their footsteps.

Townsend also belongs in the tradition of people-oriented business writing. His humor should not blind one to the underlying seriousness of his purpose.

Given that over 30 years have passed since its publication, the book still retains its freshness and originality, and its insights into the blind deficiencies of too many organizations remain sadly apt.

For More Information

Townsend, Robert. *Up the Organization: How to Stop the Corporation from Stifling People and Strangling Profits*. New York: Knopf, 1970.

Valuation
by Tom Copeland, Jack Murrin, and Tom Koller

Prompted by more intensive competition, the restructuring of industries, and ever more sophisticated stockholders, managers are checking over their company portfolios more critically than ever before in order to find out precisely where value is being created or destroyed. At a time when stakeholder value is gaining ground and stock options play an ever more important role compensating key employees, value-oriented portfolio structuring and resource allocation are central factors in strategic thinking.

Getting Started

The authors provide management with the necessary equipment to help them identify the sources and extent of value appreciation and depreciation within the company. In a series of theoretical analyses based on capital market research, they present the discounted cash flow (DCF) method and supplement their explanatory material with numerous case studies drawn from business practice.

Contribution

Company Value and Company Strategy. Companies, say the authors, need competitive strategies not only for the familiar goods and services markets, but also for the market in the disposal rights of companies. This is where the success of efforts to increase company value, which derives from cash flows, will be felt. Managers must pursue active value-management policies.

There are two stages in the development of a value-oriented policy: a restructuring that frees up the values locked into the company; establishing priorities for enhancing value.

Managers should regularly create and make use of opportunities to increase value. In this way they can avoid having to react under pressure later.

Company Value on a Cash Flow Basis: A Guide for Practitioners. The procedure that combines best with the objective of long-term value enhancement, the authors suggest, is the discounted cash flow (DCF) method.

The DCF method has the following advantages:

- The bases for valuation are free cash flows, as only these are available for servicing invested capital.
- Future expectations are systematically taken into account.
- Capital structure, financing costs, and risk are fully covered, so that the whole debit side of the company balance sheet is taken into consideration.
- An objective yardstick for comparing strategic options is created.
- Almost all the information needed to calculate the value of the company can be derived from existing and projected figures given in the company accounts.

In accordance with the DCF "component model," the value of a company's equity capital is equivalent to the value of various cash flows that lead ultimately to the cash flow to stockholders (dividends, stock repurchases, stock issues). This, say the authors, has four advantages.

1. Evaluating the relevant components of the company helps to identify and

understand the individual sources of investment and finance that influence the value of the company.

2. It identifies operating drivers with the greatest prospects for enhancing value.

3. It can be applied at various levels and combined with investment accounting.

4. It is sufficiently differentiated to cope with the complex situations and can be conducted using simple data-processing technology.

Using the DCF Component Model to Value a Company.

- **Stage one: analysis of historical performance.** First the relevant components of free cash flows are determined. Then a comprehensive profile of past performance is drawn up. It provides important clues to forecasting future performance.

- **Stage two: determining capital costs.** The first step is to establish the capital structure of the company. From this the weighting factors for the weighted average cost of capital (WACC) formula can be derived. Next, external capital costs are determined. Finally, equity capital costs are assessed, a process best conducted using the capital asset pricing model (CAPM) or the arbitrage pricing model (APM).

- **Stage three: prognosis of future performance.** Here the assumptions and scenarios relevant to a prognosis of the company's economic situation and competitive position in its industry are worked out. Forecasts also need to be made for the decisive drivers of value: growth and return on capital.

- **Stage four: estimating continuance value.** First the most suitable DCF method to apply must be decided on. The choice is between the long-term detailed prognosis, the continuing-value formula taking account of growing cash flows, and the value factor formula. The time frame for a detailed prognosis is established. The parameters are then assessed: these are the operating result after tax, free cash flow, the return on new investment, the growth rate, and the WACC. Finally, the continuing value is discounted to the present.

- **Stage five: calculation and interpretation of results.** The final phase comprises the calculation and checking of the value of the company, the interpretation of the results in the light of the circumstances surrounding the decision.

This method of calculation, the authors say, is also suitable for valuing companies under more complex framework conditions. It allows the options price theory to be applied to both their assets and their liabilities.

Context

Insufficient attention to value has meant that the value of companies worldwide has been reduced without this becoming apparent in their published accounts. This development prompted the consulting firm McKinsey to conduct extensive research that ultimately resulted in the DCF method. This book, whose three authors are partners at McKinsey, supplements accounting disciplines with a comprehensive plan for company evaluation. It was hailed on its appearance by finance experts worldwide as a must-read for managers, security analysts, and investors alike. The new edition shows how the system can be applied in the valuation of companies from the New Economy.

For More Information

McKinsey & Co., Tom Copeland, Jack Murrin, and Tim Koller. *Valuation: Measuring and Managing the Value of Companies.* 3rd ed. New York: John Wiley, 2000.

The Visual Display of Quantitative Information

by Edward R. Tufte

The book is widely regarded as one of the most authoritative guides to the visual presentation of statistical information through charts, graphs, and other graphic devices. It draws on the work of experts in the field and includes hundreds of examples of good and bad design.

Getting Started

Statistical graphics are used to communicate complex information clearly through words, numbers, and pictures. The author reports that, each year, somewhere between 900 billion and 2 trillion images of statistical graphics are produced, demonstrating the importance of the subject. Excellence, he believes, should lead the viewer to think about the content and explain complex ideas with clarity, precision, and efficiency.

Contribution

Tufte illustrates how graphics should tell a story in a way that ordinary statistics cannot do. He points out that good graphics must be based on sound data sources. However, graphics can sometimes be used to distort data. He distinguishes between perceived visual effects and attempts to deceive. Design variations, such as changing scale, can also distort information.

> Tufte illustrates how graphics should tell a story in a way that ordinary statistics cannot do.

The author suggests two ways to avoid distortion:

- the representation of numbers should be directly proportional to the numbers themselves;
- clear labeling should be used to remove ambiguity.

Tufte argues that it is a mistake to think that graphics should be used because data is intrinsically dull. This, he claims, is responsible for overelaborate graphics produced by designers who may not understand the significance of the numbers. The use of graphics should not be treated as decoration.

The author sets out principles for good design:

- above all else, show the data;
- erase nondata information;
- erase redundant data information.

He also suggests that presentation can be inspired by combining words, numbers, and pictures.

Context

The author is regarded as an authority on the presentation of statistical information. The book was based on a series of seminars on the use of statistical graphics. This, he believes, is an underdeveloped field. Most books on graphics concentrate on design technique, rather than on the information the graphics are communicating.

Tufte's collaboration with statistician John Tukey set out to bridge the gap. The collaboration, he believes, made the subject intellectually respectable.

As well as giving the subject a more intellectual dimension, Tufte also uses the book to demonstrate the tradition of excellence in graphics since the 18th century.

For More Information

Tufte, Edward R. *The Visual Display of Quantitative Information.* 2nd ed. Cheshire, CT: Graphics Press, 2001.

The Wealth of Nations
by Adam Smith

Many books are claimed to be classics or seminal works: *The Wealth of Nations* is indisputably both. It is a broad-ranging exploration of commercial and economic first principles. In it Adam Smith laid the philosophical foundations for modern capitalism and the modern market economy. There are few economists over the last 200 years—and fewer politicians of a free-market persuasion—who have not been influenced by it. Smith has helped shape the economic policies of British prime ministers and chancellors of the exchequer from the days of Lord North (1770–82) to those of Margaret Thatcher—and even Tony Blair.

Getting Started

Adam Smith was a Scottish philosopher. He was professor of logic and professor of moral philosophy at Glasgow University, but left his university posts in order to travel on the continent as tutor to a young nobleman. In France he was greatly influenced by a school of philosophical economists known as the "physiocrats." Returning to his native town of Kirkcaldy in Fife, he spent ten years preparing *An Inquiry into the Nature and Causes of the Wealth of Nations*, which was published—a significant coincidence perhaps—in the year of the signing of the Declaration of Independence, 1776.

His central thesis is that capital can best be used for the creation of both individual and national wealth in conditions of minimal interference by government. The "invisible hand" of free-market competition ensures, in his view, both the vitality of commercial activity and the ultimate good of all a nation's citizens.

Contribution

The Invisible Hand. According to Smith, conscious and well-meaning attempts to better the lot of a nation and its population are generally doomed to failure. The unintended cumulative effects of self-interested striving are far more effective. As he puts it: "Every individual is continually exerting to find out the most advantageous employment for whatever he can command . . . [and] necessarily labors to render the annual revenue of the society as great as he can. He generally neither intends to promote the public interest nor knows how much he is promoting it. He intends only his own gain, and he is in this, as in many other cases, led by an invisible hand to promote an end which was no part of his intention."

Value and Labor. The value of a particular good or service is determined by the costs of production. If something is expensive to produce, then its value is similarly high.

"The real price of everything, what everything really costs to the man who wants to acquire it, is the toil and trouble of acquiring it. What everything is really worth to the man who has acquired it, and who wants to dispose of it or exchange it for something else, is the toil and trouble of which it can save himself, and which it can impose on other people."

"What is bought with money or with goods is purchased by labor, as much as what we acquire by the toil of our own body. They contain the value of a certain quantity of labor which we exchange for what is supposed at the time to contain the value of an equal quantity."

The Division of Labor. Smith's legacy to scientific management was the concept of the division of labor.

"The division of labor occasions in every art a proportionable increase of the productive powers of labor. The separation of different trades and employments from one another seems to have taken place in consequence of this advantage."

> Smith's legacy to scientific management was the concept of the division of labor.

"Men are much more likely to discover easier and readier methods of attaining any object when the whole attention of their minds is directed towards that single object than when it is dissipated among a great variety of things."

Context

For a book that is over 200 years old, there is a surprisingly modern-sounding ring to a great deal of what *The Wealth of Nations* has to say. This is mainly owing to the acuteness and lasting value of Smith's analysis—the book was the first comprehensive exploration of the foundations, workings, and machinations of a free-market economy—but also to the familiarity of many of its basic concepts. *The Wealth of Nations* continues to have a role as a right-wing manifesto, a gloriously logical exposition of the beauty of market forces. And the appeal is not only to the right wing in politics.

Smith's system of demarcation and functional separation provided the basis for the management theorists of the early 20th century, such as Frederick Winslow Taylor, and practitioners such as Henry Ford. They translated the economic rigor of his thinking to practices in the workplace, though in ways and to a scale that Smith could never have imagined.

History has, however, put its own limitations on Smith's theorizing.

• Physical labor is no longer so important.
• The 20th century saw the emergence of management as a profession. It is barely acknowledged by Smith.
• Smith wrote without knowledge of the power and scope of modern corporations, let alone the power of brand names and customer loyalty.
• He also wrote in harder times when self-interest was not a choice but a necessity.

Nevertheless, as Gary Hamel commented: "Revisionists be damned. Citizens from Prague to Santiago to Guangzhou to Jakarta owe much of their new-found prosperity to the triumph of Adam Smith's economic ideals. [He] laid the philosophical foundations for the modern industrial economy. Enough said."

For More Information

Smith, Adam. *The Wealth of Nations*. Amherst, NY: Prometheus Books, 1991.

The Will to Manage

by Marvin Bower

Marvin Bower is the man who did more than anyone else to create the modern management consulting industry. The book gives a valuable insight into the management practices that made McKinsey and Company such a long-lasting success.

Getting Started

Marvin Bower's success grew from his principle that building trust with clients is critical to consulting success. The interests of the client should precede increasing the company's revenues: if you look after the client, the profits look after themselves.

He also believed that using values to help shape and guide an organization is extremely important. One of those values is that regard for the individual is based not on title, but on competence, stature, and leadership. Instead of experienced consultants, McKinsey recruited graduate students who could learn how to be good problem solvers and analysts. The company also developed "virtual" project teams, bringing in the best people in the organization wherever they were based in the world. Clear, simple employment policies and change through empowerment helped to maintain high professional standards.

Contribution

A New Way of Looking at Consultants. Bower did not change the name of his company, McKinsey, as he shrewdly decided that clients would demand his involvement in projects if his name was up in lights. His vision was to provide advice on managing to top executives and to do it with the professional standards of a leading law firm. Due to a belief that in all successful professional groups, regard for the individual is based not on title but on competence, stature, and leadership, McKinsey consultants were associates who had engagements, rather than mere jobs, and the firm was a practice rather than a business.

Building Trust with Clients. The entire ethos of McKinsey was to be very respectable, the kind of people C.E.O.s naturally relate to. Bower's gospel was that the interests of the client should precede increasing the company's revenues: unless the client could trust McKinsey, the company could not work with them. If McKinsey looked after the client, the profits would look after themselves. High charges were not a means to greater profits, but a simple and effective means of ensuring that clients took McKinsey seriously.

Other central principles were that consultants should keep quiet about the affairs of clients, should tell the truth, and be prepared to challenge the client's opinion. They should only agree to do work which is both necessary and which they could do well. Using values to help shape and guide an organization was extremely important.

New Patterns of Recruitment. Instead of hiring experienced executives with in-depth knowledge of a particular industry, Bower recruited graduate students who could learn how to be good problem solvers and consultants. This changed the emphasis of consulting from passing on a narrow range of experience to using a wide range of analytical and problem-solving techniques.

Developing Virtual Project Teams. Another element of Bower's approach was the use of teams. He thought of McKinsey as a network of leaders. Teams were assembled for specific projects, and the best people in the organization were brought to bear on a particular problem, no matter where they were based in the world. McKinsey's culture fostered rigorous debate over the right answer, without that debate resulting in personal criticism.

Clear, Simple Employment Policies. The company's policy remains one of the most simple: seniority in McKinsey correlates directly with achievement. If a consultant ceases to progress with the organization, or is ultimately unable to demonstrate the skills and qualities required of a principal, he or she is asked to leave McKinsey.

> The company's policy remains one of the most simple: seniority in McKinsey correlates directly with achievement.

Change through Empowerment. "There have been thousands of changes in methods, but not in command and control. Many companies say they want to change, but they need to empower people below. More cohesion is needed rather than hierarchy," Bower said in 1995.

Context

Under Bower's astute direction, McKinsey became the world's premier consulting firm. Recent years have also seen the structure and managerial style of the company receiving plaudits. McKinsey is special because it has developed a self-perpetuating aura that it is unquestionably the best. Marvin Bower was the creator of this organizational magic.

American Express chief, Harvey Golub, says that Bower led McKinsey according to a set of values, and it was the principle of using values to help shape and guide an organization that was probably the most important thing he took away.

For More Information

Bower, Marvin. *The Will to Manage.* New York: McGraw-Hill, 1966.

Author Index

THE
ULTIMATE BUSINESS
LIBRARY
Essential resources for anyone and everyone in business

BUSINESS: THE ULTIMATE RESOURCE
Introduction by Daniel Goleman

"The closest we have to a business bible" *(USA Today)*, *Business: The Ultimate Resource* includes over 100 original best-practice essays from the world's leading thinkers and practitioners, over 300 practical checklists, a world almanac, listings of over 3,000 information resources, and much more.

HARDCOVER
ISBN 0-7382-0242-8

BEST PRACTICE
Defining the World of Work

Ideas and Insights from the World's Foremost Business Thinkers
Introduction by Rosabeth Moss Kanter

Featuring 100 essays and interviews, *Best Practice* captures the state of the art in management thinking and practice today.

PAPERBACK
ISBN 0-7382-0822-1

THE ULTIMATE BUSINESS DICTIONARY
Defining the World of Work

Over 6,000 entries. Features a multi-lingual glossary; abbreviations, acronyms, and business slang; world economic data; listings of international stock exchanges and trade organizations; and worked examples of finance and accounting terms.

PAPERBACK
ISBN 0-7382-0821-3

THE BIG BOOK OF BUSINESS QUOTATIONS
More than 5,000 Indispensible Observations on the World of Commerce, Work, Finance, and Management

A compendium of the most memorable, insightful, and amusing quotes on business, leadership, and the economy.

HARDCOVER
ISBN 0-7382-0848-5
Available July 2003